AWAITING THE HEAVENLY COUNTRY

AWAITING THE HEAVENLY COUNTRY

The Civil War and America's Culture of Death

MARK S. SCHANTZ

CORNELL UNIVERSITY PRESS

ITHACA AND LONDON

Title page: George N. Barnard,
"Battle of New Hope Church, Georgia, No. 2."
Photographic Views of Sherman's Campaign (1866).
Courtesy of the Library Company of Pennsylvania.

First published 2008 by Cornell University Press
Printed in the United States of America

Library of Congress Cataloging-in-Publication Data
Schantz, Mark S. (Mark Saunders), 1955–
   Awaiting the heavenly country : the Civil War and
America's culture of death / Mark S. Schantz.
      p. cm.
   Includes bibliographical references and index.
   ISBN 978–0–8014–3761–8 (cloth : alk. paper)
1. United States—History—Civil War, 1861–1865—
Casualties—Social aspects.   2. Death—Social aspects—
United States—History—19th century.   3. War and society—
United States—History—19th century.   I. Title.
   E468.9.S33 2008
   973.7'1—dc22

                                                  2007048089

   Cornell University Press strives to use environmentally
responsible suppliers and materials to the fullest extent possible
      in the publishing of its books. Such materials include
   vegetable-based, low-VOC inks and acid-free papers that are
      recycled, totally chlorine-free, or partly composed of
      nonwood fibers. For further information, visit our
         website at www.cornellpress.cornell.edu.

Cloth printing   10 9 8 7 6 5 4 3 2 1

FOR NANCY AND MARY-CANDLER

Contents

List of Illustrations

Acknowledgments

Many people have made this book a pleasure to write. At the American Antiquarian Society in Worcester, Massachusetts, I thank especially John Hench, Nancy Burkett, and the extraordinary services rendered by Joanne D. Chaison and her staff. In particular I express my gratitude to Laura E. Wasowicz, Curator of Children's Literature, and to Georgia (Gigi) Brady Barnhill, Andrew W. Mellon Curator of Graphic Arts. Gigi went the extra mile, offering me her unparalleled knowledge of the nineteenth-century memorial lithography and sharing with me many slides of the work that she has collected over the years. That the visual arts play such an important role in this project is due in large part to her unfailing helpfulness and energy. At the Library Company of Philadelphia, too, I found ready and enthusiastic assistance. Special plaudits go to Jennifer Ambrose, James Green, Cornelia S. King, Phillip S. Lapsansky, and Erika Piola for enriching my work in numerous ways. Jim Green did a great service in introducing me to Dr. Carol Soltis, whose work on Rembrandt Peale and his painting *The Court of Death* has deeply informed my thinking. Along the way I also received expert help from reference librarians at the New York Public Library, the Schomburg

Center for Research in Black Culture, the New York Historical Society, the Historical Society of Pennsylvania, the Library of Congress, the University of Mississippi, and the Arkansas History Commission. Closer to home, I acknowledge the exceptional reference staff at the Bailey Library of Hendrix College. Peggy Morrison worked wonders with her interlibrary loan skills, collecting pamphlets and photocopies that I would not have dreamed were accessible.

Outside of my research nexus, I received encouragement, support, and wise counsel from numerous quarters. I benefited greatly from attending a 1998 Summer Institute on the history of death in America sponsored by the National Endowment for the Humanities. Held at Columbia University under the enthusiastic and able leadership of David and Sheila Rothman, this institute laid the groundwork for many of the ideas and issues explored in this book. I thank all of my fellow participants for stimulating my thought, for suggesting possible source materials, and for being great scholarly pals. Presenting an early formulation of the outline for this book at the Southern Historical Association's annual meeting also galvanized my efforts. Drew Gilpin Faust, Charles Reagan Wilson, and Bertram Wyatt-Brown all offered supportive words as well as cogent critiques. A sabbatical leave and faculty project grant offered to me by Hendrix College allowed me the blessing of time and space in which I could finish my research and complete a draft of my manuscript. I must also point to my students at Hendrix College, who over the past years have taken my courses on the American Civil War and Reconstruction and on the history of death in America. I have learned more than I can say from them. And while I cannot identify each individual student who has contributed an insight that shifted my thinking on a particular topic, I can acknowledge them collectively for their dedication, intelligence, and good cheer. Dear friends and colleagues have also sustained this project by listening to me spin out ideas, by reading snippets of prose, by suggesting sources, and by reminding me that this was a book worthy of writing. Jay Barth, Lloyd Benson, Steve and Martha Goodson, Steven Hornsby, Ian King, Rebecca Resinski, John Rodrigue, Sylvia Frank Rodrigue, Allison Shutt, Martha Sledge, and Mart Stewart have all, in different ways, made this a better book.

I could not have asked for more from my colleagues at Cornell University Press. This book project has lived through three excellent editors, Peter Agree, Sheri Englund, and now Alison A. Kalett. Alison has been a steadfast supporter of this project, offering me thoughtful readings of chapters and helping me to stay focused on its broad interpretive significance. Special credit also goes to those outside readers who read my manuscript for Cornell, Susan Juster and David Waldstreicher. Both of them lavished me with amazingly detailed reports that have made this a much stronger book. I also want to acknowledge Cameron Cooper, Susan Specter, Karen Hwa, my copyeditor, Cathi Reinfelder, and others at the Press for their work on the book.

My wife, Nancy, and my daughter, Mary-Candler, have kept me firmly grounded in the joys of the present even as I have explored the shades of the past. For that great gift, and for more to come, I dedicate this book with love to them.

AWAITING THE HEAVENLY COUNTRY

Introduction

Living under the shadow of postmodernity, where all historical "facts" are dimly perceived, at least one reality appears horribly luminous: that 620,000 men lost their lives in the American Civil War. Whether we think of the American Civil War as a "total war," a "destructive war," or simply as a "hard war," students of it agree on its singularly bloody impact.[1] Beginning with the battle of Shiloh in April 1862, major engagements routinely produced casualty rates that rivaled those of Waterloo.[2] Suicidal charges—from those in front of Marye's Heights at Fredericksburg, to Pickett's Charge at Gettysburg, to Fort Wagner, to Cold Harbor, to Franklin—punctuate the narrative of the war from start to finish. And in virtually hundreds of smaller fights, men slaughtered each other with a zeal we still grope to comprehend. In ways that continue to startle even avid students, the sheer destructiveness of the Civil War worked profound transformations on American society.[3]

Answers to the question of why so many men perished in the war have typically been mapped on terrain occupied by military and political historians. This is both meet and salutary. Surely developments such as the rifled musket and trench warfare contributed to the stunning level of carnage.[4] Outdated tactics, perhaps honed in the Mexican War, and the sheer stupidity of generals also played a part.[5] Wretched conditions in field hospitals and in disease-infested winter camps, too, plagued the armies.[6] The deeply held political convictions of the soldiers themselves also contributed to the destruction. James M. McPherson insists that average soldiers on both sides of the conflict understood that the war was about competing conceptions of liberty.[7] After an exhaustive study of the diaries and letters of the combatants, he concludes that soldierly rhetoric about duty, honor, and patriotism "was the same in the war's last year as in its first."[8] Thus, for reasons they only barely understood, such as the sinister effects of microbes, and for reasons they grasped with clarity, such as the causes for which they fought, Americans made a war of catastrophic proportions.

While these military and political explanations of the enormous cost of the Civil War are clearly of great importance, they do not consider the wider cultural matrix in which the war was fought. They ignore what, in my view, must be a paramount consideration in helping us to understand the Civil War: the ideas and attitudes Americans held about death in the middle of the nineteenth century. For if we assume that the ways in which a culture comprehends death shapes the behavior of its members, then we need to understand how antebellum Americans thought of death if we are to gain greater insight into what they did in the Civil War. If soldiers recited the phrase "death before dishonor" as a common mantra, then we need to know not only what they thought about the ideas of honor and dishonor (subjects about which we know quite a bit) but also what they thought of death itself.[9]

The argument of this book is that Americans came to fight the Civil War in the midst of a wider cultural world that sent them messages about death that made it easier to kill and to be killed. They understood that death awaited all who were born and prized the ability to face death with a spirit of calm resignation. They believed that a heavenly eternity of transcendent beauty awaited them beyond the grave. They knew that their heroic achievements would be cherished forever by posterity. They grasped that death itself might be seen as artistically fascinating and even beautiful. They saw how notions of full citizenship were predicated on the willingness of men to lay down their lives. And they produced works of art that captured the moment of death in highly idealistic ways. Americans thus approached the Civil War carrying a cluster of assumptions about death that, I will suggest, facilitated its unprecedented destructiveness.

In accenting the power of culture to condition behavior, I do not suggest that Southerners and Northerners set out *consciously* to kill themselves because they knew they would all meet again in heaven or because they grasped that their deaths might be politically valuable or aesthetically pleasing.[10] Culture operates in more subtle, but no less powerful, ways. What I argue here is that how people behaved on their deathbeds, what they thought about heaven, how they thought their memories would be preserved, what they read and wrote about death, and how they imagined death in their mind's eye, did create a wider cultural climate that facilitated the carnage of war. To ignore this powerful combination of forces in American life, it seems to me, is to sidestep one of the most pervasive concerns of the antebellum era—that is, the fundamental confrontation with death. And if we agree that the cultural universe that humans make can, in turn, modify and direct their behavior, then it seems reasonable to conclude that what Americans thought about death is relevant in understanding how they behaved in time of war. In our own day, one might think about how ideas of a heavenly paradise fold into the political behavior of suicide bombers in various parts of the globe. While we can certainly not push the parallel between these shadowy figures and the soldiers of the Civil War era too far, we can suggest, at least, that ethereal assumptions about the nature of eternity can influence the nitty-gritty world of politics in this realm.[11]

This book unfolds as a series of interconnected, interpretive, and, I hope, provocative essays. It is not intended to capture in any encyclopedic way all that might be said about the ways Americans comprehended death in the decades leading up to the Civil War. Because death was of such pervasive interest in the antebellum era, to write a comprehensive treatment of American attitudes toward it in this period would require one to read almost everything written or created for a span of some sixty years. Indeed, while I did the research for this volume, virtually every librarian or colleague who helped along the way pointed me in the direction of literally truckloads of source material that might inform the project. That reality itself should give us pause. That Americans of the early republic found in death such a rich reservoir of meaning alerts us to the wide cultural chasm that separates their world from our own. While contemporary scholars may debate the degree to which modern America is a death-denying culture, we may say with greater certainty that nineteenth-century America was a death-embracing culture.

Scholars of the sectional crisis in American history—those who sift among the ruins for the political, social, economic, and religious materials that ignited the Civil War—will find in these pages an implicit argument for the unifying power of death in America. In analyzing the attitudes of Southerners and Northerners, the enslaved and the free, men and women, I have been struck more by similarities than differences. While the culture of death in antebellum America was no doubt variegated and diverse—drawing in various degrees on the evangelical Protestant fervor of the Second Great Awakening, the culture of the Greek Revival, and the currents of Romanticism, to name only a few major sources—it nevertheless cannot be teased apart in any sensible or predictable way along the deep divides of race, class, or gender. This surprised me. As a scholar trained up in the ways of the "new social history," I expected to find these subterranean fissures to be operating powerfully in the ways in which Americans greeted death. It may well be the case that future scholars will detect such differences. For now, however, my reading of the evidence sustains the old cliché that death is the great equalizer among human beings. There is considerable irony in the observation that a shared body of cultural assumptions and attitudes about death helped to sustain a war that fractured a nation.

In some ways, the interpretation offered here complicates the overarching master narrative of the Civil War that has emerged in the last couple of decades. Articulated in powerful and sophisticated ways by historian James McPherson and filmmaker Ken Burns, this telling of the tale has become the reigning paradigm through which many Americans see the conflict. It is fundamentally a narrative of heroism on all sides, with the forces of authentic liberty and American nationhood triumphing in the end. "This story has become common sense to Americans," observes historian Edward L. Ayers, "emancipation, war, nation, and progress all seem part of one story, the same story."[12] This modern narrative retains the faint glimmer of what David W. Blight has called the "reconciliationist" memory of the Civil War. In the late nineteenth and early twentieth centuries, he argues, white Americans north and south closed ranks to rebuild the nation at the cost of pursuing equal rights for African Americans.[13] The newer narratives constructed by McPherson and Burns clearly depart from the older "reconciliationist" view in that they position the story of African American liberty at the center of the Civil War. Yet, they also share a fundamentally optimistic view of the war, one that sees its outcomes as inevitable (emancipation as the natural outgrowth of the heritage of the American Revolution) and progress for the nation as the end result. In contrast, this book suggests the possibility that the great destructiveness of the Civil War might be seen, in part, as the product of cultural attitudes and assumptions about death that may seem alien to our world. It answers Edward Ayers' call for a "new revisionism" that "would place more distance between nineteenth-century Americans and ourselves, the very distance that lets us see ourselves more clearly."[14] If this book affords us a glimpse into the cultural universe inhabited by Americans in the middle of the nineteenth century and provides us with a fresh perspective on the cost of the Civil War, then it will have succeeded.

❖

CHAPTER ONE

"Emblems of Mortality"

The generation of Americans who fought the Civil War understood that they could not escape the embrace of death. Nor did they particularly wish to. They knew that death was the inevitable portion of all who live. In 1846, readers from New Haven, Connecticut, to Charleston, South Carolina, could examine the pages of the latest reminder of their own certain mortality. Based on the "dance of death" tradition that stretched back to early modern Europe, the pamphlet *Emblems of Mortality* articulated a worldview that we moderns find nearly impossible to conjure. In a series of engravings and facing pieces of text, the skeletal figure personifying Death literally grasps "all ranks and conditions" of people— sometimes by clutching bits of their clothing and sometimes by more insinuating or even violent means. Often pictured with his symbolic hour-glass, the figure of Death begins by inviting the pope to consider his grave and concludes by carrying off the humble husband and wife to await the Last Judgment. In all, *Emblems of Mortality* depicts forty-three different scenes. Each one reveals the workings of Death on the powerful and the weak, the rich and the poor, the virtuous and the criminal, the rulers and the ruled.

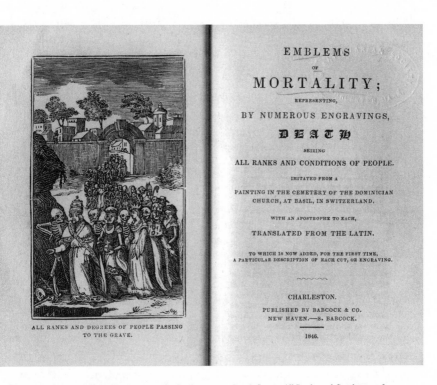

ALL RANKS AND DEGREES OF PEOPLE PASSING
TO THE GRAVE.

Fig. I. *Emblems of Mortality; Representing, By Engravings, Death Seizing All Ranks and Conditions of People. Imitated from a Painting in the Cemetery of the Dominican Church at Basil, Switzerland. With an Apostrophe to Each, Translated from the Latin. To which is now added, for the first time, a particular description of each cut, or engraving.* Courtesy of the American Antiquarian Society, Worcester, Mass.

The figure of Death in *Emblems of Mortality* may well have possessed special resonance for Americans of the early nineteenth century. Death is a man of many disguises. He is the trickster, the confidence man, the hustler par excellence—all characters of significant contemporary interest.[1] He sneaks up on the figure of the "Empress" disguised as a woman and invites her to view an open grave. Dressed as a "Count," Death surprises his quarry "to strip him of all honorable distinctions which may be about him."[2] Sometimes visible and sometimes invisible, Death stalks his victims. In this grim work, he is not impressed by money or power or even by virtue. As Death grapples with a "Gentleman" we see that Death "has seized him by laying hold of the splendid garment he wears, and is dragging him away in spite of all opposition."[3] Wealth and status could not protect one from death. In a world in which the Market Revolution was creating unprecedented concentrations of wealth in both the North and the South, the figure of Death as a great social equalizer may have appealed to the many Americans left behind in this quest for profit.[4] Death also emerges in *Emblems of Mortality* as an entertaining figure, perhaps even one of art, culture, and sentiment. He is depicted frequently with musical instruments—a lute, a trumpet, drums, a violin, bagpipes, and a shepherd's harp. Death carries off his duties with an unmistakable aplomb and skill. It is one of the ironies of *Emblems of Mortality* that the personified figure of Death emerges as an intriguing living being.

Emblems of Mortality represents only one specimen, albeit an important one, of the multitude of ways Americans conceptualized death in the early republic. Encounters with death surface in almost every conceivable source with which historians of this period have worked—in crime novels, poetry, diaries, newspapers, public health reports, slave narratives, sermons, lithographs, paintings, speeches, and photographs. It's hard to know what to make of this outpouring of evidence. Thirty years ago, historian of popular culture Lewis O. Saum warned against making facile generalizations about the apparent obsession with death in the decades before the Civil War. "The risk of idle supererogation or even impertinence," he observed, "looms large in any effort to explain the superabundant musings and dotings on death."[5] Saum's insight stands. Doing history is always a tricky business, but in the case of studying death the problem may be compounded by a virtual avalanche of source material. If we can say one thing about death in the early nineteenth century, though, we might argue that it emerges not simply as *a* peripheral topic of historical investigation but as *the* major story.

Entering the world of nineteenth-century conceptions of death may be vexed by our modern tendency to avoid the topic altogether. The degree to which contemporary American culture is death-denying remains an open question. In his series of landmark essays in 1974, acclaimed French historian Philippe Ariès argued that the modern West had now entered the age of the "forbidden death." So fearful are we moderns of our own mortality, Ariès argued, that "death has become unnamable."[6] Other historians have softened a bit Ariès' notion that talk of death would send modern westerners scurrying for cover. In a recent treatment of the history of the modern American funeral home, Gary Laderman concludes that "the American way of death is motivated not by fears or disavowals, but by attachments and fixations; it is more like a cult of the dead than a symptom of a culture in denial."[7] How else are we to make sense of the presence of images of death in popular films, advertisements, and television programs such as HBO's *Six Feet Under*? Living in the twilight of the collapse of the Twin Towers on September 11, 2001, and the subsequent "war on terror," one might argue that discussions of death are now, more than ever, part of American public discourse. But even here, our modern dance with death does not approach, either in its intensity or in its sweep, the confrontation with death evident in the early nineteenth century.

This chapter surveys the ways in which antebellum Americans died and offers an interpretation of how they sought to navigate that passage. The central argument is twofold: first, I argue that Americans in the early republic encountered death in myriad and intimate ways; second, I suggest that their culture provided them with powerful narratives that helped them navigate its passage. Death was intimately familiar to early nineteenth-century Americans. They had seen it in their homes and witnessed it in their streets. They had washed the corpses of loved ones and laid them out in their parlors. They had seen bodies wasted by epidemics piled in city gutters. They had watched at the bedsides of friends as spirits had departed. The very pervasiveness of death in antebellum America trained up an entire generation to see it not as something to be avoided, but as the inevitable destiny of humanity. Americans also taught each other how to die. Evident in all kinds of narratives of death—diaries, funeral sermons, private correspondence, and public writing—Americans created social frames for death that made it not only comprehensible but instructive, redemptive, and glorious. When secession came in 1860, they were ready to put their lives on the line.

The great demographic transformation that catapulted Americans toward modern life expectancy and mortality rates was a product of the decades that followed the Civil War and not those which preceded it.

Americans growing up between 1820 and 1860 straddled two epochs—one characterized by early death, rampant epidemics, and life expectancy and mortality rates that were nearly medieval, and one characterized by major public health advances, antiseptic surgery, and antibiotics that dramatically raised hopes for longer and more robust lives. Although the quantitative data is sketchy at the national level, scholars have converged on the finding that Americans coming of age before the Civil War might expect to live into their mid-forties.[8] At the most. Some scholars have suggested that in the 1840s and 1850s, life expectancy in America may actually have dipped slightly in comparison with the earlier part of the nineteenth century.[9] If this is true, then the generation of Americans who stood on the cusp of the Civil War knew death even better than did their parents.

The explosive economic growth that characterized antebellum American society contributed to the pervasiveness of death. The expansion of cities, for example, contributed to greater public health problems. "City dwellers in the eighteenth and nineteenth centuries," writes Christian Warren, "faced significantly higher risk of premature death than their rural contemporaries."[10] The cholera epidemic of 1849 took its most serious toll "in the infant cities of the West, with no adequate water supply, primitive sanitation, and crowded with a transient population."[11] The developing American infrastructure of canals, waterways, turnpikes, and railroads served to introduce new pathogens to communities that had previously been more insulated. In her study of Nantucket, Massachusetts, Barbara J. Logue discovered that a growing network of economic prosperity and trade "was accompanied by an increased risk of death and disease."[12] The snaking paths of commerce along the Mississippi River exacerbated the spread of yellow fever in the South during the catastrophic outbreaks of the 1850s.[13] As immigrant laborers moved throughout the nation they, too, carried disease along with their hopes for a better life. Analyzing the outbreak of yellow fever in Charleston, South Carolina, in 1852, the *Southern Quarterly Review* announced that "it is the introduction of these strangers among us that brings yellow fever. If we had no strangers, there would be no such disease."[14] Perhaps shrill in its condemnation of "strangers," this journal article nevertheless correctly linked an increasingly mobile labor force to the spread of disease and death.

As *Emblems of Mortality* made clear, death could appear in many forms. "Innumerable are the avenues of death," wrote Massachusetts minister Edward L. Parker in 1822, "and in ways little thought of by mankind, may they be called to depart out of the world."[15] Yet some forms of death could assume a grisly predictability. The early deaths of their children stung deeply antebellum Americans. As they grew to adulthood, they confronted death in the form of smallpox and scarlet fever and in cholera and yellow fever epidemics. If they survived these scourges, Americans could yet be cut down by consumption (the disease we know now as tuberculosis), the most ubiquitous of killers in the early nineteenth century. Americans knew that death was omnipresent and readily acknowledged that fact. Mary Edmondson, a young woman from northern Mississippi, captured a formulaic phrase familiar to many Americans when she wrote in her diary of hearing about her cousin's death. On January 24, 1854, she observed that "'In the midst of life we are in death.' For oh <u>how hard</u> it is to realize that one so recently with us amid gay and happy scenes can so soon have put on Angels wings for Heaven."[16] Mary Edmondson understood that death, however difficult it was to bear, was an integral part of life.

From the first moments of life, antebellum Americans confronted the specter of high childhood mortality rates. The case of Dr. Calvin Martin of Seekonk, Massachusetts, was surely a dire example of what thousands of other American families had to endure: In the winter of 1821, he lost three children in the space of a single month. "Let those present, who are parents," intoned Otis Thompson in a funeral sermon preached in Martin's home, "prepare to part with their children. This is a dying world. Parents must expect, that, if they should not be deprived of the residue of their own years, to follow some of their children, to the grave."[17] In our own day, we may tend to see in the deaths of children a horrific inversion of what we take to be the natural order of things—parents should not have to bury their children. But nineteenth-century Americans lived and thought differently. The natural order of things, if there were such a thing, validated Thompson's assertion that parents had best gird themselves for the prospect of early loss. It is difficult to overestimate the significance of this idea—that the young might well be expected to die before their parents—in the midst of a culture heading for war. Examining merely a sample of reports from the Philadelphia Board of Health during the

1830s gives us a sense of the prevalence of early death. The death of stillborn infants alone ranked among the top three causes of death in Philadelphia from 1834 to 1837, outstripped only by scarlet fever (in some years) and, of course, by consumption.[18] These stillborn deaths do not include those young children who died after only one year of life. By almost any sensible measure, the death of a child was a commonplace occurrence in the mid-nineteenth century.

Americans faced the deaths of their children not only with eyes moistened by tears but also with hearts steeled by optimism. Take, for instance, the case of Salem, Massachusetts, resident Pickering Dodge. Following the death of his infant son, Dodge labored during some of his "leisure hours" over the winter of 1841 to produce a memorial volume entitled "A Tribute to the Infant Dead" for his wife, Anna. He presented it to her on the occasion of their fifteenth wedding anniversary. The volume contained transcriptions, each done in a steady and meticulous hand, of 185 poems and literary pieces on the subject of death. He included with this thick volume a table of contents with the names of the poems and their page number, each neatly labeled. It is difficult to conjure the image of a grieving parent, sitting in the bitterness of a New England winter, working with compulsive neatness on such a massive instantiation of loss. Completing the volume, though, may have afforded Dodge a way to gain control of what was clearly an uncontrollable situation. And, on the dedication page, he sounded a note of hope. "We look upward with the eye of faith and confidence," he wrote to Anna, "to that happy Paradise, where he now rests pure and spotless in the presence of his God."[19] The presumed innocence of children and their certain place in the world to come offered solace to parents seeking to make sense of their tragedy.

Knowing well the especially fragile states of the young, parents did not shrink from the duty of preparing their children to face death. The children's literature of the antebellum period looked at death with a frankness born of experience. *The Tragi-Comic History of the Burial of Cock Robin*, one of the most popular of all children's books, instructed children in the manner of funeral rites. Following the death of Robin, Jenny Wren arranges the funeral of her beloved, employing a sparrow to carry a funeral invitation to the other birds of the forest: "Miss Jenny Wren begs the favor of your Company to attend the funeral of Cock

Robin."[20] All of the birds take their parts as Cock Robin's funeral proces-sion unfolds in the text and in illustrations. *The Mount Vernon Reader* for 1837 ("designed for middle classes") included a lesson in which a young student asks, "Mother, What is Death?"[21] *The Infant Library* speller from the 1840s inexplicably concluded with a little illustration entitled "An Officer's Funeral" with the note that "when an officer in the army dies, his body is attended to the grave by his brother officers, and by soldiers marching to slow and solemn music."[22] In the 1850s, the American Sun-day School Union published a tract entitled "Heaven" for children that featured a dialogue between a mother and a young child about to die. "Is it not dreadful to die?" asks the young boy. "It is not dreadful to such as love God and do all they can to serve and please him," replies his mother.[23] In such ways did parents seek to ensure their children would be instructed in the ways of death in the hope of a future beyond the grave.

As they grew into adulthood, epidemics preyed on parents and chil-dren alike. We have solid evidence from numerous quarters documenting how diseases could lay waste to entire communities. Elizabeth Fenn's study of smallpox in the Revolutionary era estimates that at least 130,000 Americans fell to that disease as the contending armies served as agents of contagion.[24] This death toll far exceeded the 25,000 or so battle deaths incurred by Americans as a result of the Revolutionary War. Lau-rel Thatcher Ulrich's brilliant interpretation of the diaries of Maine mid-wife Martha Ballard uncovered the ravages of an outbreak of scarlet fever in Hallowell, Maine, in 1787.[25] A yellow fever epidemic in 1793 forced thousands of Philadelphians to flee their city like refugees and nearly crippled the government of the United States. Charles Rosenberg's path-breaking study of cholera has examined catastrophic outbreaks of that disease in 1832, 1849, and 1866.[26] Yellow fever raised its head again in the early 1850s, wiping out more than 12,000 New Orleans residents in 1853 alone.[27] With startling unpredictability, disease could devastate both town and country.

To live under the siege of an epidemic was to experience a level of chaos and destruction that approached the carnage created by warfare. The Quaker diarist Elizabeth Drinker recorded an intimate glimpse of the 1793 yellow fever outbreak in Philadelphia that outstrips by far her account of the damage inflicted by the Revolutionary War. Drinker's favored term for yellow fever was "the disorder" and her observations chart its course.[28] She noted that "the dead are put in their Coffins just as they die without changing their clothes, or laying out, are buried in an hour or two after their disease."[29] She reported closed shops, stacks of coffins, and panic. "The inhabitants of Phila. were fast moving into the City before this storm," she wrote, "'tis said there were upwards of 20,000 had left their dwellings, and retired to the Country."[30] In a city of some 40,000 residents, more than 4,000 died and more than half had taken to the road. In 1832, similar scenes of disorder took place in New York when cholera broke out. "Cartloads of coffins rumbled through the streets, and when filled, returned through the streets to the cemeteries. Dead bodies lay unburied in the gutters," writes historian Charles Rosenberg, "and coffin-makers had to work on the Sabbath to supply the demand."[31] In 1849, the situation seemed even worse. Unable to keep pace with burying the dead, New York officials transported them to Randall's Island where they "were deposited in a wide trench some hundred yards in length, one body on top of another to within a foot or two of the surface."[32]

In December 1853, *Debow's Review* published an omnibus article summing up the dreadful impact of the yellow fever epidemic in New Orleans from earlier in the year. Again and again the article called attention to the problem of "the unburied dead." Based on accounts culled from other New Orleans newspapers, the editors decried dead bodies "lying piled on the ground, swollen and bursting their coffins, and enveloped in swarms of flies."[33] As in New York, burial trenches were deployed to hold the dead. "The mode of burying the dead in cemeteries was this:—Long furrows, as in a ploughed field, were made, about 18, or at the most 24 inches in depth," declared the article, "It was not deep enough to be called a trench."[34] City officials had to cope with the deaths of hundreds of residents in a single day. Standing in the muck and stench, "stoical negroes, too, who are hired at five dollars per hour to assist in the internment, stagger under the stifling fumes."[35] Looters attacked unprotected shops, and dead bodies tumbled out of abandoned carriages. Some residents committed suicide rather than wait for the disease to take its course. Given the descriptions the story contained, the editors exaggerated only slightly when they announced that this was "one of the most destructive epidemics that has ever visited the shores of the New World."[36] A special tabulation of losses published at the close of "The Epidemic Summer" cataloged a total count of 12,151 dead buried in a dozen cemeteries throughout the city.[37] This staggering total does not include the cost exacted by the disease as it moved up the Mississippi River.

Such scenes of mass death, burial trenches, and refugees call to mind parallels with Civil War battlefields. The casualty rates incurred by Civil War armies in major engagements—sometimes up to 30 or 40 percent of combatants—were certainly rivaled by the ravages of epidemics. The New Orleans death count, more than 12,000 from the summer of 1853, for example, would have been far greater than the total number of Confederate dead who fell at Gettysburg in the summer of 1863.[38] The burial trenches of 1849 New York predated the use of the same technique used by Union General U. S. Grant following the battle of Shiloh in April 1862. Even the loss of 4,000 lives in the 1793 yellow fever epidemic in Philadelphia (more than half a century before the Civil War) represented almost the total number of casualties on *both sides* at the First Battle of Bull Run in 1861.[39] Although it is certainly true that the sheer carnage of the Civil War dwarfed anything that Americans had experienced to that time (or since), it is equally true that Americans entered the war as products of a culture that had intimate experience with the workings of death on a large scale. They could comprehend, and had experience with, some of the most gruesome scenes that war could offer.

Death came to many Americans, however, not in spectacular epidemics but instead in the unpredictable form of consumption. According to historian Sheila M. Rothman's brilliant study, "during the first half of the nineteenth century consumption was America's deadliest disease, responsible for one out of every five deaths."[40] Although it struck with particular force the young and the female, consumption took a heavy toll across the American population. Todd Savitt's investigation *Medicine and Slavery* in Virginia reveals that consumption and various respiratory diseases were leading causes of death among whites, slaves, and free blacks as well.[41] Whomever it struck, consumption was a devilishly complex disease. Sometimes manifesting itself in a cough, sometimes a fever, and then disappearing for years at a time, patients and doctors struggled to even define when a sufferer had entered the final stages of the disease. The fickleness of consumption prompted doctors and patients to cast about for treatments that confronted the hereditary and environmental causes that were thought to trigger the disease in the first place. Those diagnosed with consumption might live weeks, months, or even years—responding by turns to differing climates and activities. To die at the hands of consumption meant to live with uncertainty.

As Sheila Rothman has shown, however, "invalids" diagnosed with consumption in the early nineteenth century still had vital social roles to perform.[42] For male invalids (a term, incidentally of military origin) the chief goal was to "improve"—either one's health, one's community, or, in the best scenarios, both. When they could afford it, male invalids traveled to warmer climes (such as Cuba) or took sea voyages (whaling voyages were favored) or tried their hand at manual labor. Others launched social reform efforts and hurled themselves into the heady evangelical work of temperance reform, education, and abolitionism. Female invalids continued to have children, raised families, and prepared their young ones for the day when they would depart this earth. To be an invalid in antebellum America was not to be a passive patient. It was to be a person with special duties and precise obligations, the fulfillment of which were made all the more imperative by the unpredictability that accompanied their disease. The "narratives of illness" that the invalids composed reveal that they dealt with their disease in a social context in which duty to self, family, nation, and God trumped even the best advice of physicians.

One could say that consumption endowed the invalid sufferer with a certain kind of moral cache in antebellum America. Invalids might be seen as more spiritual, more full of sentiment, more authentic even, than those of more robust health. When Harriet Beecher Stowe wrote that touchstone of all antebellum deathbed scenes, the death of Little Eva in *Uncle Tom's Cabin,* she traded on images of the young, female consumptive that were already familiar to thousands of Americans. Although actual death from consumption was a ghastly affair, narratives of death at its hands often emphasized the piety, purity, and heroism of the invalid rather than gruesome physical details of the death. It was characteristic of this romantic and evangelical age for writers to mask the suffering of bodies and focus attention instead on the glorious flight of the soul to heaven. "This attitude idealized spiritual continuity after death," writes historian Gary Laderman, "and minimized any ultimate, enduring significance for the corporeal body."[43] As we shall see, more Americans did worry more about the fate of their corporeal bodies in heaven than Laderman suggests, but he is correct in identifying the spiritual framework many Americans used to comprehend death.

This fundamentally religious way of viewing death led some consolation literature to extol the virtues of consumption as a disease. Take, for example, the comments made by Daniel C. Eddy in his book *Angel Whispers; or the Echo of Spirit Voices Designed to Comfort Those Who Mourn* (1857).[44] Rather than complain about the evident horrors of the disease, Eddy looked on the bright side in a chapter entitled "Advantages of Consumption." Articulating the antebellum assumption embedded in *Emblems of Mortality,* Eddy began noting that "death does not come in the same form to all men. He varies his assaults, and to some appears under more awful circumstances than others."[45] From Eddy's perspective, however, death by consumption was superior to death by other means in four major respects. "Consumption," he explained, "gives time for reflection and thought."[46] Turning the dreadful uncertainty of the progress of the disease to salutary ends, he wanted suffers to take the extra time to prepare well for death. Unlike others struck down by accident or plague, consumptives could ready their souls for eternity. Second, Eddy maintained, "consumption is seldom, to any great extent, accompanied with pain."[47] It is hard to know what to make of this statement, for surely Eddy's readers had seen friends and relatives at close hand, coughing up blood and wasted by fever. At the same time, we know that early Americans experienced the "defining force of pain" in their lives in ways that we may not be able to appreciate.[48] So, in the context of the 1850s, death by consumption may not have been the most painful of diseases. Eddy went on to celebrate the fact that consumption "seldom dethrones the reason."[49] The point was critical for "the possession of intellect is essential to the service of God." If the narratives composed by many consumptives themselves offer clues as to the veracity of this statement, we might give Eddy credit here. For such narratives of illness are often both cogent and moving.[50] It is Eddy's final "advantage" of consumption that is more likely to raise an eyebrow for us: "Consumption ends in Death."[51] From his perspective, death by consumption left no room to deceive the sufferer; it drove home the point that all must die. The certainty of the consumptive death, for Eddy, made authentic conversions more likely because the invalid could be sure of the fate that lay ahead. Armed with a Christian heart and a rational mind, the consumptive could face death and prepare for eternal life.

In some sense, the antebellum American embrace of death may appear Janus-faced and, perhaps, woefully inconsistent. On the one hand, we have grimly naturalistic accounts of disease and death, often offered up in accounts of epidemics. As we have glimpsed, descriptions of rotting corpses and exploding coffins are the stock in trade of such accounts.[52] Moreover, as scholars have made clear, the early nineteenth century witnessed an increasing medical interest in the living body and in the cadaver.[53] Anatomical study and the dissection of corpses provoked controversy and may also have served to sharpen emerging distinctions of class in America. Side-by-side with these scientific efforts to grapple with death stood the currents of evangelical religion. We thus have men like Daniel Eddy obscuring the workings of death on the body in order to validate the significance of the soul. And we might add to this mix of cultural forces the Greek revival with its notions of heroism, and the exaltation of youthful deaths evident in the literary trends of Romanticism. Hence Americans drew on many traditions and languages and concepts as they faced death. Just as death came to Americans in many different guises, so too did Americans deploy many different cultural resources as they prepared to die. So what may appear on the surface to be emblems of cultural confusion emerge instead as multiple sources of strength that individuals could use to confront the prospect of dying. Ironically, Americans were so well armed with models of "good deaths" that death itself was made to seem instructive, redemptive, and even glorious.

On the eve of the Civil War, Americans had settled on the essential components of what they considered the "Good Death." According to historian Drew Gilpin Faust, to die well was to die in the fullness of age in the arms of family and friends.[54] Nestled at home, the dying person could confront the transcendent importance of death and utter last words that would reveal not only the disposition of their soul but also serve as a spiritual lesson to those who attended the death. The corpse would then be cared for by relatives and buried with respect. North and South, according to Faust, these fundamental assumptions about the "Good Death" abided. So powerful were these assumptions that Civil War soldiers and their families sought to keep them alive in the midst of a conflict that challenged them in unprecedented ways: Men died in vast numbers away from home, and their corpses were treated as little more than "sticks of wood."[55] I would suggest, however, that narratives of the "Good Death" in antebellum America were even more capacious than they appear in Faust's treatment. Indeed, Americans celebrated the deaths of the old, the young, and those cut down in their primes. They also made room in their narratives for those who died away from home—including Mexican War veterans. They celebrated particularly political martyrs who died in the service of a higher cause. Above all, Americans celebrated a disposition of resignation and acceptance in the face of death.[56]

In the twin deaths of John Adams and Thomas Jefferson, antebellum Americans learned well how the titans of the Revolutionary era met their end. Sandwiched between the commemoration of the mythic deaths of George Washington and Abraham Lincoln, no two public figures received greater attention than did Adams and Jefferson when they both departed on July 4, 1826, on the fiftieth anniversary of American independence. Not surprisingly, the virtually simultaneous passing of these two political leaders sparked an avalanche of eulogies and public reflection. As Andrew Burstein has observed, "eulogies of dead leaders helped citizens, at vulnerable moments, come to terms with uncertainties they perceived in their world."[57] But they did something more. The deathbed scenes described in the Adams–Jefferson eulogies also provided Americans with scripts for how to confront, and embrace, death itself.

Perhaps the most common observation made by eulogists following the deaths of John Adams and Thomas Jefferson was that the hand of Providence could be detected in the passing of these two great men on the anniversary of American independence.[58] "Stupid must be the mortal who does not see in the death of Jefferson and Adams, the hand of Being, who controls the destinies of men," announced Sheldon Smith from Buffalo, New York.[59] "As their lives were the gifts of Providence, who is not willing to recognize in their happy termination," asked Daniel

Webster, "as well as their long continuance, proofs that our country, and its benefactors, are objects of His care?"[60] Speaking to the House of Representatives, Attorney General William Wirt asserted that "the hand of Heaven was kindly manifested even in the place of birth assigned to our departed fathers. Their lots were cast in two distant States, forming links in same chain of extended colonies."[61] For Wirt, the happy combination of leaders from Virginia and Massachusetts was clearly a portent of divine intervention. Samuel Smith, speaking in Baltimore, Maryland, went even beyond Wirt in outlining the uncanny parallels in the political carriers of the two men—both were ministers to France, both returned to America, both had served the country as vice-president and president. "And may we not believe that an All-seeing Providence, as a mark of approbation of their well spent lives," he asked, "has been mercifully pleased to grant their last prayer" that they might live to see the day of independence one more time.[62] In the deaths of Adams and Jefferson, then, Americans could see the hand of God, favoring both the nation and his two faithful servants. The moment of death thus revealed the workings of Providence on the nation as well as the spiritual disposition of the dying one.

Eulogists framed the deaths of Adams and Jefferson in ways that drew in equal parts on Christian and classical traditions. William Staughton and Stephen Rowan both took as their funeral texts 2 Samuel 1:23, likening Adams and Jefferson to the Old Testament figures of Saul and Jonathan: "Lovely and pleasant were they in their lives—in their death they were not divided; they were swifter than eagles, they were stronger than lions."[63] At the same time, speakers drew on the language of classicism to praise the two men. Both Rowan and Samuel Knapp yearned for an "American Homer" to step forth for this sort of august occasion, a poet who could do justice to epic leaders.[64] The goal of liberty for which the two men fought like brothers was celebrated by Wirt in unequivocal terms: "What were the selfish and petty strides of Alexander, to conquer a little section of the savage world, compared with this generous, this magnificent advance towards the emancipation of the entire world!"[65] Samuel Smith dared to say even more. Commenting again on the concurrent deaths of the two men, he said that "had such a coincidence occurred in the days of ancient Greece, to two of their great men, they would have been placed among the lesser deities."⁶⁶ Staughton argued that "to recommend the virtues, and purpose the examples, of the illustrious dead, was the constant practice of the ancient Egyptians, of the Greeks, and of the Romans. The primitive fathers of the Christian Church adopted the measure, and it appears, at any early period, to have been in use among pious Jews."⁶⁷ Adumbrating the rhetoric of the rural cemetery movement (explored in more detail in chapter 3), eulogists of Adams and Jefferson placed themselves in traditions of death that knit together the classical and Christian worlds.

Eulogists also accompanied their audiences to the deathbeds of the two leaders. But they made little attempt to harmonize with each other regarding what actually happened there. Speakers took considerable license in relating their deathbed stories, generating narratives that sometimes varied greatly or emphasized different features of the two deaths. Even the all important "last words" of Adams and Jefferson differed in these accounts. Such factual discrepancies did not seem to dampen the enthusiasm of listeners and readers—for what they seemed to be after in these narratives was not unvarnished historical truth but some measure of meaning. The various deathbeds offered up in the Adams–Jefferson eulogies speak to the rich meanings with which antebellum Americans endowed the deathbed.

Let us glimpse first "the venerable sage of Monticello." Speaking in Salem, Massachusetts, William Emmons provided a tidy and compact version of Jefferson's death. Noting that Jefferson had wanted to witness the coming of the "Nation's Jubilee, and when he heard the rejoicing of the people, in the language of the Prophet he exclaimed, 'Now, O Lord, let they Servant depart in peace.' And bowed his head and died."⁶⁸ In capturing Jefferson's spirit of pure resignation and his prayerful posture, Emmons secured the core of the Jeffersonian deathbed. He also gave the Jeffersonian deathbed more of an evangelical twist than the "venerable sage" might have appreciated. William F. Thornton's address added the important ingredient of Jefferson's expression of concern for his only surviving daughter. Speaking from Jefferson's native Virginia, Thornton's deathbed reveals Jefferson saying, "I have done for mankind all that I could; I now resign my soul, without fear, to my God—and my daughter to the country."⁶⁹ Slaves entered some accounts of Jefferson's end. Staughton explained that Jefferson had addressed some parting words to his "servants," speaking to them "in the tone of a father,"—the irony of this last phrase evidently escaping the speaker.[70] Wirt took a different approach. In his rendering of the deathbed, Jefferson's mind drifted back to scenes of the Revolution. Like a veteran haunted by scenes of battle, "he talked in broken sentences, of the Committees of Safety, and the rest of that great machinery, which he imagined to still be in action." Still, Wirt said, Jefferson had his wits about him most of the time—"his reason was almost constantly upon her throne."[71] At the moment of death, Wirt reported, Jefferson was cogent enough to muster up Latin: "'Nunc Domine dimittas.' Now, Lord, let they servant depart in peace! And the prayer of the patriot was heard and answered."[72] John A. Shaw, a eulogist speaking in Bridge-water, Massachusetts, seemed more interested in Jefferson's last writings than in his last words. He reported in some detail on Jefferson's response to an invitation from citizens in Washington, D.C., that he appear there on July 4 to celebrate American independence. Quoting extensively from Jefferson's elegant reply, Shaw reported that "it is one of the last paragraphs he ever penned, but it shows the vigor of his mind at the last hour, and is replete with such sentiments as republicans should ever cherish."[73] Daniel Webster eschewed the question of last words and last writings altogether by offering up this account of Jefferson's last moments: "Could it be so—might it please God—he would desire—once more—to see the sun—once more to look abroad on the scene around him, on that great day of liberty. Heaven in its mercy fulfilled his prayer. He saw that sun—he enjoyed its sacred light—he thanked God for his mercy, and bowed his aged head to the grave."[74] Webster thus gave his audience a deathbed script with real dramatic action and hints of what Jefferson's interior state might have been.

There seemed to be more concord among eulogists on what transpired on the John Adams deathbed. Like Jefferson, "the Patriarch of Quincy" clung to life in hopes of seeing another dawn of Independence Day. Most agreed that at some point Adams had roused himself to exclaim "Independence forever!" before he slipped away. But there were certain other elaborations. William Emmons explained that when Adams had been informed that he had last to the 4th of July, he announced, "It is a great, a good day."[75] Wirt suggested that Adams spoke more after he announced "Independence forever" adding that Adams had exclaimed, "'O save my country—Heaven! He said—and died!"[76] Alfred Johnson Jr. noted (as have modern commentators) that Adams had said "Thomas Jefferson survives" shortly before his final words.[77] John A. Shaw, as he did with Jefferson, recorded the last written words of John Adams—again, coming in response to a request to attend the independence festivities in Quincy, Massachusetts. But unlike Jefferson, Adams had written a warning to his fellow citizens into his final reply. Assessing the anniversary of American independence, Adams noted that it would be "destined in future history to form the brightest or blackest page, according to the use or abuse of those political institutions by which they shall, in time to come, be shaped by the human mind."[78] Writing from his father's bedside, John Quincy Adams added a note in his diary that other eulogists had not captured—his father's last words had been addressed to his granddaughter Susanna, "Help me, child! Help me!"[79] Eulogists for the crusty Adams let this little snippet of human frailty pass without comment.

Almost to a man, the eulogists praised the spirit of resignation and acceptance with which the great leaders accepted death. Henry Potter, speaking from Fayetteville, North Carolina, put these words in Jefferson's mouth shortly before his last day: "Acquiescence (he had said ten days previous to his death) is a duty, under circumstances not placed among those we are permitted to control."[80] In a broader sense, this spirit of resignation validated at an exalted level the prosaic antebellum conviction that death comes to us all. As eulogist Caleb Cushing explained in Newburyport, Massachusetts, "Death is above, below, around us. The very air we inhale may be loaded with its fatal influences." Death could, he said, "cut short the frail thread of life, and blast its fair prospects with a breath."[81] Stephen Rowan agreed. "There are passages to the grave," he said, "from every age and condition of life—from every spot of ground—and every moment in time."[82] Among many virtues and accomplishments, what made John Adams and Thomas Jefferson such able ambassadors for the "Good Death" was the fact that they embraced it.

The flurry of memorials, speeches, commemorations, and sermons simultaneously defeated the reality of death by ensuring that the deeds of the two great patriots would live beyond the grave. "They are gone to the grave," admitted Felix Grundy in Nashville, Tennessee, "yet shall they live, and although their bodies perish, still in the recollection of their country their deeds will survive."[83] Sheldon Smith agreed that the patriots had achieved a measure of immortality. "Deathless be the names of Jefferson and Adams," he exclaimed.[84] There was a bittersweet enjoyment to death, then, evident in the savoring of the fame that would follow close on its heels. Speaking of the deaths of the Revolutionary patriarchs, Peleg Sprague of Hallowell, Maine, conceded that "we contemplate their departure without anything of the bitterness of despair, and with little even of the poignancy of grief, with a soothing sadness and a melancholy pleasure."[85] Melancholy pleasure? Indeed. Within five years of the death of Adams and Jefferson, Massachusetts jurist Joseph Story would offer an oration dedicating the new and celebrated rural cemetery at Mount Auburn. In his 1831 dedicatory address, something of a manifesto for the entire rural cemetery movement, Story insisted that "the mourner will revisit these shades with a secret, though melancholy pleasure."[86] Mourning the past accomplishments of the dead could well be a source of civic strength as well as personal edification and even pleasure. To savor the benefits of mourning emerged as an important component in the antebellum culture of death.

The posture of acceptance evident in the deaths of Thomas Jefferson and John Adams suffused the deathbed scene of another antebellum patriarch—James Forten Sr. of Philadelphia. At the time of his death in 1842, no one had labored more assiduously or more wisely for Philadelphia's free African-American community. Starting as a teenage seaman during the American Revolution, Forten worked his way to the heart of a vibrant African community that included the likes of Richard Allen and Absalom Jones. He insisted that the fruits of equality ripened by the war for independence belonged to all Americans. In his famous 1813 work, *Letters from a Man of Color on a Late Bill Before the Senate of Pennsylvania*, Forten explicitly invoked the words of the "sage of Monticello." From Forten's perspective, the central idea in the Declaration of Independence, that God had created all men equal, was meant to be applied universally. "This idea," he argued, "embraces the Indian and the European, the Savage and the Saint, the Peruvian and the Laplander, the white Man and the African."[87] Forten's work as a leader for Philadelphia's African American community might be seen as an effort to instantiate more fully the promise inherent in the work of Jefferson and Adams.

Speaking before an assembly of young men of the Second Presbyterian Church of Colour, Rev. H. S. Glocester held up Forten's life as a model for imitation.[88] Taking as the text for his funeral sermon a passage from 1 Kings 2:2, Glocester developed in some detail the virtues held in common by both King Solomon and James Forten. Like Solomon, Glocester said, Forten had embodied intelligence, punctuality upon his duty, energy, and perseverance. Just as Jefferson and Adams' eulogists compared these two patriots to Jonathan and Saul, Glocester drew Forten as a modern day Solomon—a judicious and prized leader for his people. After a life of service dedicated to the community, Glocester observed that Forten "had at last, by the wise providence of God, been removed from the active and painful scenes of this mortal state; but his memorial shall remain with us; his name will not easily or soon be forgotten."[89] In Glocester's hands, the name of Forten and his deeds would stand in immortality.

As he brought his oration to a conclusion, Glocester drew his listeners near Forten's deathbed. Here he reported a scene blending great dignity with the sentimental tears of bitter loss. Sensing that his end was near, Forten gathered his friends and family to impart some last words of guidance. "He was always composed," Glocester related, "and would, most affectionately, press home upon them their everlasting concern, telling them that here they had no abiding place, and begged them to attend, in the midst of business, to the one needful thing." With his eyes fixed upon the world to come, Forten brought his friends close. While they "were bathed with tears, he in the sweetest tones said to them, 'weep not, all is well with me,' and commenced to give them his charge." Imparting advice, counsel, and encouragement to all, Forten's last words looked not to freedom in this world, but to liberation in the next. According to Glocester, before Forten "sunk quietly into the arms of death without a struggle, he announced, 'For I know that my Redeemer liveth, and that he shall stand at the later day upon the earth. And though, after my skin, worms destroy this body, yet in my flesh shall

I see God.'"[90] In Glocester's telling, Forten met death in the comfort of his family and friends and with the sure hope of bodily resurrection. As had some of the Jefferson–Adams eulogists, Glocester used the occasion of the death of a great man to remind his audience of a larger truth: All men must die. "The iron scythe of death is in motion," he reminded the young men in his audience, "and men are the grass which fall beneath its sweep. Who first, in this assembly to night, will fall beneath it, God only knows."[91] Forten's death might be seen as exemplary, for Glocester, because the aging patriarch had accepted the fundamental dictate that all men are mortal. His composure, his faith, his last words, his acceptance, his hope in the life everlasting—these were the elements in Forten's death that Glocester held up before the eyes of his young audience.

In the years immediately following Forten's death, many young American men came face to face with Glocester's vision of the "iron scythe of death." In 1846, it came in the form of the Mexican War. Although in terms of sheer battle deaths, the Mexican War was not an especially costly affair for Americans, it cast in sharp form the trials resulting from a death suffered far from home. How could the dying person organize his last moments, speak last words to his family, or be buried close at hand? The death of Henry Clay Jr. one of the most famous casualties of the Mexican War, affords us an opportunity to reflect on such questions. The younger Clay's death narrative is encapsulated to a large degree in the letters and correspondence of his even more famous father, Henry Clay, the masterful Whig politician. And there are other sources as well. Like a handful of other prominent Mexican War casualties, Henry Clay Jr.'s death was commemorated in a lithograph—in this case, one published by Joseph Ward of Boston, Massachusetts, in 1847. Here, the young and wounded Clay is pictured in a heroic pose that closely resembles that of General James Wolfe in Benjamin West's famous portrait of *The Death of General James Wolfe* (1770). Taken together, these sources reveal how such traumatizing battle deaths—incurred far from home—might yet be interpreted in ennobling and redemptive ways.

On March 1, 1847, American commander General Zachary Taylor wrote to Henry Clay with the news of the death of his son. Taylor knew well that Clay may already have heard of his son's death and sought to mollify what he called Clay's "paternal sorrow." He assured the senior

Fig. 2. Joseph Ward, *Death of Lieut. Col. Henry Clay, Jr., of the Second Kentucky Volunteers. At the Battle of Buena Vista, Feb. 23, 1847.* Courtesy of the American Antiquarian Society, Worcester, Mass.

Clay that his son had become part of Taylor's "military family" and that his actions had been "manly and honorable in every impulse, with no feeling but for the honor of the service and of the country."[92] Along with another Kentucky officer, Clay had helped to lead a counterattack against the Mexican forces and had been killed in the charge. "Gallantly did the sons of Kentucky," wrote Taylor, "in the thickest of the strife, uphold the honor of the State and of the country. A grateful people will do justice to the memory of those who fell on that eventful day."[93] As more news trickled in of the fighting, the younger Clay's heroism became even more evident. Cary H. Fry, an officer of the Second Kentucky Regiment who survived the assault, wrote that Clay Jr. "was every inch a soldier, and had he lived, would have returned home, worthy of the praise and

Gratitude of the whole Nation." With his letter, Fry enclosed "a lock of his hair, which was taken from his head as soon as he was brought into the Camp." He related, as well, details involving Clay's possessions and informed the father that his son "was buried near Saltillo"—but hoped that they could bring the corpse home for "the melancholy satisfaction" of a proper burial.[94] Such condolences from the front were clearly designed to put the senior Clay at ease with tales of his son's courage and with clear knowledge of what had happened to his body.

It didn't work. Word of his son's death initially unhinged the father. In response to letters of condolence, Clay admitted his devastation. "I was greatly attached to him," he wrote to friend William N. Mercer, "and he had high qualities, well known to me, entitling him to my warmest affections." What had been the purpose of his son's death, he wondered. "Oh God!" he exclaimed to Mercer, "perhaps the object is to detach us altogether from this world, as possessing nothing on which to fasten our feelings and affections, and to point to, and prepare us for, another and a better world."[95] The death of his son was an especially bitter pill for Clay to swallow because, like many in the Whig Party, he considered the Mexican War a misguided adventure undertaken to sate the appetite of southern slaveholders for more land. Staggering in his grief, Clay admitted that "the consolation would be greater, if I did not believe that this Mexican War was unnecessary and of an aggressive character. My poor son did not however stop to enquire into the causes of the War. It was sufficient for him that it existed in fact."[96] Here is a portrait of a father, wrestling with headstrong patriotism of his boy.

In response to a flood of condolence letters, Henry Clay came to admit that his son desired to die in combat. "I know he preferred to meet death on the field of battle," he wrote to John M. Clayton, "in the service of his Country."[97] To Mary S. Bayard he noted that "it is indeed some consolation to me to know that he himself preferred, as I would have chosen, that, if I were to be deprived of so great a blessing as he ever was to me, he should expire on the field of battle, in the service of his Country."[98] To William Mercer he wrote in almost identical phrasing: "It is indeed some consolation to me to know, that he himself preferred, if death must come, that his life should be terminated on the field of battle in the service of his Country."[99] It may be tempting to ascribe Henry Clay's evolving position on his son's death to rationalization; that is, the only way for him to embrace so crippling a loss would be for him to enfold it in the flag of volition. His son died because the boy had desired it. And, furthermore, Clay could tell himself, the death had been suffered in service to his nation, regardless of the rectitude of the particulars of the conflict involved. More certain, however, is the reality that Henry Clay and his family did not face their son's death alone. For they, too, were wrapped in a community that offered them love, support, and the comforting assurance that their son had died a heroic death in the service of his country.

From many quarters came public validation of their son's death. On April 10, 1847, the "People of Louisville" announced a series of public resolutions voicing their appreciation for those killed at the Battle of Buena Vista, including, especially the younger Clay: "To the City of his adoption he was endeared in life by many virtues, and the sad story of his unyielding valor, & chivalric death, will long be remembered & treasured by her sons."[100] From Philadelphia, Pennsylvania, came word that citizens admired the younger Clay's "noble Gallantry which characterized his conduct on the Field of Battle."[101] Maryland Whigs, too, at their convention of July 1847, adopted a resolution expressing sympathy to the senior Clay and his family.[102] Henry Clay could, and eventually did, take solace in the fact that his son had died a patriot's death. As he put it, expressions of condolence and respect such as these helped him bear his loss "with becoming resignation."[103]

The production of the Joseph Ward lithograph sealed Henry Clay Jr.'s image as an authentic hero. Framed by his fellow soldiers, he lies on the ground in the pose of General James Wolfe—a posture that, given the popularity of Benjamin West's work in America, would have been clear to many observers. Clay has been wounded in the leg and the bullet hole is neatly rendered in a manner common to other lithographs of fallen Mexican War figures. Clay's horse, too, is down and displays a slightly larger wound. That Clay was eventually killed by the stab of a bayonet (as noted in the Clay correspondence) is denied in this version of his death.[104] Here, in fact, he is not dead but caught in the act of speech. He is handing a pistol to one of his comrades uttering what we might take to be his last words: "Leave me and take care of yourselves," he says. "Give these Pistols to my Father, and tell him I have done all I can with them, and return them to him." Published condolence letters and letters from Clay's comrades immediately following his death do not say anything about last words or about a brace of pistols, but they clearly became important emblems in the narrative of his death. On July 23, 1847, the father acknowledged to Thomas B. Stevenson that he had received from one Captain Cutter (a member of the Second Kentucky Regiment) "a brace of pistols" that had belonged to his son.[105] So the pistols—along with locks of hair, memorial jewelry, and eventually a splendid coffin for burial at home—became symbols connecting the dead hero to his home.[106] They thus connected father and son after death. As instruments of war and of honor, the pistols served to verify the heroic nature of the young man's death.

Heroic death in antebellum America could also be embodied by those suffering with consumption as well as those cut down in war. While these deaths did not occur on the field of battle, they nevertheless demonstrated the spirit of submission that Henry Clay Jr. had instantiated. Consider, for example, the death narrative of Mrs. Susan Huntington of Boston, Massachusetts. As presented in her *Memoirs* (which are really a series of letters and writings edited and arranged by the Christian writer James Montgomery), Huntington sought after Christian peace as her death approached.[107] As she sank deeper into her illness at her country home, Huntington asked her physician if there were any hope remaining. "His answer was in the negative." Montgomery wrote, "She received it, with some feeling, but with submission and thanked him for his kindness in being so explicit." She returned at once to Boston "to set her house in order, in preparation for death."[108] According to Montgomery, Huntington had been troubled by the notion that she "might never have been truly humbled for sin" and that her piety had been shallow and perhaps an illusion.[109] Facing her doubts, however, she came to a greater sense of the certainty of her salvation and of the prospects of heaven. About a month before her death, she acknowledged that "I have had no rapturous views of the heaven to which I hope I am going, no longings to depart. But I have generally been enabled to feel a calm submission, and to realize the fullness and preciousness of the Saviour. I desire to feel perfect resignation to the will of God, because it is his will."[110] Watching at her deathbed, her minister reported that Huntington maintained her posture of faith until the end—cogent, intelligent, and comforted by the prospect of salvation. The narrative of Susan Huntington emerges as a model for how Christians, even those struggling with doubts, might overcome their fears and face death with an authentic spirit of acceptance.

Charles T. Torrey, abolitionist and consumptive, manifested another variation on the theme of deathbed victory. Born in Scituate, Massachusetts, in 1813, Torrey had been educated at Yale and Andover Theological Seminary before becoming a minister and an abolitionist lecturer. In June 1844, Maryland authorities arrested Torrey for aiding fugitive slaves. He was convicted to a term of six years in prison and knew well that his illness would prevent him from living again as a free man. But an account of Torrey's last days in prison reveals that he appears to have relished the idea of dying as a "martyr" for the abolitionist cause. "Those who had the privilege of conversing with him," wrote Rev. William W. Patton, "testify that his soul was perfectly prepared to die, and even looked forward to death with rejoicing."[111] According to other witnesses, Torrey did not waver in his embrace of death. As he passed from this world into the next, "where the wicked cease from troubling the weary are at rest, where prisoners rest together and they hear not the voice of the oppressor," Torrey voiced his deepest political convictions.[112] According to Patton's account of his deathbed, Torrey announced that "it is better to die in prison with the peace of God in our breasts than to live in freedom with a polluted conscience."[113] If the death of Susan Huntington revealed a triumph of faith over doubt, the death of Charles T. Torrey revealed a triumph for freedom over slavery. Each had died with their eyes fixed on a transcendent prize.

Models of acceptance and conviction in confronting death could also be found in abundance in the antebellum South. Perhaps no southern death attracted more attention in the decades before the Civil War than did John C. Calhoun's on March 31, 1850. Capping off more than three decades of public service, Calhoun died in Washington, D.C., during some of the most contentious political debates in American history. Given his status as one of the nation's most brilliant political minds and as a staunch spokesman for the political interests of the South, it is not surprising that Calhoun became a celebrity in death. In the weeks following his death, Calhoun inspired artist Clark Mills to produce a famous death mask. "Numerous busts and paintings were commissioned," write Clyde N. Wilson and Shirley Bright Cook, "likenesses were for sale in all the bookshops of Charleston and elsewhere. During the course of 1850 a lifesize wax image, a painting with accompanying musical composition, a 'panorama' and a 'diorama' featuring Calhoun were exhibited."[114] Ironically, it was in death that John C. Calhoun may have at last fallen victim to the kind of hustling, commercial ethos that he had spent much of his life trying to hold in check. Still, given his posthumous popularity, we might safely assume that the details of his demise would have been of great interest across the South.

Joseph A. Scoville offered up the bedrock account of John C. Calhoun's deathbed scene in "The Last Moments of Mr. Calhoun's Life" in a letter composed on the day of the death itself. Scoville's account accents a man in full possession of his intellectual faculties who died without pain. Shortly before his death, Calhoun had asked for a little wine, but this had failed to rally him. "He then breathed quietly," Scoville recalled, "except a slight rattle in his throat, his eyes retaining their brightness, and his countenance its natural expression, until the last breath (which was drawn with deep inspiration,) when his eyes suddenly became dim. They were immediately closed by Mr. Venable. His countenance was that of one who had fallen quietly asleep. He was conscious to the last moment." Scoville's account records the presence of John C. Calhoun Jr. and a host of other Southern political leaders in the death room—James L. Orr and Daniel Wallace among them. No women appear. This masculine environment for Calhoun's death and its locus outside the immediate domestic circle evoke the kinds of deathbeds Southern men would soon experience in wartime. Indeed, Scoville deliberately framed his narrative of Calhoun's death within a national political context. He noted that Calhoun's mind had moved to the recent congressional debates and that he "had expressed his confidence that there would soon be but one sentiment—that the Southern people would unite as one against Northern aggression. His confidence in the Southern people was unwavering to the last."[115] Like Patton's account of Charles T. Torrey's death, Scoville used the occasion of John C. Calhoun's death to validate a dying man's political testament.

Accounts of John C. Calhoun's last moments do not smack of the kind of evangelical Christianity that animates many antebellum narratives of death. Neither Joseph Scoville nor John C. Calhoun Jr. mention last prayers, glimpses of heavenly bliss, or talk of salvation and the disposition of the soul. This is not to say that Calhoun lacked religious conviction. His wife, Floride, on hearing of the death of her husband wrote immediately to her daughter Anna (who was in Brussels) with the advice to "begin from this hour, to give your children religious instruction. Tell them how calmly and resigned, their Grandfather died." She went on to insist that her husband had thought more deeply about matters of faith than had many "public professors" of religious sentiment.[116] So faith may have been an element in the Calhoun death narrative, but it was not one highlighted by key witnesses to the event. Instead, John C. Calhoun's son brought to bear another potent tradition available to antebellum Americans as they confronted death: classicism. He wrote that his father had "met death with calm dignity; silent because he had no past regrets to recount, and thoughtful and dignified because he was a Philosopher, who had no fear of the king of terrors."[117] By invoking the figure of the philosopher, the son's account resonates with Plato's account of the death of Socrates in *The Apology*. Here Socrates argues that the true philosopher has no reason to fear death because we either pass on into oblivion and eternal sleep or we might encounter the shades of those who have already died, opening up endless opportunities for edifying conversation. Either way, death holds nothing for the wise man to fear. Like Scoville's account, John C. Calhoun Jr.'s account of his father's death stressed the potency of his mind rather than the purity of his soul.

Anna Maria Calhoun Clemson, John C. Calhoun's daughter, also deployed classical language in speaking of her father's death. Shortly after hearing from her brother Patrick regarding details of the death, Anna wrote back to share her thoughts. "Our noble father," she confided, "can never be restored to us. We shall never look upon his like again. In all history I find no man who combined so much talent, heart, philosophy, & simplicity. Truly do you say that his death is one of the noblest on record." She went on to validate another component of the classical variation on the notion of the "Good Death"—the glorious nature of a death suffered in the full stride of life rather than one suffered in the

throes of compromising infirmity. She found in the soundness of her
father's mind and his strong reputation a kind of beauty: "So glorious is
the spectacle of such a man," she wrote, "in the full splendour of his intellect, & at such a critical period, sinking in the grave, like the setting sun
in unclouded splendour, amidst the tears of a nation. His life & death
are bright and encouraging examples to every one." She regretted that
she had not had the "sad pleasure" of mourning for her father at home,
but she looked forward to the prospect in the weeks ahead.[118]

The narratives of some antebellum Americans displayed not merely
philosophical resignation in the face of death, but an absolute yearning
for it. As presented in a funeral sermon by Rev. Moses D. Hoge of Richmond, Virginia's Second Presbyterian Church, Mrs. Caroline E. Morris
was one such seeker. A wife and mother of four young children, Morris
might not seem the archetypal figure wanting release from the earthly
world. Yet Hoge's sermon cast her in this role. "Death had literally no
terrors, no glooms, for her," he wrote, "There was no shrinking back
from his approach."[119] From his perspective, Morris's "dying chamber
presented a beautiful and impressive illustration of a heavenly-descended
hope." Recording dialogue from the deathbed, Hoge noted that Morris
had announced, "On my own account I have no desire to live, and I can
resign all that is dear to me on earth into the hands of God."[120] Hoge
went on in his oration to hold up Caroline Morris's unalloyed embrace
of death as a model for his congregation to emulate.

It was her faith alone and "no cold stoicism, no disgust with a life
whose happiness was exhausted, which caused her to feel that it was better to depart and be with Christ. Oh! No."[121] Perhaps aware of the dangers of the portrait he was drawing, Hoge did not want his listeners to
hold cheap the things of this world, but only to relish more highly the life
of the world to come. God's grace, he said, had "elevated her above all
fears of death and made the parting hour one of serenity and peace."[122]
Hoge invited his congregation to lives of faith and holiness that would
cause them to face death as Caroline Morris had—not as something to
be feared, but "as a welcome friend."[123]

James Jackson, a young African American boy in Boston, appears to
have greeted death in exactly such warm terms. A memoir published in
1835, composed by his teacher Miss Susan Paul, shows the zeal with which

a pious child might confront his mortality. The narrative of Jackson's death stretches across almost twenty pages of this brief memoir, and his exemplary deathbed behavior was likely the reason for its publication. If antebellum Americans valued submission in the face of death, then it would be difficult to imagine a more prized death than that accomplished by a boy not quite seven years of age. Upon hearing of the serious nature of his illness, Jackson was heard to protest the news that he might well recover: "No; I do not want to get well, I would rather die; for then I shall go and be with God, and the blessed Saviour."[124] The narrative drew repeated comparisons between the hardships and evils of this world and the bliss that would await believers in the next. "O, I want to go away from this wicked world," Jackson exclaims, "and live always with the blessed Saviour in heaven. There is nothing wicked there."[125] And again: "O, how glorious it will be, to be a saint in heaven—to be holy, and not to be with the wicked people."[126] In meeting his death, Jackson showed no fear and retained his mental agility until the very end. As Paul describes Jackson's last moments on earth, we see him singing a hymn with those gathered around his deathbed. The moment of his death is presented in such a way as to show how closely linked were this life and the life everlasting: "James still looked as if his heart was full of joy, but his eyes began to grow dim, his hands were cold, and in a few moments all was calm."[127]

It strains modern credulity to think of a child dying with such composure, faith, and sheer earnestness. And we may offer analysis that serves to explain away the thirst for death evident in the story. The narrative closes with an appeal to readers to consider young James's death so that "you will not injure any person who is poor, or in distress, or colored."[128] There is a need in this narrative to present James Jackson as the most pious and accepting of all sufferers, revealing that a young African American boy might best encapsulate the Christian patience of his day. Is there here an assertion that a young African American boy is the prime exemplar of Christian forbearance? The repeated talk of the wickedness of the present world may also have been a veiled reference to the deteriorating state of race relations in the antebellum North and to the sheer level of violence perpetrated against African Americans. The death narrative may have served, then, as a subterranean form of social protest. So awful are conditions for African Americans on earth, it suggests, that the life of heaven is even more appealing. We might question the veracity of the narrative on other grounds, too. The death of pious innocents was becoming a trope in early American literature—indeed, Harriet Beecher Stowe could have drawn on this kind of narrative when she wrote the famous deathbed scene of Little Eva in *Uncle Tom's Cabin* nearly twenty years later. So, perhaps, Paul exaggerated and embellished the truth in the narrative in the interests of literary convention.

These observations may help us to contextualize the death narrative of James Jackson, but they do not diminish the force of its embrace of death. When we read this story in the light of other antebellum narratives—from those of Thomas Jefferson and John Adams to Susan Huntington and Caroline Morris—its tale of submission and resignation is entirely congruent with these sources. What is striking and surprising here is the common element of acceptance across the divides of race, region, age, and gender. That the narratives of Caroline Morris, a Presbyterian from Richmond, Virginia, and James Jackson, a young African American from Boston, Massachusetts, should share so much invites us to think of the pervasiveness and power of these narratives across antebellum America. That Charles T. Torrey and John C. Calhoun should be praised for their firmness of mind and their dedication to a higher cause as they faced eternity should tell us something about the didactic nature of the deathbed, both north and south. Of course these narratives of death are not identical. The classical context evoked in the Calhoun evidence is quite different from the evangelical impulse evident in the accounts of Caroline Morris and James Jackson. But the thread of acceptance, submission, and the embrace of death unites these diverse accounts in myriad ways. That this theme could find so many forms of expression—from the classical to the Christian—helps to explain its appeal. By the time secession emerged as a political fact, Americans had been well schooled in the necessity of resigning themselves to the reality of death.

Standing on the precipice of the Civil War, no one in America accepted death's grip more willingly than did the abolitionist John Brown. Such an attitude literally bursts forth from his writings and actions. In 1858, according to historian Bertram Wyatt-Brown, Brown had written to an abolitionist colleague that "I have felt for a number of years, in earlier life, a steady, strong desire to die."[129] In 1859, the suicidal raid at Harper's Ferry, Virginia, showed that Brown was not just talking. His trial and eventual execution gave expression to the very values of acceptance and resignation glimpsed in the narratives of death considered in this chapter. As polarizing as Brown was as a political figure in the sectional conflict, his behavior in the face of death appealed even to some Southerners. Governor Henry Wise of Virginia admired his resolve: "He is a bundle of the best nerves I ever saw," Wise admitted in 1859, "cut and thrust, and bleeding and in bonds."[130] In a letter to his wife sent December 2, 1859, Thomas J. Jackson, the future "Stonewall," praised Brown's "unflinching firmness" in the face of death. "I was much impressed with the thought that before me stood a man, in the full vigor of health, who must in a few minutes be in eternity," wrote Jackson, "I sent up a petition that he might be saved."[131] As if to return the favor, Jackson's Northern adversaries would praise the devout manner of his own death at the battle of Chancellorsville in May 1863.[132]

The massive national response to John Brown's raid, arrest, and execution showed that he had touched a raw nerve in antebellum America. In political terms, we can say that Brown's actions comprised the first act in what historian James McPherson has called "the Revolution of 1860."[133] It sparked the counterrevolutionary impulse among southern politicians to break away from the Union before it was in the grip of the dangerous and radical Republicans. But Brown's death also touched something deep in the culture of antebellum America. In his forthright acceptance of death—indeed, in his yearning for death—John Brown emerges not as a madman but as a synecdoche. Brown was a compelling figure, I would suggest, not because he may have been a manic depressive or a lunatic or even a civil rights advocate, but because he represented (albeit in exaggerated form) the antebellum embrace of death. John Brown's corpse itself had become an "emblem of mortality" in a wider cultural universe that acknowledged and submitted to the reality of death.[134]

❖❖❖

CHAPTER TWO

"The Heavenly Country"

Antebellum Americans could face death with resignation and even joy because they carried in their hearts and heads a comforting and compelling vision of eternal life. For them heaven was not an ethereal, dreamy state of the soul or a billowy universe of unspecified dimension. It was, instead, a material place, a land, a country in which individual bodies and souls would be perfected and the relations of family and friendship restored. Speaking before the Charleston Baptist Association at Orangeburg, South Carolina, in 1809, John M. Roberts voiced the tonic note in what many would come to see as a standard refrain: "the heavenly country is infinitely better than any earthly country."[1] Although he was not the originator of this new idea of heaven, Roberts summed up an essential idea that others would expand. In 1857, Sarah Gould compiled numerous writings on heaven in a book entitled *The Guardian Angels, or Friends in Heaven* published in Boston, Massachusetts. "We believe Paradise to be our fatherland; our parents and patriarchs; why should we not haste and fly to see our home and greet our parents?" she asked. In heaven, she insisted, the departed would find "the glorious choir of the Apostles" and the "innumerable company of the martyrs, crowned on account of their victories in the conflict of suffering." Here, too, would be "pure virgins," the "merciful," and the "blessed poor." "To these, dearly beloved children," she sang, "let us hasten with strong desire, and ardently wish to be with them, and with Christ."[2]

The most famous of all deathbed scenes in antebellum America, that of Little Eva in Harriet Beecher Stowe's 1852 novel *Uncle Tom's Cabin,* gave popular expression to the blessed quality of the passage to heaven. Surrounded by family and servants, Little Eva's death chamber itself gave a foretaste of the glorious world to come. "Over the head of the bed was an alabaster bracket," wrote Stowe, "on which a beautiful sculptured angel stood, with drooping wings, holding out a crown of myrtle leaves."[3] Eva speaks in loving ways as she departs and takes solace from the fact that she will see Uncle Tom and Mammy in heaven. Throughout the process of her death, Little Eva was "so placid and bright" that observers could hardly believe "that it was death that was approaching. The child felt no pain."[4] Anesthetized by her glimpse of heaven, Eva was not rendered insensible. Rather, she tried, in her last words, to offer a piece of what she saw to her family and friends. Just before her death "A bright, a glorious smile passed over her face, and she said, brokenly,— 'O love,—joy,—peace!' gave one sigh, and passed from death to life!"[5] Stowe thus placed before her readers the cardinal concept that death was not really death at all; that a more beautiful life awaited believers on the shores of a land whose faint and shimmering outlines could be detected even on this earth.

This chapter explores in more detail what antebellum Americans thought about heaven. As Colleen McDannell and Bernhard Lang describe, nineteenth-century Americans stood on the cusp of what they term "the emergence of a modern heaven."[6] According to them, it was the eighteenth-century Swedish scientist and theologian Emanuel Swedenborg who defined the contours of this new paradise. The modern heaven could be distinguished by four key features: (1) its proximity to earth; (2) its sheer materiality; (3) its insistence on progress and growth; and (4) its emphasis on the reconstituting of human communities, including both families and wider civic institutions. This was, in some sense, a "thoroughly anthropocentric view of heaven" that accented human experience rather than the contemplation of divine presence.[7] Americans came to see this new heavenly environment as compelling in at least three respects. First, they defined the landscape of heaven itself in ways that stressed both its natural beauty and the glorious life that all would live once they arrived. Second, they understood their existence beyond the grave in essentially material terms. Resurrected persons would live on not only in spirit but in the full possession of perfected bodies. Finally, they clung to the comforting notion that loved ones would clasp hands again in heaven. Because identifiable bodies would be preserved, the notion of "heavenly recognition" seemed almost self-evident to those who imagined life beyond death. Heaven thus emerged in the antebellum imagination as a place of dazzling and luminous appeal, inhabited by complete human beings who would live in harmonious accord with one another.[8]

Graphic depictions of heaven on everything from dedication pages to missionary certificates to commercial advertisements insisted that heaven was close at hand, just beyond the cover of clouds. An 1807 engraving from a book of poetry pictures a winged angel perched above the clouds "pouring down Heaven's liquid blessing" upon the earth (fig. 3). We cannot know exactly what the mysterious "liquid blessing" contained, but we can infer that the artist conceived that heaven and earth could be connected by a material substance. A membership certificate for the New Jersey Society for promoting the Abolition of Slavery reveals an abolitionist and a kneeling slave standing before a break in the clouds that sheds heavenly light on the Bible, opened to a passage from Isaiah (fig. 4). Another certificate from a Methodist Missionary Society in New York shows a frenzied apocalyptic scene that features an angel swooping down to earth, trumpet sounding and Bible in hand. The angel is welcomed with outstretched arms by a family of kneeling slaves who observe its approach (fig. 5). An advertisement from "John Ashton, Importer & Manufacturer of Musical instruments of every description" shows a heavenly tableau of characters who are overseen by an angel with a Greek temple standing in the background (fig. 6). Another early nineteenth century engraving shows a group of soldiers kneeling before an image of Napoleon, who is himself receiving swords from "Alexander & Caesar" while he ascends to the clouds (fig. 7). One has the impression that if antebellum Americans looked hard enough, they could glimpse the outlines of heaven floating above them.

Tisdale pinx.   *Leney sculp.*

Mercy's Angel
pouring down
Heaven's liquid blessing   *Echo 1, page 4.*

Fig. 3. Frontispiece, Richard Alsop, *The Echo, with other Poems* (New York: Printed at the Porcupine Press by Pasquin Petronius, 1807). Courtesy of the American Antiquarian Society, Worcester, Mass.

Fig. 4. Certificate for the members of the New-Jersey Society for the Abolition of Slavery, ca. 1810. Courtesy of the Library Company of Philadelphia.

Fig. 5. Nathaniel Currier, certificate for the Missionary Society of the Methodist Episcopal Church, ca. 1835. Courtesy of the Library Company of Philadelphia.

Fig. 6. Thomas Sparrow, advertisement for John Ashton, Importer and Manufacturer of Musical Instruments, ca. 1830. Courtesy of the Library Company of Philadelphia.

Fig. 7. *Alexandre & Cesar la recovient dans les cieux,* ca. 1821. Courtesy of the Library Company of Philadelphia.

Foretastes of heavenly life were indeed accessible to those who contin-ued to inhabit the earth. In a sermon entitled "the Kingdom of Heaven," Massachusetts Congregationalist minister William H. Furness argued that "the spirit of the heavenly world, the spirit of truth and God, is blowing around us like the wind, invisible, mysterious like air."[9] Like Little Eva, those on their deathbeds were held to possess special knowl-edge of the world that loomed ahead. "The expiring believer," wrote Augustus C. Thompson in his 1854 book *The Better Land; or The Believ-er's Journey and Future Home,* "does not see death: he sees the heavens opened, and Jesus Christ standing at the right hand of God."[10] Thomp-son argued that Christ was physically present at the moment of death, "stray beams of his lustre often fall on the dying believer before his soul leaves its tenement."[11] Some Americans claimed to have visited heaven by means of visions. One Missouri diarist, whom we know only as "Eliza-beth Princess of Light," wrote of her experience of a "Heavenly vision, whilst standing by the grave of Thomas H. Benton." On April 16, 1858, Elizabeth explained that she "beheld a numberless multitude of Angels hovering around in a circle" and that they then took Benton and his little grandchild with them to heaven. "My joy was great earth seemed to be the Abode of Angels," she recalled, "I had seen therefore I knew that my spirit too would alike be wafted to its heaven of rest by Angel hands."[12] Thus could angels descend to earth, and humans ascend to heaven. For some Americans, the boundary between heaven and earth was blurred, flexible, and likely to be pierced at any time.

Fascination with the world of spirits percolated in the minds of antebellum Americans. The rise of the Spiritualist movement in America in the 1840s gave institutional expression to the idea that living beings could commune with spirits of those who had departed. Grounded in the teachings of Emanuel Swedenborg, the American Spiritualist move-ment took off with the publication of the revelations of Andrew Jack-son Davis, who in March 1844, claimed to receive direct intelligence from the spirit world while in a "strange abnormal state."[13] Although we might tend to think of the movement as a caricature—linked to those who heard spirit rappings on tables in upstate New York—it cap-tured considerable support outside those who identified themselves as Spiritualists. "There was, in other words," as Bret E. Carroll has argued, "a truly popular interest in the spirit world in antebellum America."[14] We know that Spiritualist publications could be found from New York to Harmony Grove, Arkansas, to New Orleans, Louisiana.[15] Belief in the spirit world manifested itself in slave cabins and secluded arbors throughout the American South.[16] In 1862, following the death of their son Willie, Abraham and Mary Lincoln succumbed to the temptation to contact his spirit. According to David Herbert Donald's biography, Abraham Lincoln had a series of deep conversations with Presbyterian minister Phineas D. Gurley in the aftermath of Willie's death. "Gently the clergyman comforted with the assurance that Willie was not dead but lived in heaven," writes Donald, "Lincoln may not have believed him, but he wished to believe him."[17] While Donald paints Lincoln's religious views in essentially fatalistic terms, it is nevertheless true that the president could conceive of and hoped for a future life for his son.

If they could agree that the heavenly world stood near at hand, Americans exercised considerably more liberty in offering up descriptions of the eternal environment that awaited them. At an obvious level, the freedom that Americans exercised in writing about the heavenly landscape makes sense—who, after all, could verify or dispute the specifics of such analysis? The unknowable quality of heaven itself invited speculation. Heaven was a tabula rasa upon which Americans could inscribe their most profound hopes and aspirations. As poets, novelists, and theologians grappled with heaven, they loosed their imaginations, sometimes basing their ideas in dreams, sometimes in rational thought, sometimes in the authority of the Bible. But however they described it, Americans agreed that heaven was, above all, a real place of surpassing beauty.

In 1830, Dr. Richard Emmons of Philadelphia published a poem in which he offered a view of heaven that was simultaneously pastoral and political. In "Description of Heaven," he described "rivers of nectar" and "emerald valleys" replete with innocent lambs and the songs of "birds of rare cadence."[18] Here, too, was a lake in which the "translated" souls washed away their sins—"when freed from earth they burst their prisoning clay." Emmons's heaven also imbibed a hierarchical character as he described a three-tiered place that included realms for the new human occupants, the angels, and the "Deity unseen." Emmons populated his heaven with a variety of historical figures, focusing attention especially on the heroes of the American Revolution. Here were George Washington, Joseph Warren, Benjamin Franklin, John Hancock, John Adams, and Patrick Henry, among others. The inhabitants of Emmons's heaven were men (the only females mentioned are the goddess figures of Columbia and Fredonia), and they listen attentively while the patriot leaders offer up odes to civic virtue and freedom. Emmons thus painted a kind of neoclassical heaven for his readers, one in which legions of revolutionary heroes strolled the pastoral landscape discussing important political ideas. Given the recent passing of figures such as Thomas Jefferson and John Adams in 1826, it is perhaps not surprising that Emmons's heaven would concentrate so heavily on the memory of the Revolutionary era fathers. By the end of the 1830s, living connections with the revolutionary generation had faded almost entirely.

If Richard Emmons tapped into the classical universe in constructing his heavenly realm, then George Wood's 1858 tale *Future Life; or, Scenes in Another World* took his readers on a journey into a mystical dream world. Above all, Wood's heaven is a land of free artistic expression. His story follows the adventures of two characters, Peter and Mrs. Jay, as they explore the wonders of their new home. The visitors are struck first by the wafting tones of harmony from an angelic choir as they sweep out of a cathedral across a lake. The fantastical "Palace of the Redeemed" stands at the side of the lake. "The grounds were beautifully laid out," wrote Wood, "and were adorned with statues, which seen in the shadows of twilight amid the shrubbery of the garden, were often mistaken for living beings of surpassing beauty and grace."[19] Wood's heaven reveals the existence of a "Metropolitan City" sitting on a high plateau near the "glassy lake of pure water." The City itself, because of its location near the equator, possessed a "cool and bracing" climate that proved ideal "for the prosecution of the higher branches of art."[20] Most notable, perhaps, among the arts was music. In one of Wood's most fantastic scenes, Handel, Haydn, Mozart, and Beethoven collaboratively perform a glorious heavenly anthem.[21] As they traverse the heavenly landscape, Peter and Mrs. Jay encounter Christian martyrs and heroes of the early faith, from St. Perpetua to St. John Chrysostom. These conversations are invariably framed with descriptions of sublime landscapes, magnificent sculptures, or music of intoxicating beauty.

As it turns out, the inspiration for Wood's *Future Life; or Scenes in Another World* was a dream. The narrative itself concludes with the revelation that the character Peter has dreamed up the entire episode and that he is still alive (and therefore impoverished) living in this world. At the conclusion of his book, Wood tacked on a number of explanatory appendices, including one claiming to contain the dream of a North Carolina clergyman, James B. Finley. According to Wood's rendition, Finley had been visited by "angel guides" who had taken him on a visit to the "gates of Paradise."[22] Here he saw "a broad sheet of water, clear as a crystal, not a single ripple on its surface, and its purity and clearness indescribable. On each side of this lake or river, rose up the most tall and beautiful trees, covered in all manner of fruits and flowers, the brilliant hues of which were reflected in the bosom of the placid river."[23] Elements of this description are seen in the opening passages of *Future Life*. Wood's book was of a piece, then, with others in antebellum America for whom visionary experience constituted a key authority for the knowledge of heaven.

The Rev. H. Harbaugh, pastor of the First German Reformed Church of Lancaster, Pennsylvania, brushed aside considerations of heaven that were not grounded in a level-headed understanding of the scriptures. It is doubtful that anyone in antebellum America wrote more extensively about heaven than did Harbaugh, producing three hefty volumes on the subject in the space of seven years.[24] Harbaugh sought to present heaven in as responsible a way as he could, drawing on both scriptural passages and on the reasonable inferences he thought one could draw from them. He insisted, above all, that heaven was a material place. When Jesus told his disciples that he was going before them to prepare a "place" for them, Harbaugh said, the Lord meant what He said. Harbaugh reasoned, a "local, material" heaven would be absolutely essential for the bodies that would identify us there. "It could not be a suitable abode for the saints," he argued, "if it were not a local, material heaven. The saints will have bodies."[25]

The closest analogy for heaven, Harbaugh speculated, might be the descriptions of Eden in the book of Genesis. As would surely be the case in heaven, Eden was free from sin and therefore its fabulous beauty would be edifying, rather than distracting. "Nature in Paradise," he wrote, "in the form of earthly scenery, was not polluting or degrading, but rather elevating to holy minds."[26] Moreover, he thought, human beings were constructed in such a way that they would possess the need for beauty even after death. "Our imagination," he wrote, "which needs scenery for its health and development, is not a profane faculty."[27] If God had created scenes of beauty on earth, why would he not spread before us even more spectacular vistas in heaven?

Harbaugh speculated that heaven would be even more beautiful than Eden. Eden offered a foretaste of heaven, but it might not tell the whole story. Harbaugh knew that humans thought in analogies and metaphors so that the idea that we would find in heaven "trees, streams, mountains, &c, I will not affirm, but much less will I deny."[28] What if the laws of physics that animated our earthly universe, such as those of "attraction and gravitation" did not exist in heaven? What if the friction that caused decay did not exist in heaven? Harbaugh thought that this was possible, if not likely. "Then life would be most gloriously free!" Harbaugh sang, "In that case there could be no such thing as decay."[29] He thus conjured an eternity free from the processes of time, corruption, and decay that characterized life on earth. Freed from the shackles of sin and from the ravages of decay, humans might live gloriously in eternity.

The perfected heaven that Harbaugh saw stretching before him would differ from earth in other significant ways. In elaborating on these points, Harbaugh wrote almost as if he were composing a travel guide for visitors about to embark on a journey to an exotic land. In the first place, he noted, there would be no night in heaven. "There no dark night-sides of nature cover the lovely face paridisean realms," he exclaimed. "No cycles in the heavenly worlds ever cause the joyous life of the saints to ebb back from waking energies of bliss into dull stupor, under the overshadowings of darkness and gloom!"[30] At times, Harbaugh seemed to be arguing from the perspective of a physicist, explaining that the regular motion of the planets may not be part of the heavenly universe. Simultaneously, the elimination of night from heaven also contained a strong metaphorical and theological component. In banishing darkness from heaven, God simultaneously destroyed dark thoughts, doubt, sorrow, and even death itself. Rev. Rufus W. Clark, in his 1853 text *Heaven and Its Scriptural Emblems*, explained it this way: "No night in heaven! Then no sad partings are experienced there;—no funeral processions move, no death-knell is heard, no graves are opened."[31] Rather, radiant saints would "walk the golden streets of the eternal city, surrounded with perpetual brightness, breathing an atmosphere of heavenly purity, and free to enter the palaces of our King, or climb to heights over which no shadow ever passes."[32]

The saints would experience these and other enjoyments in a heaven without seas. Harbaugh and Clark believed that biblical testimony spoke against the existence of oceans in the eternal and timeless world. Streams, lakes, and even rivers would add to the blessed scenery of heaven, but passages such as Revelations 21:1 spoke against the survival of the seas. Aside from scriptural authority, it just didn't seem to make sense to have oceans in heaven. "The sea not only contracts man's activities," wrote Harbaugh, "confines him to places, hinders and endangers the intercourse of nations, but also presents wide wastes unfit for the abodes of man."[33] Moreover, the cycles of drought and flood that existed on earth would not be of much use in heaven—plants would stay in a permanent state of bloom. "What a Paradise is that," announced Harbaugh, "where no leaf withers, and where no flower fades!"[34] Rufus Clark pressed home that assault on the seas from a different perspective. "The sea is the emblem of change," he wrote, "It is never perfectly at rest."[35] As such, it symbolized the radical contingency and flux of temporal life: "Change, instability, and disappointment, are inscribed upon everything pertaining to our earthly existence."[36] These vicissitudes and trials would be abolished in heaven. The seas would, quite literally, have to give up their dead.

The heavenly landscapes described by antebellum Americans were thus places of transcendent beauty and great variety. Some passages captured elements of Romantic pastoralism—lush green fields, gently rolling hills, and quiet streams abounded. Other heavenly imaginings emphasized the sublime and magisterial quality of heaven—its ability to awe with tall mountain peaks and brilliant light. Other visions of heaven emphasized a stronger human hand at work on the landscape—it could be a place where artistic achievement would warrant pride of place; a place of music, choirs, and sculpture. Some ideas about heaven pointed to the magnificence of great cities; others venerated a more agrarian ideal. Some passages about heavenly life emphasized strong elements of continuity with our existence on earth—people could walk, talk, and see with their own eyes. Yet other passages—those in which the night and the seas would be abolished—stressed how radically different life would be in a place where decay and death did not exist. Heaven may have been so powerfully appealing to antebellum Americans precisely because of the freedom it gave them to conjure perfect worlds that suited individual imaginations. If, as James McPherson has so eloquently argued, all participants in the Civil War fought to realize their particular vision of freedom, then no place on earth could rival heaven as a domain for its expression.[37]

Theologians and intellectuals devoted considerable attention not only to broad interpretations of the heavenly realm, but they also thought deeply and obsessively about the nature of the resurrection bodies the saints would possess when they arrived there. As Caroline Walker Bynum has demonstrated, debate about the resurrected body has been central to western Christianity since the beginning.[38] Probing the mysteries of St. Paul's foundational passages in 1 Corinthians 15 proved critical not only for Christian thinkers of the Patristic age but for antebellum commentators as well. What did it mean for Christians to think about themselves as "spiritual bodies" once they were in heaven? If Christians were to be totally transformed at the final sound of the trumpet, in what sense would they remain with their individual identities intact? In other words, how would God strike the balance between change and continuity in dealing with the resurrected body? Moreover, there remained the thorny problem that Bynum identifies as the "famous chain consumption" dilemma.[39] As corporeal remains decayed on earth, these fragments in turn nourished the lives of plants and animals. Humans then consumed as nourishment these plants and animals thus imbibing in tiny particles the bodies of those who had lived before. And this in turn conjured the horrible problem of a sort of cannibalism. With the corporeal matter of humans spread throughout the world and body parts jumbled up among countless individuals, how could individual bodies be sorted out with any certainty at the resurrection? These were not matters of idle speculation for the earliest Christians or for their antebellum American counterparts. All of these issues raised questions about the coherence of human identity in heaven and thus cut to the core of how the faithful constructed ideas of the afterlife.

To a degree that has not been fully appreciated by scholars, nineteenth-century American intellectuals confronted questions about the resurrection body with brio and a lively appreciation of the arguments made by their ancient predecessors. Perhaps surprisingly, church fathers such as Irenaeus of Lyon, Tertullian, Origen, and Augustine discovered new life in America in the decades before the Civil War.[40] Writers on the subject of the resurrection body aligned themselves along something of a rough continuum. On one end of the line stood those who considered the resurrection body to be almost entirely spiritual. To them it made little sense, either scientifically or theologically, to posit the endurance of the flesh in heaven. Others staked out a more moderate, centrist position. They used traditional Christian metaphors—such as the growth of a seed or the transformation of an ugly insect into a beautiful butterfly—to imagine how both the transformation and the continuity of the individual might be manifest in heaven. Other thinkers had little patience for anything other than the idea that the saints would rise in the very bodies in which they had died. On balance, it would be fair to say that antebellum Americans tended to favor strongly materialistic ideas about the resurrection body. For the most part they were willing to risk intellectual inconsistency and left any unresolved issues resting in the hands of God's providence.

In his 1837 treatise, *An Essay on the Identity and General Resurrection of the Human Body,* Samuel Drew unpacked 1 Corinthians 15 in such a way as to insist on the endurance of human identity in heaven, but he doubted that it could have much to do with flesh and blood. Drew wanted to take seriously the idea that humans would have some sort of body in heaven, but he doubted that we could conceive what that would be like. Bodies would exist, he said, but they would not be like the ones we had on earth. Still, they would preserve something essential, perhaps some atomic trace or hidden essence that had always contained our identity. In basic terms, Drew's solution to the problem of the resurrection body seemed to be to reinterpret and minimize what the human body was on earth in the first place. "Body, therefore, must even now, in its refined and philosophical sense," he wrote, "consist in something different from flesh and blood."[41] As much as Drew wanted to argue for the reality of the resurrection body he could not get around the biblical pronouncement that "flesh and blood cannot inherit the kingdom of God, nor corruption inherit incorruption."[42]

If Samuel Drew tiptoed carefully around the question of human identity, Professor George Bush of The New York City University took direct aim at the notion that actual bodies would populate heaven. In three excruciatingly detailed and strongly argued works published in the mid-1840s, Bush dismantled the arguments presented by the materialists.[43] Displaying his expertise as a professor of biblical languages, Bush dove first into the Bible and produced evidence to jettison the idea that a corporeal resurrection had ever been taught. He was willing to consider resurrection in strictly spiritual terms, but that was all. The resurrected body, he maintained, "has nothing to do with the gross material particles which enter into the composition of our present earthly tenements."[44] The soul survived. The body died. In the end, Bush found that the "judgment of reason would be, *that a spiritual body is developed at death. By spiritual,* in this connexion, we mean refined, subtle, ethereal, sublimated."[45] It is little wonder, then, that some of George Bush's theological adversaries placed him in a genealogy of heretics that stretched from the early Gnostics up through the Spiritualist Emanuel Swedenborg.[46]

Throughout his work, Bush was aware that he was ruffling the feathers of those who believed that fully human bodies basked in heavenly light. He was nimble in defending himself against those who thought that his work abandoned the idea that there could be no "mutual recognition of the departed saints in heaven."[47] From Bush's point of view, this was nonsense. Perhaps sarcastically, he speculated that "if we can conceive the possibility of two individuals of the caterpillar tribe recognizing each other as caterpillars, we can readily conceive of their recognizing each other as butterflies."[48] Bush of course knew that he was trading on a familiar metaphor for the resurrection—that of insect transformation— to make a surprising point. If insects might recognize one another, why couldn't humans? "What should prevent the developed spiritual body of one human being instantly recognizing that of another," Bush wrote, "when their state relatively to each other is the same after as before the magnificent transition."[49] Even though Bush proved willing to challenge the reigning paradigm of material resurrection, he continued to think that his notion of spirit resurrection did not rule out the cardinal principle of heavenly recognition.

In his 1860 tract, *The Anastasis of the Dead, or Philosophy of Human Immortality,* James Lewis wrestled with the problem posed by the "chain consumption" argument and found that it tilted against ideas of literal bodily resurrection. It was common knowledge, he said, that "no natural fact is better established than this, that an entire transformation is going on perpetually."[50] Fields and forests, Lewis maintained, were also burying grounds and, later, upon them would grow grains that would sustain future generations. "The bodies of the ancients," he concluded, "are thus incorporated with those of the moderns."[51] Lewis admitted that God, in his "Omniscience" and "Omnipotence" might gather up the particles of a few of the saints and reconstitute their bodies in total. But "to do this last for every individual of the race, can but be perfectly *im*possible."[52] Lewis thus tried to walk a razor's edge, admitting that God probably could reassemble some humans out of dispersed atoms, but to reconstitute the whole human race seemed a task too extensive even for the Almighty. Besides, Lewis asked, which human individuals would God select to reassemble? Citing an argument known to other theologians, he noted that humans themselves are in a constant state of flux—and that the atoms that composed the frame of "John Smith" when he was but a boy would certainly not be the same as those that constituted him at age seventy. So, which John Smith would then be resurrected? Finally, Lewis went beyond science to agree with Bush that evidence from the Bible showed the material resurrection to be unsubstantiated. Turning again to 1 Corinthians 15, Lewis emphasized that Paul had said that humans are sown with a "natural body" but would be raised in a "spiritual body." The two bodies could not be the same ones. Otherwise why would Paul have spent time differentiating the two ideas? Still, after demolishing the theory of the literal bodily resurrection, Lewis continued to admit that a few saints may have been made whole. But this should not raise widespread hopes for similar treatment. "Though certain bodies of saint are declared to have arisen, and to have come out of the graves, &c., on the occasion of Christ's resurrection," wrote Lewis, "it by no means follows that a like honor awaits the bodies of all our race."[53] So did Jason Lewis straddle the theological fence—admitting that bodily resurrection might be possible for some, but unlikely for most.

That even critics of the literal and material resurrection pulled their punches suggests how powerful and pervasive ideas of the physical resurrection were in antebellum America. Proponents of the corporeal afterlife often deployed metaphors from the Christian tradition to explain their thinking, and most stopped short of insisting on complete continuity between dead bodies on earth and the living saints in heaven. In a sense, the materialists wanted to stake out a middle terrain—one that acknowledged the bodily resurrection but made room for transformation and perfection in heaven. Harbaugh himself articulated this sort of argument by triangulation in his 1853 book, *The Heavenly Home*. He attacked those, like the infamous "Prof. Bush," who argued that "the future body is something entirely different from the present body."[54] At the same time, he took on those who tended toward the opposite extreme, "the attempt to preserve such a gross and carnal identity of the present with the future body."[55] Both extremes were wrong. "The scriptural idea," wrote Harbaugh, "lies between these two extremes, including the truth that is in both."[56] In the end, though, even the moderates left no doubt about where they ultimately stood. "The body is not merely a companion to us," Harbaugh said bluntly, "it is a part of us."[57]

Arguments based in Christian metaphor provided both the elasticity and the precision that the materialists needed. Perhaps the most popular metaphorical argument for corporeal resurrection deployed the idea of "The Insect Transformed."[58] This line of reasoning traced the metamorphoses of earthy worm or grub into chrysalis and then into a glorious butterfly. The notion of progressive development revealed here could be appealing for two reasons. First, the radical change from homely worm into beautiful butterfly was dramatic enough to suggest the utter transformation of human beings as they entered eternity. At the same time, however, the insect argument was effective in demonstrating a continuity of identity. It was, after all, the same creature that evolved through three different stages of growth. Therefore we might reasonably assume that if insect identity remained constant throughout radical change, then discrete human identity would be preserved in heaven. George Burgess, the Episcopal Bishop of Maine, gave voice to this double-edged appeal of the insect analogy when he spoke of what happened to Christian bodies after death. "But, vast as the change is," he wrote, "all that are in the graves shall come forth; each body the same, by a law of identity, with that which slept; the same, yet another, as the butterfly, the soaring emblem of immortality, is the same with the worm and the chrysalis."[59]

Materialists also used the seed metaphor to describe the delicate balance between human continuity and transformation after death. Planted in the earth, seeds sprout and grow into grain or into tress of tremendous beauty, vastly changed but still containing the "germ" that made each plant unique. In such ways could humans comprehend the change that would await them in the resurrection. The danger inherent in the seed argument, as Caroline Bynum has shown, is that it evokes the problem of organic decay and death in the midst of a discussion of eternal life. This issue was not lost on antebellum commentators such as Rev. Harbaugh. In his discussion of the seed analogy, Harbaugh admitted that new life could not proceed without death; this was the lesson of nature. "The new plant is not the old grain," he wrote. Yet, whatever sprang from a seed could not be "something entirely new and different, made independently of, and separate from the old grain; but it is evolved out the old, and remains still part of it."[60] The seed metaphor served, in some ways, to heighten the glorious power of God to transform something that had died into something that would never again experience decay. In speaking of the resurrected body, George Burgess explained that "it is to the body in the grave what the rich, waving tree, with its broad branches, its green foliage and its golden fruit is to the dull, dead atoms of the little seed under the furrows."[61] Even if it risked acknowledging the specter of decay, the seed analogy simultaneously served to magnify the glories of the eternal body in heaven.

Even as they sang of flittering butterflies and budding trees, antebellum proponents of the bodily resurrection still had to contend with the devilish complexity of the "chain consumption" argument. How would God sort out individual identity in the wake of millennia of human bodies decaying in the earth? Awareness of this question did work its way into the consciousness of some antebellum Americans. Consider, for example, some lines near the close of Walt Whitman's "Song of Myself" in the 1855 edition of *Leaves of Grass*. "I bequeath myself to the dirt to grow from the grass I love / If you want me again look for me under your bootsoles."[62] Whitman, both here and in his other work, was deeply concerned with organic images of decay, "compost," and then new life, but here he confronts directly the issue that fragments of the individual might literally be ground into the dust. How might individual identity be preserved in light of this dilemma?

For the Reverend N. W. Hodges, a minister from Greenwood, South Carolina, it should have been enough that we have it on "Divine authority" that particular bodies endure eternally in heaven.[63] But Hodges, in an 1837 camp-meeting sermon, went on to enlist "the aid of science" in attacking the problems raised by millions of decomposing corpses in the earth. Hodges argued smartly that matter itself, including all sorts of chemicals, might take on different appearances in different environments—consider, for instance, the ways in which water might appear in various guises. For Hodges, it seemed perfectly plausible that such chemicals "can again be collected by the power of God, who originally made them, be rebuilt, and become the future habitations of our departed spirits." Moreover, he suggested that "personal identity consists not in the same particles of matter, but in a particular form of construction of those particles." Like some who scoffed at the literal bodily resurrection, Hodges conceded readily that even in life individual bodies are in a constant state of flux, undergoing "continual waste and repairs."[64] But Hodges used this fact to suggest that there are no particles that are entirely our own to begin with; therefore, the fact that all of our decomposing particles will mix in the ground is of no great consequence. God has the ability to take various particles, he said, and to mold them into the forms of individuals. It was the arrangement of the particles into individual bodies that mattered—not the sorting out of the discrete particles themselves.

Hodges' sermon is a tour de force in defense of the bodily resurrection. He marshaled arguments from the scriptures, from science, and from "certain operations of nature" to drive his point home.[65] After navigating around the problem of decomposing particles, Hodges deployed both the seed and the butterfly analogies to complete his argument. He warned those who were ungodly to beware of their "resurrection of condemnation" if they did not mend their ways, while cheering on the pious to receive their reward beyond the grave.[66] It would be hard to find a more rousing and coherent brief treatment of this subject in the literature of antebellum America.

For some antebellum writers on heaven, the sort of close reasoning that Hodges felt compelled to offer made their heads ache. "The same body will be raised," Augustus Thompson bluntly asserted. "Without wasting time in disquisition upon what constitutes identity, suffice it to say, that notwithstanding all its mutations, the same body that is born is the one that dies, and the one which dies is that which will be raised again. It would be deemed irrelevant, in this connection, to discuss abstruse questions relating to substances, atoms, and the like."[67] In his 1853 critique of the ethereal theorizing of George Bush, Calvin Kingsley of Alleghany College threw up his hands in frustration. At the end of the day, Kingsley said, what Bush and the other rationalists failed to comprehend was that "the whole subject of the resurrection belongs to miracles."[68] "Why will men," he asked, "professing to believe the Bible, identify themselves with rationalists and infidels, in their abhorrence of anything miraculous?"[69] It seemed self-evident to Kingsley that believers would be resurrected in full possession of their material bodies. Arguments about particles and butterflies and seeds were a waste of time.

However they framed the path of individuals to heaven, antebellum writers agreed that our bodies in heaven would be vastly superior to those we inhabited on earth. In heaven, we would be free from the processes of sin and death and decay. Our future bodies would be whole and glorious and eternal. "They will be like angels in heaven," wrote Benjamin Onderdonk of New York, "they will be blessed with the immediate vision and fruition of God."[70] Richard Mant, an English writer whose book *The Happiness of the Blessed* was published in New York in 1847, thought that the saints in heaven could look forward to both intellectual and moral improvement. They would consort with angels and other celestial beings in singing the praises of God.[71] For George Burgess, writing of our spiritual bodies in heaven, "every sensation, every perception, every operation in which the mind employs the body, must then be inconceivably subtler, quicker, more comprehensive and more intense."[72] Heavenly bodies would be perfected in ways that we on earth could not yet even understand. "Who can measure the happy advantages which will flow to the saints in light by means of their glorified bodies?" asked

Rev. Harbaugh.[73] Soaring descriptions of individual capacities in heaven could unite those who might quibble over subtle points of theology.

That those who fought the Civil War marched off to battle with robust notions of the literal bodily resurrection planted firmly in their cultural universe is a matter of deep significance. We know, of course, that the war's toll of 620,000 lives made it the most costly conflict in American history. But we also know that thousands of those who were killed (and that literally thousands of those who survived) were literally blown to fragments on the field of battle. The huge lead slugs thrown by rifled muskets, the long range of field artillery, the deadly impact of canister, grapeshot and exploding ordnance all contributed in the making of thousands of mangled bodies. Witnesses to this wide-scale corporeal maiming are too numerous to rehearse here. Think of Walt Whitman's accounts of amputees in army hospitals in his prose work *Specimen Days*.[74] Think of Robert Gould Shaw's letter to his father after the battle of Antietam in which he recounted those who "were mangled and torn to pieces by artillery."[75] Think of the amputation of "Stonewall" Jackson's arm during the battle of Chancellorsville in 1863 (and of the fact that to this day the arm is buried in a separate place near the battlefield.) And consider historian T. J. Jackson Lears' observation that one of the most common sights in postbellum America was that of severely wounded amputees moving painfully along the street.[76] Giving some scope to the scale of mangled bodies in the postwar period, Wyatt-Brown writes that "in some parts of the South, a third of the veterans had lost a limb or were otherwise maimed. As late as 1879, the government of Georgia was spending $35,000 a year on artificial legs and arms. South Carolina spent $20,000 for that purpose."[77] The Civil War did not simply kill people; it ripped them apart.

A vision of heaven that literally restored bodies to wholeness may have been powerfully compelling to people in such circumstances. We do know that Civil War soldiers of all kinds wrote thoughtfully and extensively about heaven, seeing there a place that would reverse their earthly sufferings. Soldiers looked to heaven as a home where death, suffering, and separation from loved ones would be "no more."[78] We do not have evidence that soldiers consciously risked their lives and the very real possibilities of physical disfigurement because they knew that they would be fully restored in heaven. But the hearty belief in the restoration of full and glorious literal bodies in heaven could not have been far from their minds in a culture rife with the idea. That Americans in vast numbers were willing to risk being torn to bits at precisely the moment that their culture told them that heaven would make their bodies whole and sound is an idea over which we might linger with profit. For it may help to explain how and why Americans on all sides were able to endure such a grisly conflict.

Historical evidence suggests that strongly materialist notions of the resurrection have served to counter the threat of bodies ripped apart in foreign lands. Caroline Bynum has argued that the insistence of early Christian writers on the material reality of the resurrection may have had much to do with the fear that bodies martyred in the cause of the faith would be fragmented and scattered by their Roman adversaries. The insistence of early Christian writers on the materiality of the resurrected body thus served very real political purposes for the early Church. "Resurrection was finally not so much the triumph of martyrs over pain and humiliation as the triumph of martyrs' bodies over fragmentation, scattering, and the loss of a final resting place," Bynum writes.[79] Although separated by a chasm of centuries, this conclusion resonates with what we know about the problem of death in the American Civil War. As scholars such as Drew Faust and Gary Laderman have shown, concerns about the "fragmentation, scattering, and the loss of a final resting place" were forcefully articulated by those in the Civil War generation.[80] The Civil War marked the first time in American history in which large numbers of young men died (mangled and torn) far from their homes. Attempts to address this problem surfaced in the form of experimental metallic coffins and in fledgling attempts at embalming corpses on the battlefield. Both of these efforts were directed toward the preservation of the body itself in an environment that threatened its very existence. In a broader context, the belief in the reality of a heaven, in which bodies would be made whole and brought "home," may have been powerfully meaningful.

The cardinal principle of the heavenly homecoming for antebellum Americans was that individual bodies would be reunited with an eternal human community. Heaven would be a place where families, not only individual bodies, would be reconstituted. No idea about heaven was more important in the early nineteenth century than the notion of what was called "heavenly recognition": Individuals who had known each other on earth would be able to identify each other in heaven. Writings on the heavenly life from this period accent heaven as a place where human society would be reformed. While God and the angels would indeed be present, scenes of beatific visions of the divine were being replaced by scenes of cheery reunions among family and friends. For all its grandeur and transcendence, the nineteenth-century heaven had taken on the features of a middle-class parlor.

Because the Bible provided no unassailable passages verifying that believers would be able to distinguish each other in heaven, those who wrote on the subject of "heavenly recognition" took pains to explain why this would be the case. First, they suggested, some biblical stories seemed to provide indirect evidence for this idea. In the Gospel accounts of the transfiguration of Jesus on the mount, they suggested, the characters of Moses and Elias were clearly visible and identifiable to witnesses. So if Moses and Elias had retained recognizable bodies, why wouldn't other heroes of the faith?[81] Commentators argued, too, that because "we are endowed with social natures" God would surely allow for the fulfillment of those communitarian impulses in heaven.[82] As recounted in a dialogue offered in William Mountford's 1849 book, *Euthanasy; or Happy Talk Towards the End of Life,* "to know our friends again is not a fantastical or unreasonable wish; it is a hope that is quite rational, and altogether natural to us, as loving and thinking and immortal souls. Our nature is not our own making, but God's."[83] Moreover, commentators argued, even in its perfected state the earthly body would retain unique characteristics. In his 1857 tract, *Our Friend in Heaven,* James Killen explained that the change undergone by believers at the moment of death is "one of *perfect development* rather than of *essential alteration.*"[84] He went on to explain that "the resurrection body, though gloriously improved, will still be capable of being identified with its former self."[85] Thus, the witness of scripture, the dictates of human nature, and the continuity of the resurrection body itself all pointed to the existence of human community in heaven.

The endurance of relationships in heaven also provided salve to the wounds of those mourning the loss of friends and family members.

Consolation literature painted heavenly reunions as hopeful tableaus to be anticipated in the midst of present suffering. "My Christian reader, have you lost near and dear friends?" asked Rev. J. Duncan, "and did they die in Jesus? O remember they are not separated from you forever—you are going to them. They are waiting to receive you into everlasting habitations."[86] And because the faithful would be glorified in heaven, such meetings would be sweeter and more sublime than they were on earth. "It is one of God's purposes," wrote Boston divine F. W. P. Greenwood, "in taking them away, that we shall see them again, and in truer and more satisfying aspects than before."[87] Arguments like Greenwood's seemed to suggest that a few decades of separation in this temporal realm would seem almost insignificant in comparison to the eternal glory to come. Holding this thought in mind would surely ease the pain of those confronting the loss of dear ones.

While many writers on the subject of "heavenly recognition" focused rather narrowly on the happy reunion of family and close friends, some of them made more capacious claims for human community beyond the grave. "Heaven is a social state, a city, a kingdom, a church, in which there is a great assembly," said Greenwood, "an innumerable company, and in which the innocent and the good, the servants of the Eternal King, the spiritual and true worshippers of the Father, will meet together, and know each other, and never be separated any more."[88] Greenwood's heaven thus implied that some form of civil government pertained in heaven, perhaps along the lines of a gentle and benevolent monarchy. Other writers stressed frankly the role of freedom in the social and governmental relations of heaven. George Wood's futuristic work, *Scenes in Another World*, includes a snippet of dialogue in which a visitor to heaven "asked after the progress of liberty, and was happy to be informed that every advance was in favor of freedom."[89] The Reverend Rufus W. Clark went further than most in outlining his views of the kind of "moral government" that would abide in heaven. For Clark, government in heaven "respects the actions of free agents, and aims at controlling them by the power of motives. Physical force cannot enter into it."[90] God was certainly calling the shots in heaven, but He was not compelling its occupants to particular courses of action. "The homage, worship and services, that are rendered in heaven, by the saints and the angels," wrote Clark, "are all the voluntary offerings of loyal subjects."[91] What is striking in these brief samplings of writing on government in heaven is the degree to which these speculations mixed aspects of modern democratic language and the discourse of "freedom" with ideas medieval concepts such as "homage" and "loyal subjects." Heaven could mean all things to all people. But whatever particular form of governance existed there, writers agreed that some form of human organization could be glimpsed outside the circle of immediate family members and close friends. This heaven was a country, a civic polity, a nation-state. It offered not only communion with God but full citizenship for its occupants.

Evidence from a variety of quarters suggests that not even the seemingly limitless carnage of the Civil War could blast away the antebellum idea that a blessed reunion awaited believers after death. Writing of "the most poignant true deathbed scene" he encountered in soldierly correspondence, James McPherson notes the case of a sergeant in the Eighth Illinois Cavalry who fell victim after a "skirmish" near Culpeper, Virginia, in 1863. Writing to his fiancée from a hospital bed in Washington, the sergeant maintained that "if I go first I will wait for you there, on the other side of the dark waters." When his fiancée arrived at his bedside, she made note of the sergeant's last words: "We'll meet in Heaven. I'll wait for you there.... It looks light. O Lord take my spirit.... Gusta kiss me,—kiss me closer. You will love me always wont you Gusta."[92] We also know that as the military defeat of the Confederacy appeared more and more likely, Southern troops gripped tightly to the promise of the Gospel. Confederate armies experienced waves of revival activity in 1863 and 1864 at the moment when their hopes for ultimate temporal victory dimmed.[93]

The death of Confederate General "Stonewall" Jackson following the battle of Chancellorsville in 1863 brought forth much talk of heavenly reunions. Versions of Jackson's reported last words—"let us pass over the river, & rest under the shade of the trees"—conjured images of a heavenly passage.[94] According to Charles Royster's analysis in *The Destructive War,* Jackson had been prepared for this spiritual journey for quite some time. In December 1862, he reported to his colleague General John Bell Hood "that he did not expect to live through the contest. Moreover, that he could not say that he desired to do so."[95] Indeed, Jackson had longed for the peaceful reunion with family members that would await him after death. "Jackson often had said he knew he was saved," writes Royster. "Anticipating a happy eternity in heaven, where he would never part with family, had long been his main escape from loneliness—the loneliness that had recurred since his boyhood and that the fame of Stonewall had both alleviated and deepened."[96] The widespread mourning that accompanied the procession of Jackson's funeral train toward Lynchburg, Virginia, was alleviated by the notion that the general had already achieved his heavenly reward. Speaking at the First Presbyterian Church of Lynchburg, James B. Ramsey insisted that Jackson's death "was emphatically a translation from the high places of his earthly fame, to the infinitely higher places of heavenly glory."[97] The death of the Confederacy's most beloved general crystallized assumptions about heaven that percolated throughout that society.

Beyond the battlefield, popular literature produced during the Civil War extended the antebellum concern with heavenly topics articulated by writers such as Harriet Beecher Stowe. Alice Fahs' study of the sentimental narratives claiming to capture a "soldier's thoughts at the moment of death" reveals that dying men looked beyond to an eternal world.[98] What Fahs' calls "dying soldier" poems not only situated men within their family circles but also in the context of the Christian faith.[99] If soldiers dreamed of being reunited with their families, dying soldiers could look only to heaven as the arena in which that meeting could take place. Although these poems were highly idealized and romanticized, they indicate that notions of heavenly family reunions continued to have emotional appeal in the midst of war.

Perhaps no single piece of Civil War literature captured the lure of heaven better than did Augusta Jane Evans' 1864 novel, *Macaria; or Altars of Sacrifice*. With some twenty thousand copies circulating, Evans' novel was probably the single most popular piece of literature in the Confederacy. And in presenting its readers with the comforting prospect of heaven, Evans' *Macaria* serves in some ways as the counterpoint to Stowe's *Uncle Tom's Cabin*. One of the key threads in *Macaria*'s narrative—the relationship between Irene and the young soldier Russell—is laced with heavenly discussion. As she watches Russell prepare for war, Irene begs him to protect his faith so that they may be assured of a heavenly reunion if Russell were to fall in combat: "Will you promise to read the bible I give you now—to pray constantly for yourself? Will you promise to meet me beyond the grave?"[100] It is this promise of a future life that animates Irene's willingness to "sacrifice" Russell and her relationship with him to the Confederate cause. Thus Russell could still "win deathless glory on the battle-field," and the two lovers could be reunited in heaven for all eternity.[101] This notion of heaven enables both Irene and Russell to complete their duties on earth, deferring their romantic dreams. Russell complies with Irene's request and vows "to spend the residue of my life as to merit your love, and the hope of reunion beyond the grave."[102] The account of Russell's death in a field hospital constitutes the climax of the book; here he reveals that he has made good on his promise to live a godly life. Strengthened by Russell's convictions, Irene announces that she can "bear loneliness" if she can be assured that "we shall soon meet in Heaven, and spend Eternity together."[103] Although his duty to the Confederacy separated them temporarily, Russell also looks forward to "a sure hope of happiness beyond the grave. There, though separated in life, you and I shall be united by death."[104] Just as Little Eva, Uncle Tom, and Mammy will be united in eternity, so too will Russell and Irene. While the political agendas of *Macaria* and *Uncle Tom's Cabin* are worlds apart, they nevertheless speak in unison regarding the certain reunion of the faithful in heaven.

Both in the North and in the South, strongly materialist conceptions of the afterlife managed to survive the war. Following Abraham Lincoln's assassination in the spring of 1865, a carte de visite appeared that depicted "Washington Welcoming Lincoln Into Heaven" (fig. 8). In the upper-left-hand corner, the image portrays a band of angels with wings, bathed in light, and reaching out to welcome the two presidents home. Washington holds a wreath of victory to bestow upon Lincoln, and the two men embrace each other as they move toward the heavenly light. On one level, this image may be read as another specimen of the rituals of political reunion and order that accompanied the national confrontation with Lincoln's violent death. "The ceremonies following Lincoln's death," Gary Laderman explains, "the long, circuitous funeral journey, and the final disposition of the body in the cemetery were rituals that represented political continuity and national order."[105] So the image may be read as a depiction of national unification—the nation's first president (a Virginian and a slaveholder) welcomes the martyred president (who only days before his assassination had broached the subject of black suffrage) home. At the same time, however, the depiction of this reunion is startling in that it shows both men as whole, robust, and entirely recognizable. The caption for the illustration is thus unnecessary. Who could not tell who these men were? Moreover, Lincoln's wounds are denied in this image; he appears healthy and sound as he ascends to heaven. As figures in a national transfiguration scene, both men (like Moses and Elias) are clearly recognizable and familiar. They are known, too, to the angels who stretch to welcome them home. It is clear that the artist who created this image assumed his viewers shared with him a strongly materialist notion of the heavenly reunion.

So, too, did Sergeant Berry Benson, a South Carolinian who served in the Army of Northern Virginia. In Shelby Foote's elegiac account of Benson's war narrative (recited by Foote in the Ken Burns' Civil War documentary), the Confederate veteran imagines that he and his fellow soldiers might be reunited in heaven—this time to fight again, but without the horrible finality of death. "And after the battle," the account concludes, "then the slain and the wounded will arise, and all will meet together under the two flags, all sound and well, and there will be talking and laughter and cheers, and all will say: Did it not seem real? Was it not as in the old days?"[106] Encapsulated in heaven, even soldiers who at one time had tried to kill and maim each other would talk, embrace, and reminisce about old times. It would be difficult to find a more trenchant example than this of the transformational power of the nineteenth-century vision of the afterlife.

This robust vision of a glorious life beyond death—one distinguished by a luminous environment, complete bodies, and the restored ties of kinship and friends—must have possessed great significance for the Civil War generation. This compelling and pervasive view of heaven likely served to insulate soldiers and their families from the horrors of the battlefield. Protected by visions of a glorious afterlife in heaven, these men and their families could look beyond their present suffering to an eternal world of bliss and perfection. As Steven E. Woodworth writes in his treatment of the religious views of Civil War soldiers, "Death held

Fig. 8. *Washington Welcoming Lincoln into Heaven*, 1865. Carte de visite. Collection of the author.

few terrors for those who were prepared to meet it."[107] Sociologist of religion Peter L. Berger argues in his classic book *The Sacred Canopy* that "every human society is, in the last resort, men banded together in the face of death. The power of religion depends, in the last resort, upon the credibility of the banners it puts in the hands of men as they stand before death, or more accurately, as they walk, inevitably, toward it."[108] As soldiers of the Civil War era gathered in mass ranks, they held no banner higher than the one that proclaimed that they would all live again, gloriously, in eternity.

❖❖❖

CHAPTER THREE

"Melancholy Pleasure"

On September 24, 1831, Judge Joseph Story pronounced the dedicatory address for Boston's freshly created Mount Auburn Cemetery. He was the man for the job. An associate U.S. Supreme Court justice and a professor of law at Harvard, Story possessed a brilliant legal mind as well as rhetorical flair. His potent intellect, however, had been chastened by profound sorrow. As he labored over his speech, Story's son suspected that his father was wrestling with the death of a daughter, "the fifth child lost in fifteen years." Working on the address provided Story with some solace even as it sharpened his sense of the impermanence of all human life. Although he recognized the transience of all earthly striving, Story had been deeply involved in efforts to improve the local Boston community and had "played a leading role in the development of Mount Auburn."[1] The effort had paid off. In one of the little valleys of the newly appointed cemetery a "temporary amphitheater" had been constructed, and an audience of about two thousand people had gathered to hear his words. After a prayer had been offered and a special hymn sung, he stepped forward to deliver his address.[2]

Story began by considering the duty that the living had to care for the dead. This duty, he said, was not new. There existed in humanity a deep, subterranean, and universal desire to provide for those who had passed on and to commune with them. "As we sit down by their graves," Story explained, "we seem to hear the tones of their affection, whispering in our ears."[3] Throughout human history, he said, evidence of this urge to honor and to learn from the dead could be glimpsed. Story then traced a historical lineage that revealed the development of this memorial impulse in various cultures and times. He pointed to the burial customs of Old Testament patriarchs (especially Abraham's burial of his wife Sarah), those of the "aboriginal Germans," the Egyptians, the "ancient Asiatics," the Greeks, the Romans, and their "Moslem Successors"—all of them had sought to create burial sites outside their cities in which "the dead enjoy an undisturbed repose."[4] In this way, Story connected the efforts of a small band of civic reformers to the unfolding of a grand historical narrative. A burial plot of seventy-two acres in Boston, Massachusetts, now stood in an unbroken line that could be traced back to the towering pyramids of ancient Egypt. This was both heady and romantic stuff. It now fell to Story and his contemporaries to carry forward this global tradition of protecting the dead from urban corruption by establishing Mount Auburn.

The creation of the cemetery was critical in that it served as the repository for human history and tradition. "Our Cemeteries rightly selected, and properly arranged," Story explained, "may be made subservient to some of the highest purposes of religion and humanity."[5] The cemetery offered its visitors a liminal spiritual terrain—poised somewhere between heaven and earth—in which the lessons gleaned from the dead would be all the more striking and powerful. According to Story, standing "upon the borders of two worlds" was the ideal posture in which persons could cultivate an emotional disposition that would allow them to learn from the past.[6] And without this concrete and palpable connection to past generations, human beings would be lost. "The deeds of the great," explained Story, "attract but a cold and listless admiration, when they pass in historical order before us like moving shadows."[7] Cemeteries were needed because they provided visitors with a "didactic landscape" in which they could encounter more directly those who had passed before them.[8] In this sense, Story saw the cemetery as a steadying and conserving force in the midst of swirling and perilous change, as a way to anchor the present to the past.[9]

Nature provided the perfect cover for the effort to preserve the habitations of the dead. "Here is the thick shrubbery to protect and conceal the new made grave; and there is the wild-flower creeping along the narrow path, and planting its seeds in the upturned earth," said Story.[10] In heralding the supremacy of a natural setting for the rural cemetery, he did not mean to point to a wilderness environment untouched by human hands. To the contrary, Story hoped that Mount Auburn and other cemeteries like it would take advantage of both "natural and artificial scenery" to achieve its effects.[11] Cemeteries were to include meandering paths, careful landscaping, manicured grounds, and appropriate monuments and works of art to seal the memory of the past in the present. Indeed, the Massachusetts Horticultural Society had already taken pains to craft Mount Auburn's landscape with "flowers, and trees, and walks, and other rural ornaments."[12] What Story and his comrades had in mind, then, accords with what historian Leo Marx has called "the middle landscape"—a kind of pastoral ideal situated somewhere between the howling forces of raw nature and the corrupting taint of refined civilization.[13]

The impact of the rural cemetery would be to work a transformation in the hearts of the living. Throughout his address, Story emphasized the emotional states that would take root in cemetery visitors. To mourners, especially, "the reminiscences of the past" would provide "sources of pleasing, though melancholy reflection."[14] The cultivation of melancholic states was not presented by Story and his contemporaries as something for which one might seek spiritual counsel, advice, or (in the modern world) therapy. It was rather a disposition to be savored, for it made one open to receive the lessons of the past. In the cemetery, Story said, mourners would visit the departed "shades with a secret, though melancholy pleasure."[15] The goal of the cemetery was, in Story's words, to help us "cultivate feelings and sentiments more worthy of ourselves, and more worthy of christianity."[16] There was for Story, and the advocates of the rural cemetery movement in general, something mystical, emotional, and pleasurable to be achieved in a visit to a proper cemetery. The laying out of landscapes and the placing of monuments was thus calculated to work changes in the emotional life of the human soul.

In the three decades following Story's 1831 landmark address, countless other Americans would catch his passion for the creation of rural

cemeteries. Rural cemeteries sprang up from Brooklyn, New York, to
Cave Hill, Kentucky, from Pittsburgh, Pennsylvania, to Savannah, Georgia, and from Bangor, Maine, to Little Rock, Arkansas. One contemporary noted that by the end of the 1850s there was "hardly a city or town of
any size in the union which does not possess its rural cemetery."[17] Unlike
other major reform movements of the antebellum era—abolitionism, the
drive for women's rights, or temperance, for example—those who championed the rural cemetery appear not to have encountered any serious
organized opposition. Nor was the movement for rural cemeteries confined to a particular region of the country. Perhaps Story had been right:
Perhaps the inclination to shelter the dead and to learn from them was
universal. Nestled safely in picturesque landscapes and tucked away from
the scenes of profane commerce, the rural cemetery conferred on Americans the promise that their memories would be cherished in perpetuity.

This chapter explores the rise of the rural cemetery movement with
an eye toward examining how it served as a vehicle for the expression
of public memory and national history. It charts the arguments used for
the establishment of rural cemeteries and explores how promoters cast
them as useful instruments of civic improvement. It also argues that
rural cemeteries were institutions dedicated largely to the preservation
of masculine accomplishment. Grounded as the rural cemeteries were in
the world of the Greek revival culture in antebellum America, it is not
surprising that they would serve as vehicles for the preservation of martial and civic achievement. To the generation of men who would grow
up to fight the Civil War, this may have produced a powerful incen-
tive to risk their lives. For not only could they hope to live gloriously
with friends and family in heaven; they could look forward to being
remembered in the memory of the nation. Like the heroes enshrined
in Homer's *Iliad* or those documented by Thucydides in his work on
the Peloponnesian War, American boys could look forward, in death, to
imperishable glory.

Advocates for the rural cemetery movement, however, often began
their arguments for reform on less lofty ground. They looked first to
what they viewed as the deplorable condition of urban burial grounds
and the lamentable neglect of graves even in the countryside. The expansion of cities in the early nineteenth century had left municipal graveyards

and even church burial plots with more business than they could comfortably handle. For people concerned with the integrity of the human corpse, both in this world and in the next, the overcrowding of graveyards spelled trouble. "Who would wish to be buried," asked Bostonian reformer Joseph Buckingham, "in a close city and crowded graveyard, to be deranged and knocked about, separated and disjointed, long before the last trumpet sounds?"[18] Moreover, the noise, bustle, and timbre of urban commerce seemed to intrude on the sleep of the dead. Cemeteries were needed to insulate graves from the annoying clatter of this world. As Baltimore civil leader Charles F. Mayer noted at the dedication of the Loudon Park Cemetery, "here the dead must have an unobtruded domain—a reigning calm—where no sounds invade, laden with purposes of worldly engagement, and reverberated from hard and unpitying paths of interest."[19] Bellamy Storer, Esq., speaking from Covington, Kentucky, added his voice to the chorus of those wanting to disentangle the living from the dead. Familiar contact with burial grounds, Storer argued, had the tendency "to produce indifference to the high and solemn associations which should be connected to the dead."[20] For Storer, the promiscuous mixing of dead corpses and living bodies contributed to a lackadaisical attitude on the part of the latter toward the sacred resting places of the former. Add to these arguments the abiding concern that crowded urban burial places spawned epidemic disease and noxious aromas, and the case for the rural cemetery seemed unassailable.

But advocates for the rural cemetery did not stop there. They spoke at length about the crying need for cemetery reform even in the nation's small towns and farming communities. For here, too, lurked serious problems facing the proper internment of the dead. Perhaps the most pressing issue in the countryside stemmed from prevailing patterns of land tenure. As one farming family sold their land and moved on to more fertile acres, the new owners would have no knowledge or care in preserving the graves of the previous owners. "The homestead passes into the hands of thoughtless, and, perhaps, heartless strangers," lamented South Carolina statesman James L. Orr. "The enclosure falls, and time and season level the little mound. Soon it is forgotten that the dead sleep there; and over the bones of the once owner of the mansion, groves and broad fields around, cotton and corn grows."[21] Implicit in the indictment of rural burying practices seemed to be the assumption that unvarnished country folk did not possess the refinement or the energy to maintain burial plots. As one Maryland reformer put it, "How often have I stopped to note the village grave-yard, occupying a cheerless spot on the side of the road! Its ragged fence furnishing a scant barrier against the intrusion of passing cattle, or beasts still more destructive."[22] The prospect of livestock rooting around in human graves was serious enough in Little Rock, Arkansas, to draw the attention of the town council. On March 7, 1843, it prohibited city burials outside of the newly established Mount Holly Cemetery and passed an ordinance declaring that "no cattle, hogs, horses, or other animals are permitted within the enclosure."[23] Although the source of the threat to the integrity of the corpse was different, a common desire to minimize the physical disruption of the body was central in the minds of cemetery reformers from Boston to Little Rock.

By the 1840s and 1850s, the rural cemetery had emerged as a jewel in the crown of any enlightened community. Broadly speaking, the rural cemetery movement might be seen as another dimension in the process of "refinement" that historian Richard L. Bushman has identified as a major motif in the antebellum era.[24] The creation of a kind of "gentility"— one based in the cultivation of melancholic states, as Story's oration suggests—was inherent in the rural cemetery movement. Moreover, as we shall soon see, promoters of the rural cemetery made deft use of the historical past in presenting their case for reform in the present. This process accords with Bushman's observation that "gentility did its part not by appealing to modern liberal and capitalist values but by drawing on the aristocratic past."[25] Here again, in condemning the spirit of commerce as an impediment in the proper mourning of the dead, the rural cemetery developed as an institution of refinement in American culture.

The degree of concord, both in the South and in the North, on the advantages of the rural cemetery seems remarkable. During a time in which the territorial expansion of slavery was driving a deep wedge into the nation's political life, both Northern and Southern cemetery reformers were speaking from the same text. Uttering comments that would have pleased Massachusetts Justice Story, South Carolina Senator James L. Orr announced in 1855 that "every town and village should have its cemetery—enclosed with substantial iron railing—laid out in plats and walks, and planted in flowers and evergreens, and in some neat, simple monument be erected over every grave. This would be showing that respect and affection for the memory of the dead due by a civilized and christian people."[26] Prominent cemeteries in both regions of the country swapped architects. When the proprietors of the Holly-wood Cemetery in Richmond, Virginia, cast about for an architect, they looked no further than the celebrated John Notman. Fresh from his renowned work at the Laurel Hill Cemetery in Philadelphia, Pennsylvania, Notman went right to work. Adapting to his new Virginia environment, he explained to the cemetery company that it was customary to name cemetery roads after common trees and plants or after local civic leaders. "If you have the tomb of Chief Justice Marshall on a section of road," Notman explained, "what more appropriate name than Marshall Avenue?"[27] Even in prickly South Carolina, cemetery reformers were happy to give their Massachusetts counterparts a solid round of applause. Charles Fraser, in his dedication speech for Magnolia Cemetery in Charleston, pointed to Mount Auburn in Boston as the model for all such places. "If all the other cemeteries in this country are has happily suited to their object as Mount Auburn, near Boston," intoned Fraser, it would provide clear evidence of God's "Providence in designating the sites of our great cities."[28] Dedicated in 1850, the creation of Magnolia Cemetery coincided with furious sectional debate over the Fugitive Slave Law in the U.S. Congress. But on the afternoon of November 19, Charleston civic leaders stood arm-in-arm with their brothers in Boston.

In crafting their calls for reform, advocates of the rural cemetery looked to Europe for inspiration. Close at hand, they could lay hold of the tradition of English landscape gardening. Linked to the English "graveyard poets" of the eighteenth century, English gardens provided Americans with various models of the contemplative landscape. Thomas Jefferson's 1771 plans for Monticello were influenced by English examples, as was his design for his friend Dabney Carr's grave site. He buried Carr "under a large elm where they had often read together; he inscribed the gravestone with a verse from the *Iliad* paraphrased by Alexander Pope."[29] As the new nation sought to find its distinctively American artistic and cultural voice, English examples proved durable. The Old Gray Cemetery, dedicated in 1852 in Knoxville, Tennessee, was named for the English poet Thomas Gray (1716–1771) who had written "Elegy Written in a Country Churchyard."[30] More compelling in the minds of cemetery reformers was the example of the Père Lachaise Cemetery, dedicated in Paris in 1804. Americans pointed to Père Lachaise—with its well-appointed monuments—as the epitome of how the dead might be buried near the city but outside its confines. "The example of Pere la Chaise has ruralized the burying places of Europe," said John H. B. Latrobe at the dedication of the Mount Olivet Cemetery in Baltimore, "and Mount Auburn has had the same influence in America."[31] In 1837, the designers of Philadelphia's new Monument Cemetery sought unabashedly to copy the model of Paris. They boasted that "the location of the Cemetery will be the same in reference to Philadelphia as that of Pere la Chaise to Paris, while the ground is exceedingly verdant, dry, and finely situated."[32] Both England and France provided rural cemetery advocates with specimens of a usable past.

Beyond the use of modern European precedent, rural cemetery reformers pointed to what they thought was a virtually universal human desire to care for and to remember the dead. Following the template that Joseph Story had placed before them at Mount Auburn, other cemetery dedication orators argued that human nature itself demanded cemetery reform. Problems involving the overcrowding of urban graveyards or even the depredations of roaming livestock were real enough. They needed to be addressed. But undergirding calls for the rural cemetery was an understanding of human nature that stressed that the need to memorialize the dead was an inherent part of what it meant to be alive.

Spokesmen for the rural cemetery movement celebrated relentlessly the human instinct to cherish the dead. "It has been the care of all ages of the world, and of all nations of men, to mark with tokens of affection and respect, the disposition of the remains of the dead," exclaimed Massachusetts governor Levi Lincoln at the dedication of Worcester's rural cemetery in 1838.[33] Speaking from Columbus, Ohio, in 1849, Rev. James Hoge insisted that "the poetry, the history, and the customs of ancient nations, almost universally, exhibit similar respect for burial places."[34] At the opening of Green Mount Cemetery in Baltimore, John P. Kennedy claimed that "it is a natural sentiment that leads man to the contemplation of his final resting place."[35] From Savannah, Georgia's Laurel Grove

Cemetery, Henry R. Jackson traced the urge to memorialize the dead to "the universal cravings of our nature" for some sliver of immortality.[36] To be buried with our friends and loved ones, said John McLean in Spring Grove Cemetery in Cincinnati, Ohio, "is the feeling of our nature, all history attests. It is found in all countries, civilized and uncivilized."[37] Striking a blow for the inherent goodness of the natural man, McLean explained "that this impulse was not learned in schools. It pervades all bosoms, in all ages and countries."[38] Speaking from Cave Hill, Kentucky, Edward P. Humphrey was only a little more guarded in his assessment of the memorial impulse—"this sentiment of reverence towards the dead is, except among barbarous tribes, a universal sentiment."[39] Everywhere rural cemetery advocates looked, they detected evidence that human beings yearned to remember those who had passed before them.

As they deployed language that included phrases such as "universal sentiment" and "feelings of our nature" and "universal cravings of our nature" rural cemetery reformers tapped into the philosophical vocabulary of the Enlightenment. One thinks here, especially, of the opening lines of Thomas Jefferson's Declaration of Independence with its invocation of "self-evident" truths and the universal human endeavor to secure "life, liberty, and the pursuit of happiness." For Jefferson and for the avatars of the rural cemetery, there was such a thing as an enduring, abstract, and universal conception of human nature. We might conjecture that "the sage of Monticello" would himself have been an exhibit in the rural cemetery argument for the universality of the memorial impulse. We know that Jefferson channeled significant energy into the ways in which his own legacy would be recalled. Before his death he designed the memorial for his own grave, noting especially his authorship of the Declaration of Independence, Virginia's Statute of Religious Freedom, and his founding of the University of Virginia.[40] It may be tempting from a postmodern perspective to dismiss as naïve pretensions that purport to have identified a universal human nature that would apprehend self-evident truths. Yet, it is important to see how advocates for rural cemetery reform laced their appeals with exactly this sort of sweeping confidence.

Any fair examination of the historical record, reformers said, would sustain their claims of a pervasive human desire to preserve and to honor the domains of the dead. Again following Story's lead, they laid out a predictable chain of historical evidence that demonstrated the human memorial impulse. Although this master narrative varied from speaker to speaker, the essential points of the argument from history might be summarized as follows: First, the patriarchs of the Old Testament demonstrated a clear and distinct resolve to care for their own dead. In 1844, speaking from Winchester, Virginia, William Clark pointed to Abraham's burial of Sarah "in the cave of the field of Machpelah" as a crucial piece of evidence in this regard.[41] Second, the story then advanced to the classical world, where speakers considered the burial customs of ancient Greece and Rome. Here the Greeks earned unrivaled accolades. "In no place that we read of," crowed Charles Fraser from Magnolia Cemetery, "was greater respect paid to the dead than in Athens."[42] Complementing the inheritance of Western classical antiquity, antebellum Americans also pointed to what they had learned from the ancient Egyptians. E. B. Wilson, speaking at the dedication of the Riverside Cemetery in Grafton, Massachusetts, praised the Egyptians for constructing tombs so durable that "their sepulchral monuments continue to this day."[43] Perhaps hoping to imitate this feat, the designers of Mount Auburn had placed a massive Egyptian-style gate at the entrance to their cemetery.[44]

As they carried their grand narrative closer to the present, cemetery orators cited still other examples of the human need to dignify the dead. The many burial mounds scattered throughout North America proved that the Indians had venerated their ancestors. Daniel Appleton White, speaking at Harmony Grove Cemetery in Salem, Massachusetts, claimed that the "pilgrim fathers of Plymouth" had left a description of "a rural cemetery of the Indians, which might well be imitated by many of their civilized successors."[45] John H. B. Latrobe noted that it was not only the Jews, Romans, and Greeks who had honored their dead, but that "Etruscans, Gauls, and ancient Germans, had no places where the dead were indiscriminately buried, but each family had a place for itself."[46] The Muslims and the Turks also received a few favorable reviews. "The Mohammaden burying grounds are situated in much frequented roads," expounded Latrobe, "so that all who pass may be reminded of praying for the dead buried there."[47] "Even the Turks," admitted Wilson M'Candless at the dedication of the Allegheny Cemetery in 1849, "paid commendable attention to the burial of the dead."[48] At Cave Hill Cemetery, Edward Humphrey went so far as to single out the ancient Peruvians for their skills in the work of embalming. They were, he said admiringly, "no less skillful than the Egyptians in this singular art."[49]

American reformers thus placed themselves in the lineage of a long train of human cultures and civilizations that had memorialized the dead. Places such as Père Lachaise and Mount Auburn, then, stood in an unbroken line stretching back to antiquity. Advocates of the rural cemetery emerged as conservative innovators—they wanted to reinvigorate a worthy respect for the dead that had always been inherent in human nature. In his pioneering 1974 article on the rural cemetery movement, Stanley French first argued that it was a "conservative cultural uplift movement during the Age of the Common Man."[50] There is still much truth in this conclusion. The reformers did try to instill certain versions of "refinement" and cultured sentiment in those who visited the cemeteries. But the reformers also sought to place both the dead and the living in a vast historical narrative, one that connected them to the deep past even as it pointed them to the future.

Cemetery orators deftly wove together Christian themes and theological concerns with the largely non-Christian tale they told. In some ways, the emergence of Christianity completed and complemented the natural and universal human tendency to venerate the dead. Christian burial practices as such received only passing notice in the cemetery orations, but the rural cemetery itself was seen in fundamentally religious ways.[51] Cemetery orators often reminded their listeners that, ultimately, heaven awaited them. As we saw in chapter 2, this abiding concern for heaven was pervasive in antebellum America. As a liminal ground—between death and eternal life—the cemetery served as an institutional reminder of the resurrection of the body. At the dedication of the Ever Green Cemetery in Gettysburg, Pennsylvania, in 1855, Methodist minister J. H. C. Dosh declared that "we do not idolize the departed, nor would we cling too devotedly to their mortal remains; 'knowing that these *vile* bodies shall be changed,' and shall come forth from their graves glorious and immortal bodies."[52] At Spring Grove Cemetery, John McLean spoke extensively about the nature of the perfected and glorious resurrection body. "We should view the grave," he said, "as the opening portal of Heaven."[53] Proper burial, said Bellamy Storer, would help Christians find solace in the face of grief. "In the spirit of this animating assurance, we may joyfully resign our mortal remains to the tomb," he averred, "for it becomes no other than the house of God—the very gate of Heaven."[54] Indeed, the natural setting of the rural cemetery validated it as a symbol of new life—embodying each year the cycle of the seasons and the fresh growth that inevitably followed on the heels of winter. Thus did cemetery orators dovetail Christian theology with the secular history that they presented.

Given what we know about rising racial hostility in America during the 1830s, 1840s, and 1850s, the narrative unfolded by the cemetery reformers seems, at first blush, to be surprisingly inclusive. As American race theorists saw black inferiority validated by the "scientific" study of human skulls, cemetery reformers held up the Egyptians as worthy models for imitation. As the grim spectacle of "Indian Removal" proceeded apace in the 1830s, some could look to Indian burial grounds as illustrations of early rural cemeteries. As a demanding evangelical Protestantism swept the nation, leaving behind a hearty anti-Catholicism in its wake, cemetery reformers could find room to praise pagans and Muslims. In some ways, then, the rural cemetery stood squarely against the racial and nativist tide in antebellum America, for it embodied a willingness to value the traditions and customs of a diverse collection of cultures.

The inclusiveness promised by the cemetery stopped hard at its gates: It remained the dominion of white persons—mostly men—who had the funds available to purchase lots. As institutions of civic improvement, rural cemeteries were the domain of men of property and position. At every step along the way, they guided the process by which cemeteries were established—acquiring land for a site, petitioning the state legislature for articles of incorporation, organizing a board of administrators or trustees, selling burial lots, establishing necessary committees for the upkeep of the cemetery, laying out plans for its dedication, composing rules for prospective visitors. It is therefore not surprising that key civic leaders, such as judges, governors, mayors, and clergymen, were selected to deliver the dedicatory addresses.

The frankly commercial aspects of cemetery creation complicated reformers' claims that it was, literally, the "very gate of Heaven." No aspect of the market economy penetrated this sacred domain more fully than did the open selling of family burial plots. Most cemeteries put sharp limits on the lots available to individuals, preferring instead to sell substantial lots to entire families. Prices for a lot on cemetery grounds varied enormously from place to place. In 1839 at Brooklyn's Green-wood Cemetery lots went for one hundred dollars each.[55] In the same year, lots at Mount Auburn were going for sixty dollars each.[56] Despite this substantial sum, Stanley French argues that "the appeal of Mount Auburn to the lower classes was successful."[57] In lieu of cash, mechanics and farmers promised their labor and pledged to contribute "articles used in the improvement of the place."[58] In 1845, at Winchester, Virginia's Mount Hebron Cemetery, lots measuring sixteen by twenty feet could be had for the less princely sum of thirty dollars.[59] Beyond the purchasing of a lot, though, individual proprietors were charged with providing fencing and all appropriate memorials to the dead thus raising considerably their overall costs. Although death might have been seen as the great equalizer among men, the principles upon which the rural cemetery was based guaranteed that some men would be remembered more robustly than others.

Memories that celebrated the military and civic accomplishments of great men mattered most in the rural cemetery. This makes sense for a number of reasons. First, if Americans looked with keen interest to the contemporary model of Père Lachaise in Paris, they would have done so at precisely the moment when it had become jam-packed with memorials to Napoleonic generals and other heroes of the Second Empire. "By 1830," writes Blanche Linden-Ward, "over 31,000 monuments were in place, and the original look of the picturesque was nearly obliterated."[60] Moreover, at a time when the Greek cultural revival was well underway in America, it would hardly be surprising that models of military and civic virtue would be given pride of place. Finally, the rural cemetery movement came to life at the point when a living connection to the heroes of the American Revolution was being lost. As patriots such as John Adams and Thomas Jefferson exited the stage in 1826, survivors of the founding era became increasingly rare. Ancient revolutionaries, such as George Robert Twelves Hewes of Massachusetts, were trotted out in the 1830s at various July 4th celebrations and delighted crowds with tales of their exploits.[61] But in time Americans would lose touch with those who had made their Republic.

Anxiety about preserving the memory of the military heroes of the Revolution percolates through the history of the rural cemetery. One event that gave momentum to the cause of cemetery reform in Boston was the mysterious loss of the remains of patriot General Joseph Warren of Bunker Hill fame. His nephew, Dr. John Collins Warren, spearheaded an effort to find his ancestor's remains, which had been lost in Old Granary Burying Ground. After locating the skeleton—marked by a bullet hole behind the left ear—Warren spirited the remains away to a private crypt he had built in the basement of Saint Paul's Episcopal Church.[62] That the remains of such a prominent patriot might be lost, perhaps even callously discarded, served as a wake-up call for those wanting a more orderly internment of the dead. Such thoughts animated reformers at Philadelphia's Laurel Hill Cemetery. In 1840, they arranged for the body of General Hugh Mercer to be removed from a church burial ground and reinterred at the cemetery for proper veneration. "Mercer's removal to Laurel Hill," writes historian Colleen McDannell, "was not merely a step in recognizing the merits of a dead war hero. It was an effort to create sacred characters."[63] By the 1840s, revolutionary generals and war heroes were taking on the role of civic saints.

Orators frequently cited the rural cemetery as the proper locus for maintaining the memory of the great men of the Revolutionary age. In 1837, the Monument Cemetery of Philadelphia—the cemetery that forthrightly claimed to be America's version of Père Lachaise—boasted that a massive memorial to Washington and Lafayette would be constructed to serve as the focal point for the entire grounds. Local accounts noted that the Society of the Cincinnati, a hereditary group descending from Continental Army officers, had pledged some twelve thousand dollars to the massive task. The promoters of the cemetery envisaged the statue as a major selling point for the public. "The monument to Washington and Lafayette," on press notice claimed, "will distinguish this from any other Cemetery."[64] Promoters at Mount Auburn promised that their cemetery, too, would be a place dedicated "to the names and memory of great and good men." They announced that "its summit may be consecrated to Washington, by a Cenotaph inscribed with his name."[65] From Salem, Massachusetts, Daniel Appleton White admitted that there might never be another George Washington, but that at Harmony Grove Cemetery, there would be "a city of the dead, here will be found those who emulated the virtues and possessed the spirit of Washington, the benefactors and ornaments of their race."[66] Levi Lincoln at Worcester Cemetery, too, saw the cemetery as a place where future generations might learn of the singular contributions of their revolutionary sires. "The direct lineal descendants of these men among us," Lincoln lamented, "are but as a handful." Still, the cemetery would serve as witness to "Bands of devoted Christians, faithful Patriots, and self-sacrificing men, of rank and merit and moral worth, such, as in no age, was ever excelled."[67]

From Southern cemeteries, too, wafted odes to the unsurpassed heroes of the Revolution. At Mount Hebron Cemetery in Winchester, Virginia, William L. Clark promised that "the tomb of Morgan [probably Daniel Morgan, the celebrated commander of Virginia riflemen] shall be here; and a monument to the Father of his Country, appropriate everywhere, will be peculiarly so here, from his long residence in this town, during the most perilous period in its history." Then Clark directly connected the martial valor of the patriots of '76 to the bravery of the ancient Greeks. The establishment of Mount Hebron would make it "so that the youthful volunteer will have no need to make a pilgrimage to the plains of Marathon or the pass of Thermopylae, to inhale patriotic fervor. For *here,* on the graves of Morgan and the Soldier of the Revolution, shall burn unceasingly the vestal flame of Patriotism, fed by unseen spirits."[68] Clark's comments convey the appeal of history in the rural cemetery—for in it the soldiers of the American Revolution became part of a master narrative that allied them directly with the heroes of antiquity. If one follows the flow of Clark's logic, then, it would be perfectly reasonable to assume that those patriots who died henceforth would have their names amended to that same noble tradition. Perhaps no one sang more gloriously of the patriot sons of the South than did the poet William Gilmore Simms. The antebellum South's leading man of letters, Simms delivered a massive poem entitled "The City of the Silent" at the dedication of Magnolia Cemetery in Charleston, South Carolina. As the twenty-seven–page epic drew to its close, Simms delivered a Homeric inventory of the South's revolutionary heroes. Here were Moultrie, "the martyred Hayne," the "rashly brave, young Laurens," as well as the "Pinckneys, Gadsdens, Rutledges" and "Marion." Simms rounded out his list with "the wondrous man of statesmen, our Calhoun!" These were, he intoned, "great historic names that cannot die."[69] By invoking Calhoun, Simms implicitly echoed the point made by Clark and others— the list of heroes to be celebrated in the cemetery was an evolving and organic one. It awaited only the brave warriors of the current generation to be added to the roster.

In 1849, at the opening of the Allegheny Cemetery in Pittsburgh, Pennsylvania, Wilson M'Candless knew of two contemporary names he wished to add to the heroic ranks. In his dedicatory remarks, M'Candless offered up his reflections praising two local war veterans—Joshua Barney of the War of 1812, who died at the battle of Bladensburgh in defense of Washington, D.C., and James Lawrence Parker, who died in the Mexican War at the battle of Puebla, "overwhelmed by numbers."[70] In his remarks at Magnolia Cemetery, Charles Fraser also invoked the spirit of those who had been killed in the Mexican War. Identifying a cemetery landmark for his audience, Fraser explained that "the tomb beneath that spreading oak was found here when the Company became proprietors. It marks the resting place of a youthful soldier of the Palmetto Regiment, and will always be a valued trust in their possession."[71] Before his regiment left for Mexico, Fraser elaborated, the young soldier had a final conversation with this mother. What sprang from the conversation was his desire to be brought home from Mexico if he died, to be buried under that very tree. So it came to be. After serving his tour of duty, the young man "fell victim to disease"—but his memory had been honored. His body now rested at home, under the oak tree in Magnolia Cemetery, to be honored in perpetuity.

Even when they did not invoke specific wars or heroes, cemetery advocates cast their institutions as repositories for masculine accomplishment. As Joseph Story himself had said in his Mount Auburn oration, "here let the brave repose, who have died for their country. Here let the statesman rest, who has achieved the victories of peace, not less renowned than war."[72] From Savannah, Georgia, Henry R. Jackson agreed: "The characters of her distinguished citizens are a precious treasure as well to a city as to a state."[73] It was the duty of the cemetery to preserve the memory of "men of distinguished talent" for all to admire.[74] Thus the founders of the Green-wood Cemetery in Brooklyn considered their reforming efforts to be "the part of patriotism, therefore, as well as humanity."[75] Civic responsibility dictated that the memory of heroic men be preserved.

The sort of heroism that Americans had in mind owed much to the examples they discovered in ancient Greece. In the decades prior to the Civil War, as fresh colleges and seminaries sprouted across the nation, a new generation of classics scholars sought to reinvigorate the study of the ancients in America.[76] Led by Harvard College men such as Edward Everett and Cornelius Conway Felton, these scholars wanted to make the study of Greek and Latin something more than the rote memorization of grammatical formulae. Inspired by the philological approach that infused German scholarship, they cast the study of the Greek language as an avenue that led to the appreciation of an entire civilization. Indeed, scholars advanced the study "of ancient Greece as a corrective to the evils of the Jacksonian era, a remedy for political and civic corruption, materialism, anti-intellectualism, factionalism, and populist mediocrity."[77] Like the rural cemetery advocates, these scholars saw themselves as reformers seeking to bring new life to old traditions. Sometimes, as in the case of Edward Everett, classicists and cemetery aficionados were one and the same person. Rather than focusing on dry classroom exercises, professors urged their students to enter directly into the world of the past, "not so much to imitate the ancients as to absorb their spirit through the critical, historical study of authentic ancient texts."[78] Incorporating the spirit of the past into the present, according to historian Caroline Winterer, informed the project of self-making for educated antebellum Americans. "The spirit of antiquity revealed truth and beauty and so cleansed the modern soul," she writes, "it was described as something into which students entered, as though they were embarking on a journey through time."[79] What the new generation of American classics scholars championed, then, was not merely the study of the Greek language but the more ambitious agenda of "becoming Greek, literally of self-transformation through a historicized encounter with the classical past."[80]

As they sought to become better Greeks, young American college men would have encountered texts that taught them much about classical ideals of the heroic death. While we cannot trace with precision the direct influence of ancient texts on how men actually behaved in battle, we can explore the contours of the worldview these men studied. As they worked their way back into Greek civilization, as they tried to become good Greeks, they would have imbibed the idea that it was a glorious thing for young men to die heroically, at the apex of their powers. To die young, to die heroically in battle, was in some degree a way to cheat the forces of nature. An early death cut short the inevitable aging process and the gradual wilting of the human capacities that the Greeks so prized. A youthful and dutiful death also redounded to the glory of one's reputation and to the reputation of one's family. The Greek historian Herodotus provides one example of the advantages of a young and glorious death. When Solon visits Croesus, in Book 1 of *The Histories,* he tells the story of the great athletes Cleobis and Biton. Their mother is trying to reach a temple to celebrate the festival of Hera, but the oxen to pull her cart "were late in coming back from the field." Cleobis and Biton decide to jump into harness themselves. After pulling the cart a distance of six miles to the temple, they died of exhaustion. But they were much celebrated for their extraordinary feat, which simultaneously demonstrated loyalty to family, piety to the gods, and physical prowess. An adoring crowd "kept crowding around and congratulating them on their strength." Their mother, too, is showered with praise and is much honored by those assembled at the temple. Herodotus explains that the two men had "a most enviable death—a heaven-sent proof of how much better it is to be dead than alive."[81]

Homer's *Iliad,* too, could have provided young men with powerfully compelling models of how they should die in combat. As the ancient tale of the Greek siege of Troy, "the Iliad had long set the standard for inspiring narratives of wars nobly fought, and the epic had also served as a major source of knowledge about Greek mythology and early Greek life."[82] And we know that the *Iliad* had been well known and prized in America since at least the eighteenth century. Alexander Pope's edition of the *Iliad* and the *Odyssey* had sales "which totaled nearly twenty thousand copies in the year 1774."[83] Nineteenth-century classics scholars continued to revere this classic war epic. An edition of the poem by Harvard's Cornelius Conway Felton "went through a number of editions" in the decades before the Civil War. Readers, Felton said, should imagine themselves striding across the wind-swept plains of Troy where the swift Achilles and the mighty Hector did battle. "We must study ourselves into the Homeric age," he announced in 1848.[84] Some Americans took Felton's admonition to heart. In his classic novel about the Civil War, *The Red Badge of Courage,* Stephen Crane traces the thought processes of a young recruit as he yearns to join the Union cause. As he burns to enlist, the youth conceives of the modern war that draws him forward as "Greeklike struggle." The movements of massed armies and their exploits "might not be distinctly Homeric, but there seemed to be much glory in them. He had read of marches, sieges, conflicts, and he had longed to see it all."[85] The heroes of the Trojan War thus continued to be honored well into the nineteenth century.

Even a cursory encounter with the *Iliad* yields up compelling models of the youthful and heroic warrior willing to accept the risks of death.[86] Consider the words of the Greek King Nestor in Book 7. In this passage, the Greeks are considering which champion they will send forth to do battle with the fierce Trojan, Hector. Chafing at the reticence of his comrades, the aging Nestor (known as the oldest of the Greek warriors) prays that he could be young once again—for then he could claim the honor to do battle. "Oh if only—Father Zeus, Athena, Apollo—I were young again!"[87] He then reminisces for the assembly about his encounter with the massive Arcadian champion Ereuthalion—a fight that he won "as the youngest trooper of us all... I took him on and Athena gave me the glory."[88] Nestor's taunting works. After his speech, throngs of young Greeks step up to volunteer for the task. Or consider an example from Book 9. Here Achilles is weighing his prospects for sticking with the fight at Troy or for sailing home. He lays out two options. He can board his ships and return to the "fatherland" he loves and live without glory. Or, he can stick with the fight, forsake his journey back home, confront his own death, and be content with the idea that "my glory never dies."[89] But we know that for Achilles these are contrived choices. Going home is not an option. An early death and the prospect of eternal glory easily outweigh the benefits of a cushy trip away from the field of battle.

The climactic duel between the Greek champion Achilles and the Trojan hero Hector in Book 22 also provides the occasion for discussion of the virtues of a youthful death. In this case, the words come from Troy's King Priam. In the course of trying to persuade his son, Hector, not to confront the dreadful Achilles in one-on-one combat, Priam compares the deaths of the young and the old in warfare. "Ah for a young man all looks fine and noble if he goes down in war, hacked to pieces under a slashing bronze blade—he lies there dead . . . but whatever death lays bare all wounds are marks of glory." In contrast, when an old man is killed in combat "the dogs go to his gray head and the gray beard and mutilate the genitals."[90] Priam thus conjures an image of his own death that reverses the natural order of things in the Greek world—his own dogs devour his corpse, thus erasing any chance that his glory will endure.[91]

It is also essential for warriors to be remembered as individuals and to receive the appropriate funeral rights. Following his triumph over Hector, Achilles drags the corpse of his defeated enemy around the walls of Troy, heaping dishonor on his vanquished opponent. As Jean-Pierre Vernant has argued, the mutilation of an enemy's corpse is the inverse of the "beautiful death" (*kalos thanatos*) prized by the ancient Greeks.[92] The disfigurement of Hector's body at the hands of Achilles will rob it of the individuality that makes any memory of it possible. In contrast, the "beautiful death" of a warrior in the full powers of youth is one distinguished by its enduring memory. As scandalous as this apparent mutilation of Hector's corpse is, the narrative flow of the *Iliad* eventually sets to rights this outrage. Achilles comes to terms with the death of his beloved friend Petroclus (after being visited by the spirit of his dead comrade) and conducts apt funeral games. Circumventing the rage of Achilles, the gods intervene to protect the corpse of Hector—anointing it with oils—so that it may be given its proper funeral rights. Indeed, the final passages of the *Iliad* are concerned with recounting the details of Hector's funeral—his body laid on the pyre, his friends collecting his "white bones" and depositing them in a golden chest, his burial in a "hollow grave," guards being posted to maintain a vigil over the place of the dead, and the funeral feast held in his honor. Given the prominence accorded to proper burial customs in the *Iliad*, it is little wonder that American cemetery reformers were so entranced with the rituals of the ancient Greek world. The ancient Greeks epitomized the universal human impulse to care for the dead and to remember the compass of their heroic deeds.[93]

Beyond the universe of Homeric epic, the historical experience of the Greek city–states in the Peloponnesian War would also have provided antebellum Americans with glimpses of heroic and virtuous deaths. Fought between Athens and Sparta in the fifth century BCE, the Peloponnesian War was, essentially, a civil war among Greek city–states. As such, it maps with an eerie correspondence onto the American Civil War. "America as a second Athens," writes historian Garry Wills, "was an idea whose moment had come in the nineteenth century."[94] This historical parallel was not lost on Americans of that time (particularly, as we shall see below, Abraham Lincoln).

The classic account of that war, written by the historian Thucydides, features the funeral oration delivered by the Athenian leader Pericles in 431 BCE, at the close of the first year of the war. According to the account offered by Thucydides, Pericles extolled not only the values and culture of Athens but also praised those who had fallen in defense of liberty. These brave men, said Pericles, in choosing to "die resisting, rather than to live submitting, ... fled only from dishonor."[95] By choosing death rather than dishonor, ancient Athenians adumbrated a decision that would be made by thousands of young American men in the 1860s. Writing of the correspondence of Civil War soldiers, historian James M. McPherson acknowledges, "'death before dishonor' is a phrase that occurs in their letters and diaries more times than one can count. And they really seem to have meant it."[96] These Civil War soldiers seem to have taken to heart the advice given by Pericles in Athens centuries before as he praised his fallen comrades: "Take these as your model, and judging happiness to be the fruit of freedom, and freedom of valor, never decline the dangers of war."[97] True citizens embraced the defense of their homeland and could count themselves lucky to lay down their lives as a sacrifice for the state. "Fortunate indeed are those who draw for their lot a death so glorious as that which has caused your mourning," insisted Pericles.[98]

The historical record shows that Civil War soldiers were propelled by a powerful constellation of forces, some familiar to us and others that may seem alien to our sensibilities. We may well grasp that even ordinary men displayed a sophisticated and deep understanding of the cause of liberty for which they all fought. They battled, too, for more instinctive reasons, such as the desire to avenge fallen friends and comrades.[99] But the wider cultural milieu in which these soldiers fought needs to be taken into account as a force in making the Civil War such a savage and bloody affair. A vital and living part of the heritage that these troops carried with them stretched back to the wars of ancient Greece. "Many people knew the stories of the ancient world," observes historian Edward Ayers, "of the Spartan soldiers and their women. People knew how they were supposed to act in times of war and crisis. People followed the scripts and took great pleasure in speaking the lines they already knew."[100] These cultural scripts required that men put their lives at great hazard to win imperishable fame for themselves, their families, their communities, and their nations.

Like captains from the *Iliad,* Civil War commanders insisted on leading their men into battle. As a result, officers "threw themselves into a 15 percent greater casualty rate than enlisted men, and generals suffered the highest rate of all: they stood a 50 percent greater chance of becoming a casualty than did ordinary soldiers."[101] Clearly something other than military necessity was driving this sort of reckless behavior. Late in the war, even Confederate General Robert E. Lee— arguably one of the greatest strategists in U.S. military history—made himself vulnerable to death in ways that startled his brothers in arms. According to Lee biographer Emory Thomas, on four separate occasions during the fighting in the Wilderness and around Spotsylvania, Lee "was about to launch himself into the fury of combat."[102] Each time his men sent him to the rear. Whether Lee possessed some kind of "death wish" is something that historians may never know, but this urge to court death was common among Civil War officers.[103]

Tempting as it may be, we cannot assign the blame for the staggering casualty rates of the Civil War era solely to the bungling idiocy of commanders. This simply doesn't make sense. The Civil War's most savvy and brilliant military leaders, Robert E. Lee and Ulysses S. Grant for instance, were the same people who produced so many casualties. There is also a certain degree of unseemly arrogance in the argument that casualty rates were high because nineteenth-century generals were blunderers. With the advantage of historical hindsight, the same criticism could apply to civic and military leaders in any age. Moreover, another standard mantra in the Civil War literature—that the technology of warfare outstripped battlefield tactics, hence generating the high casualty rates—also does not survive close scrutiny. While this notion might offer some interpretive leverage on death rates early in the war, it is also the case that during four long years of conflict military leaders could have adjusted their battlefield tactics. They did not. Even after generals had felt firsthand the awful impact of the rifled musket, trench warfare, and long-range field artillery, they persisted in drawing up the same kinds of field orders. Perhaps even more surprisingly, their men obeyed them, and loved ones on the home front accepted these catastrophic losses as the natural cost of war. There was, however, nothing natural about this devastating loss of life. But to a people steeped in the martial and civic traditions of the Greek revival, heroic death on the battlefield was something that could be comprehended and admired.

President Abraham Lincoln shared with his soldiers and his countrymen deep connections to that Greek inheritance. In writing his famous Gettysburg Address in November 1863, Lincoln incorporated Greek models—most specifically, according to historian Garry Wills, the famous funeral oration of Pericles, which we have considered.[104] Woven into the structure of the Gettysburg Address were the two key components of the classic Athenian funeral oration: an invocation of the ancestors followed by a section giving advice to the living. Moreover, on November 19, Lincoln's companion on the speaker's platform was Edward Everett, Massachusetts politician, civic reformer, and rural cemetery advocate. Everett's two-hour oration explicitly invoked the Athenian heritage, likening the battle of Gettysburg to that of the ancient battle of Marathon (fought against the Persians in 490 BCE)—where, too, the glorious dead had been buried on the field of battle. That Everett and Lincoln would take Greek precedents to heart in composing their addresses is consistent with the cultural world of their time.

As he proceeded to Gettysburg, Lincoln carried with him an appreciation of the traditions of the rural cemetery. On May 24, 1860, Lincoln's hometown had dedicated the Oak Ridge rural cemetery in Springfield,

Illinois. His friends and neighbors there were actively involved in its creation. Coming from his political background in the Whig tradition, he would surely have appreciated this endeavor in community reform and improvement. In 1865, Lincoln himself would be buried there, at his wife's insistence, after his assassination. "So Lincoln," writes Wills, "who delivered the most famous address at a rural cemetery, was laid to rest in the same kind of institution."[105] Lincoln, too, cultivated a disposition of melancholy of the kind that Judge Joseph Story had praised in his 1831 Mount Auburn address. According to Lincoln's old law partner William Herndon, "melancholy dripped from him as he walked."[106] But Lincoln's melancholy, far from being seen as a political liability, was viewed as one of his most endearing and laudable features.

The president's brief remarks at Gettysburg in 1863 did not constitute the first cemetery address delivered there. Nearly nine years before, the Methodist clergyman, Rev. J. H. C. Dosh, had beaten him to the punch. On November 7, 1854, Dosh might be said to have delivered the original Gettysburg address at the dedication of the town's Ever Green Cemetery. Like others before him, Dosh rehearsed a litany of reasons in support of the rural cemetery movement and pointed to the triumph that awaited all those who fell asleep in Christ beyond the grave. Records of that day's festivities also preserve remarks made by one Rev. R. Hill at the "Laying of the Corner Stone."[107] Given what would soon follow on the Pennsylvania landscape, Hill's comments read now as chillingly prescient. "Nineveh, and Babylon, and Athens, and Rome, have all in passing from the stage of action, left monuments which assure posterity that they once existed," he noted. "Their wars are written in books, or else marked in hieroglyphic representations on the crumbling walls of buried places."[108] These conflicts, Hill announced, "tell us of murder, and oppression, and dishonesty, and uncleanness, and idolatry, and every species of wickedness." Nine years later, "every species of wickedness" would indeed be played out in this quiet Pennsylvania town. In three days (July 1, 2, and 3, 1863), more than fifty thousand Americans would fall as casualties of the Civil War's most deadly battle. But Hill did not stop with a gloomy assessment of the ravages of war. The tombs of the cemetery, he said, tell us something different. They speak of hope. "They tell how strong are the ties that bind us together," he sang, "of the unbroken chain which fastens mind to mind, and heart to heart."[109] The memorials and monuments at Gettysburg, for Hill, spoke of the connections that linked together past and present, the living and the dead.

Forging a living connection to the past was exactly what Lincoln was up to in the opening lines of his Gettysburg Address. As scholars have observed, Lincoln's first lines tracing the founding of the United States to the Declaration of Independence (rather than to the Constitution) contained the core of his interpretation regarding the origin of the American nation.[110] Following his predecessors in the Whig tradition, such as Daniel Webster, Lincoln insisted that the Union predated the making of the Constitution. In his First Inaugural Address, Lincoln had suggested that the Union existed as early as 1774, with the formation of the first Continental Association. The fathers of America had begun with the essential germ of an idea—that of a new republic "dedicated to the proposition that all men are created equal." It was now up to the Civil War generation to fulfill the promise of the Revolutionary generation by winning the war and by securing liberties for all citizens.

As we have seen, rural cemetery reformers had long sought to commemorate the deeds of the Revolutionary founders. Monuments to George Washington and other patriotic heroes studded rural cemeteries across the country. The memory of these great men was living in the present, available for veneration and imitation. The power of memory to shape present action was a given for cemetery champions such as Joseph Story. Lincoln, too, shared this commitment to the potency of memory as a source for action. Recall the comments he offered in his First Inaugural Address as the country seemed to move inexorably toward disaster. Hoping against hope to avert Civil War, Lincoln pulled out his appeal to the memory of the Revolutionary founders as a force that might yet hold the nation together. "The mystic chords of memory," he said, "stretching from every battle-field, and patriot grave, to every living heart and hearthstone, all over this broad land, will yet swell the chorus of the Union, when again touched, as surely they will be, by the better angels of our nature."[111] Thanks to the work of the rural cemetery, Lincoln's reference to "patriot graves" would have had a palpable reality for thousands of nineteenth-century Americans.

Lincoln and the champions of the rural cemetery also understood that the dead could teach important lessons to the living. In Lincoln's mind, the "devotion" evinced by the Union dead now commemorated on the battlefield would be inspiration for the living to continue their work. As we have seen, the rural cemetery was to instruct visitors in the lessons of history and faith. As they strolled among the monuments, trees, and gentle hills, mourners could imagine themselves communing with the spirits of the dead. As Rev. Dosh explained in his 1854 Gettysburg oration, "the monuments which affection may erect to their memory shall speak to the living."[112] Moreover, visitors would envisage themselves as part of a long and celebrated history of commemoration of the dead. They would learn, in essence, what it meant to be alive.

The president and rural cemetery reformers comprehended the profoundly spiritual dimension of the cemetery. When he spoke of the "new birth of freedom" in his brief speech, Lincoln simultaneously invoked the language of theology. Lincoln thus framed his interpretation of national freedom in words that echoed the resurrection language pronounced at rural cemeteries across the country. As historian David Donald has shown, Lincoln was no evangelical. But he did possess a kind of fatalism that trusted the nation's future to the workings of an all-powerful Providence.[113] Speaking as a Methodist clergyman, it is apt that Dosh spoke in more explicit terms about the physical resurrection that would follow internment. Invoking a capacious worldwide end to death, Dosh looked forward to the day when "cloud shall succeed cloud of the glorified, as they ascend from Europe, Asia, Africa, and the islands of the ocean, and the continent of America, the dead of Ever-Green Cemetery shall awaken unto life, and prepare to ascend celestial hills."[114] The cemetery looked simultaneously to this world and to what beckoned in the future.

Garry Wills is no doubt correct that "the dedication of Gettysburg must, therefore, be seen in its cultural context, as part of the nineteenth century's fascination with death in general and with cemeteries in particular."[115] But there is more. For in honoring and remembering the fallen, Lincoln and his contemporaries were assuring a new generation of American warriors that they, too, would be praised in the way that their Revolutionary forefathers had been. Their heroic actions, their sacrifices, their bloodshed, would not be forgotten, but would live on in eternity. Like the celebrated chieftains of ancient Greece, their glory would be eternal—not only in the next world, but here on earth. As Joseph Story had promised, visitors to the cemetery would be attuned to the whisperings and guidance of their heroic forefathers. The rural cemetery movement provided a cultural locus for the preservation of civic memory and martial valor. It assured men, North and South, that their sacrifices would never be forgotten. It was an assurance that they believed.

❖

"A Voice from the Ruins"

In February 1847, the poet known as Susan published a premonition of destruction and war entitled "A Voice from the Ruins." Although we know little about Susan as an author, we do know that she had at least a small following in antebellum America. "A Voice from the Ruins" was one of perhaps a half-dozen poems that she contributed to the *Southern Literary Messenger* of Richmond, Virginia—one of the nation's premiere literary journals. In it she placed before her readers the ghostly vision of a ruined city glittering in the moonlight. Charting the ephemeral nature of human happiness, Susan imagines that she had seen "the young and the gay" finally meet grief and pain. She glimpses a young bride—happy one minute and laid in a coffin the next. She sees, too, a "valiant knight" on his way to meet certain death on the battlefield:

> With his sword and helmet glancing bright
> And a dauntless head and heart:—
> Then came a funeral train
> With sable palm and plume,
> And the warrior's lifeless form was lain
> In the lonely chancel-tomb.

Susan's little poem ends with a moral that all earthly beauty must eventually pass away into oblivion. It is a "mournful tale, / Yet holy in its truth." In accepting the reality of death, Susan's work illustrates well the fact antebellum Americans possessed a keen sense of their own mortality. Looking back from a contemporary perspective, Susan's vision of martial death also seems prescient in light of the coming of the American Civil War.[1]

This chapter takes a sounding into this vast literature of death by exploring the death poetry that appeared in the *Southern Literary Messenger* in the years between the Mexican War and the onset of the Civil War.[2] It seeks to explain how this poetry of death provided an intellectual and artistic lens through which Americans might conjure and comprehend the carnage of war. The "cultural work" performed by death poets such as Susan paralleled the work done by the architects of the rural cemetery.[3] As the rural cemeteries instantiated a didactic landscape of memory, the poetry of death provided an imaginative landscape in which Americans could learn the lessons of life and death. First, the poets taught that death itself—particularly the figure of the corpse—might be viewed as beautiful and aesthetically pleasing.[4] Second, the death poems pointed to a life beyond the grave. By invoking the reality of heaven, death poetry salved the pain of earthly separation for its readers. Finally, the poems insisted that readers could learn much from the conscientious study of death. More often than not, the death poets held up models of historical figures—particularly those martyred in the service of a great cause—as exemplars to imitate. As Americans girded for war in 1861, the poetry they had consumed had taught them to see death as beautiful, redemptive, and socially fulfilling.

In presenting her reflection on the topic of death, the poet Susan joined dozens of other writers of the nineteenth century. Gathering momentum after the publication of William Cullen Bryant's classic work "Thanatopsis" in 1821, the subject of death became the coin of the realm in the antebellum poetic imagination.[5] Emily Dickinson accorded death a prominent place in literally hundreds of her 1775 poems, including the famous opening lines of no. 712 from 1863: "Because I could not stop for Death- / He kindly stopped for me."[6] Death also captivated Walt Whitman. As he explored images of decomposition and regeneration in poems such as "This Compost," Whitman twined the convictions of

Christianity and the insights of modern chemistry to play with the notion that in the cycle of life and death there was "an ongoing resurrection and a democratic exchange of substances inherent in nature."[7] We know, too, that a fascination with death extended well beyond canonical figures in the history of American letters such as Bryant, Dickinson, or Whitman. Nineteenth-century poetry anthologies, such as Caroline May's 1849 collection *The American Female Poets* or Rufus Wilmot Griswold's 1856 volume *The Poets and Poetry of America* bristle with poems about death.[8] Death poems surface with frequency in the collections of South Carolinian man of letters William Gilmore Simms and in the works of Cincinnati, Ohio's rising poetic star, Rebecca S. Nichols.[9] In the privacy of their own rooms, literate Americans—black and white—inscribed their copybooks and commonplace volumes with ditties on death, some original and some copied from newspapers and popular magazines.[10]

The death poets brought their readers directly to the bedsides of the dying and the dead. Like the narratives of death we have previously considered, the poetry of death fearlessly confronted the reality and inevitability of life's cessation while simultaneously holding out the promise of eternal life. An offering from June 1854, entitled "Myrilla. From my Cousins" presented in great detail the passing of a beautiful young woman. Once the "youngest flower" of her family, she now rests with "wasted feature" upon her deathbed. The reference to her "wasting" appearance may well mark the sufferer of the poem as the classic consumptive of nineteenth-century American literature. The poet then takes a step back to comment on the presence of a man—perhaps a doctor or a husband—who sits beside her: "All quietly his hand is pressed / Upon the wrist of snow" tracking the slow trailing away of her faint pulse. As the young sufferer passes into the next world, the poet validates the salvation that awaits her in "an Eternity of bliss / When time shall be no more."[11] In a similar vein, the poet "Tenella" tracks the trajectory from the reality of the deathbed to the hope of salvation in a work entitled "Lines Written at the break of day after watching all night by the corpse of a friend." Tenella's poem encapsulates the proximity of the living to the dead in the antebellum era as it illuminates the common practice of sitting up at night with those who had recently died. It also speaks to the calmness and resignation with which the friend embraced death: "So calmly did she cease to breath / So gently take her flight, / I scarce could tell when dusky eve / Had faded into night." Tenella traces the process of death as the gentle journey of a friend from earth to a better place where "Her soul is wide awake."[12] In Tenella's hands, the soul of her friend passed through the porous boundary that separated death on earth from life in heaven.

Amid buoyant talk of souls and of the afterlife, the death poets lingered over details of the corpses they considered in their works. This fascination with the dead body should not surprise us. As historian Gary Laderman has reminded us, the corpse itself occupies a liminal terrain in the human imagination, poised somewhere between death and life.[13] Corpses are, by definition, dead. At the same time, they possess features that clearly distinguish them as known individuals—before decomposition, they retain the shadow of life even in death. Curiously, though, the poets tended to avoid idiosyncratic descriptions of individual dead bodies, preferring instead to offer readers a stock set of descriptions that offered glimpses of the body's hair, hands, countenance, purity, and beauty at the moment of death. The poets provided their audience with a standard set of collective images they could deploy as they gazed on the bodies of their friends and family members. This standardized vocabulary of the dead body may have given antebellum Americans a sense of coherence and stability as they struggled to understand the mysteries of life and death.

These poetic memorials to the dead provided important precedents for the sentimental poetry that flourished during the Civil War. In reciting the beauties of the corpse, the antebellum death poets turned particularly to the bodies of young women who died in the prime of their lives, to children, and to young mothers. In much of what they offered to readers, the poets underscored depictions of death that were distinctively feminized and highly idealized. If the rural cemeteries championed primarily the memories of important men, then the death poets might be said to have preserved the memories of noteworthy women. In her analysis of popular literature during the Civil War, historian Alice Fahs has unearthed literally hundreds of what she calls "dying soldier" poems— literary efforts that "grappled with the fact of mass, anonymous death by creating idealized deaths for soldiers."[14] The genre of "dying soldier" poems that burst on the scene during wartime may well have had its roots in the sentimental literature of dying women and children that had coalesced in the antebellum years. It might not be too much to speculate that the "dying soldier" poems of the war era retained the major themes and concerns of the antebellum sentimentalists while simultaneously pulling off something of a gender reversal—the prewar subjects of beautiful young women and children were swapped for images of beautiful young men.

The poets of the *Southern Literary Messenger* celebrated relentlessly the deaths of beautiful young women in the prime of life. E. B. Hale's 1845 contribution "Weep for the Beautiful" led readers in mourning the loss of one "whose days are o'ver; / Gone e'er the bud its blossoming had done."[15] The image of a young flower cut down in the fullness of its glory proved almost irresistible to the death poets. The Reverend William Lowe used exactly such language in his brief 1855 offering, "Lines to the memory of Miss Sallie Garthwright, and respectfully dedicated to her mother." Lowe began by considering "The rose in bloom / Full of beauty and grace, / Which charms every eye that beholds it, / Soon droops to the tomb, / In its love-cherished place, / When death in his cold arms enfolds it."[16] In 1848, G. B. Wallis of Washington, D.C., traded explicitly in such natural images in her poem "In the Bloom of her Beauty She Died."[17] To the Romantic imagination, there was something compelling about the death of the young and the pure, dying in the very fullness of life. To die young was to avoid the sins, snares, and temptations of maturity and old age. The final stanza of Wallis's poem cheered the death of a young woman in precisely this way:

> In the bloom of her beauty she died,
>   Yet why should we mourn o'er her youth,
> Ere life's vain delusions had tried
>   Her heart's full devotion and truth.

To drop from the vine in full bloom gave the dead a distinctive moral and spiritual advantage over those who survived them.

Because they were beautiful and pure, the bodies of the dead commanded special attention. The death poets brought readers close to their corpses and laid them out for public viewing. "Lines on the Death of a Lovely Young Girl" composed by "A Lady of Virginia" asked readers to imagine a body resting prone before them:

> Tell of the virtues she possessed,
>> Who on the bier lies low;
> With cold clasp'd hands upon that breast,
>> Which ever felt for wo.[18]

In her 1852 poem entitled simply "The Dead," Mrs. E. H. Evans traded on a virtually identical image of the corpse. Imagining the deceased body as a monument of sorts, she wrote,

> One kiss upon her icy brow
>> And on her lifeless hands, that rest
>> Like sculptured ivory on her breast,—
> Then for long hours of lonely woe.[19]

The death poets offered up their efforts as literary memorials to the dead, every bit as important as the stone monuments that adorned rural cemeteries. In a poem entitled "Anniversary of the Death of a Friend," an anonymous poet from Utica, New York, explicitly invoked this comparison in a poem that sought to take the place of a "memorial stone / To designate they place of rest."[20] If a poem could take the place of a monument, if verse could substitute for marble, then the death poem allowed members of the Civil War generation to conjure up the dead and to celebrate them even when they died miles from home.

Part of the beauty of these bodies inhered in their peacefulness and stillness, the way in which they seemed merely to be sleeping while awaiting the final call to the resurrection. Even the bodies of strangers might be endowed with such calm. In an 1856 poem entitled "The Unknown," the poet known as "Matilda" from Grape Hill, Virginia, offered an account of the death of a stranger.[21] Significantly, Matilda's poem encapsulated a key issue that would confront writers as they witnessed death in the Civil War era—how to deal with anonymity of death on the battlefield.[22] Matilda's poem on an unknown dead woman might be seen as a precursor to wartime poems that considered more directly the fate of unknown soldiers. But the hidden identity of Matilda's dead subject did not render her less beautiful. The poem begins:

> They found her dead,
> One snowy morning on the open street,
> Her white cheek resting on the pearly sheet
>   Around her spread.
> And on her lip a peaceful smile reposed
> As if in slumber life's short dream had closed.

Matilda's poem goes on to assert that this unknown stranger did not die alone. For angels "with shining wings and white robes from above" had descended to guide her to the "better land" where family and friends awaited to greet her in heaven. As the death poets observed their subjects, they saw evidence of peace, purity, tranquility, and the life of the world to come.

Perhaps no young woman received more attention in the pages of the *Southern Literary Messenger* than did Jane Tayloe Worthington. A Virginian and daughter of a U.S. Army colonel, Worthington married in 1843 and died in 1847 "lamented by a wide circle of literary and personal friends."[23] Although known primarily for her essays, Worthington was also a poet of note who contributed a number of works to the *Southern Literary Messenger.* Not surprisingly, some of her best-known poems—such as 1845's "To an Angel in Heaven"—contemplated the subject of death. In 1847, when Worthington herself passed from the scene, she was mourned in a special section of the *Messenger* entitled "Votive Wreaths" in which a number of other death poets lamented the loss of one of their own.[24] Even a year after her death, Worthington's death continued to be the object of keen poetic interest. In 1848, New Yorker Elizabeth J. Eames offered a poignant poem in memory of this woman whom she had never met but whose poetry she had come to love. Eames celebrated the prophetic brilliance of Worthington's poetry: "Too truly did thy verse foretell the darkness, and the pall!" wrote Eames. Eames noted, too, how Worthington had passed from this earth "in the early prime of womanhood" but at the peak of her poetic prowess. She would now be remembered at the apogee of her talents, as the "prophetic child of song—Woman, and Poet true."[25] In the verse of Emeline Eames, Worthington became the ideal poetic heroine. Both in life and in death she became the archetype of the pure, spiritual, and talented young woman who departed this earth at the moment of full bloom. One can detect in the poetic tributes to Worthington the faint outlines of a template for how young soldiers would be memorialized in the context of war.

The prospect of early death was tackled even more expressly in poems that dealt with children. Given the reality of early childhood death in antebellum America (see chapter 1), it is hardly surprising that the death poets took up this subject with such vigor. Here again, they stressed the inherent beauty of the corpse. Caroline Howard's 1854 poem, "The Death of a Child" describes a child's dead body like the models used previously for young women:

> In the sleep of death, with white hands intertwined
> > Upon her breast,
> And flowers around her pallid, marble face
> > That she loved best.[26]

Again we meet the prone, peaceful, beatific body. Again we see poetic images of a "marble cheek" or a "placid face." In her poem "Little Nell," the poet known only as Amie offered one of the most complete and idealized portraits of the dead body of a child:

> Dainty ringlets of sleeping gold—
> Fingers like snow-flakes still and cold—
> Lips like faded rose-leaves white—
> Eyes like violets veiled from sight—
> Form like sculptured cherub rare,
> Cold as marble—as moonlight fare—
> Young head drooped like a lilly-bell—
> Is this thy record, oh Angel Nell![27]

Amie's description of Little Nell is dense with the stock antebellum imagery of death—from the careful description of ringlets of hair, to its evocation of flowers, to its equation of dead children with pure cherubs, to the image of skin as cold (and as beautiful) as marble. Given the pain that parents must have felt in relation to the loss of their children, it may strike modern readers as peculiar, perhaps even as perverse, that poets held the spotlight on these little bodies. At the same time, the highly formulaic and idealized descriptions of the bodies may have helped grieving parents to abstract their dead children from the suffering that they had endured.

The death poets refused to leave parents wallowing in doubt and despair. In "Thoughts on Following a Child to the Grave" one "T. V. M." of Richmond, Virginia, began by wondering about the "coffined clay" that mourners followed to the graveside. There the mourners turned from deep grief to "holy gladness" when they imagined the resurrection of the child in heaven.[28] Here, as elsewhere, the death poems of children followed the familiar trajectory from earthly death to glorious life in heaven. In "Lines by a Father on the Death of a Child (Addressed to the Mother)" the poet "R" used the innocence of his young son William as evidence that the boy would slip easily into heaven as an "angel-babe."[29] In the 1850 poem, "The Death of the First Born" an anonymous contributor imagined that the death of a child would release a young soul from suffering, thus enabling it to become "A bright Star through Eternity."[30] And, of course, heavenly reunions between child and parent could be contemplated with satisfaction. An 1857 offering entitled "The Dying Words of Little Celia" put the hope for such a happy time into the mouth of an expiring child:

> I know you will be sad, mother,
>   When I am gone from thee,
> But you'll be very glad, mother,
>   When you come up to me![31]

Pious children could thus emerge as innocents leading their parents toward the prospect of heavenly life.

In several important respects, the poem "The Dying Words of Little Celia" adumbrated standard features of the "dying soldier" poetry that emerged during the Civil War. Both forms of poetry gestured forthrightly toward eternal life; both invoked loved ones (either mothers or sweethearts); both frequently cited what were reported as the "last words" of the dying; both endowed the dying with a strong sense of the acceptance of their fate. "All of these were considered appropriate death-bed or dying thoughts," writes Alice Fahs, "and they were reiterated in numerous poems during the war."[32] In such ways did the sentimental poetry of the antebellum era provide the Civil War generation with an imaginative template with which to deal with the suffering unleashed by mass warfare. Although the scale of the carnage unleashed in the Civil War was unprecedented, Americans seemed able and willing to package that suffering in literary forms that they had learned well in the years leading up to the conflict.

Given the scale and grimness of the wartime slaughter, it makes sense that some Americans rejected outright appeals to the Romantic imagination. It is undeniably the case that some soldiers became so hardened by battle that they came to see dead bodies as something less than human. Lieutenant Henry C. Lyon of the Thirty-fourth New York Regiment recalled a battlefield during the 1862 Peninsula Campaign by saying that "we passed around, among the dead bodies and wounded soldiers apparently no more affected than would we be if we saw a number of Dead Beaves."[33] Another Union man, William Gable, considered his fallen comrades to be nothing more than "sticks of wood."[34] Pennsylvanian Sgt. Thomas Meyer, who served on a burial detail following Pickett's Charge at the battle of Gettysburg, wrote that the Confederate dead had "faces black as charcoal and bloated out of all human semblance."[35] As if writing against the Romantic poets, Rhode Island soldier Elisha Hunt Rhodes observed that "death is so common that little sentiment is wasted. It is not like death at home."[36] Examples such as these, testifying to the depersonalizing impact of mass death, could be multiplied many times over. Wartime descriptions of dead soldiers that liken them to "Dead Beaves" or to "sticks of wood" seem not to have come from the same culture that only a few years before had been transfixed by the corpses of beautiful young innocents.

And yet it is possible to detect elements of the Romantic imagination in the midst of the horrors of war. Beauty could be a part even of battle and death. How else might we explain the endurance, for example, of the colorful "Zoave" regiments of the Union Army, decked out in "bright red baggy trousers and tasseled fezzes" charging across the bloody fields of Antietam?[37] It was also the case that soldiers—even those about to put their lives on the line—could see beauty and majesty in the formations of great armies joined in battle. On December 31, 1862, Confederate John S. Jackman of Kentucky's famous "Orphan Brigade" could thus write of the battle of Murfreesboro: "The division was charging across a big field in perfect line of battle, the men yelling and cheering. Soon the Federal batteries open on them, then the musketry, and I could see men falling. Presently they opened fire, and the line was obscured in smoke. This was, I believe, the grandest scene I ever witnessed, in the military line."[38] Soldiers who witnessed Pickett's division marching out of the woods on July 3, 1863, were similarly struck by the beauty of its formation and by the perfumed and carefully styled ringlets of hair of worn by General George Pickett himself.[39] Even in the aftermath of battle, it was possible for soldiers to glimpse elements of beauty. Robert Gould Shaw of Massachusetts, who himself would become the focus of much poetic interest after his death, saw this in the summer of 1862. Surveying a battlefield strewn with bodies, he found a man from his regiment: "The first man I recognized was Cary. He was lying on his back with his head on a piece of wood. He looked calm and peaceful, as if he were merely sleeping; his face was beautiful, and I could have stood and looked at it a long while."[40] Shaw's description of this dead body resonates with the descriptions of corpses drawn by antebellum poets.

Emma LeConte, a teenaged girl who lived in South Carolina when the state felt the sting of William T. Sherman's Union troops, nevertheless recalled the devastation she had witnessed in terms that echo our poets of death. In 1865, writing from the burned-out city of Columbia, South Carolina, LeConte wrapped the devastation she witnessed in the language of the Romantic sensibility. "I must say something of that walk among the ruins," she confided to her diary, "It was very beautiful and melancholy. I wish I had a picture of that scene. Everything was still as death." As LeConte proceeded to describe her tour of the "picturesque" destruction, she invoked the idea that the white columns of a crumbling mansion brought to mind "an old Greek ruin." Walking into the night, she "reached Christ Church—it was a very pretty little church, and makes a lovely ruin. It was charming in this mystic light."[41] LeConte's fascination with the beauty of ruins is of a single piece with Susan's poem "A Voice from the Ruins" published nearly twenty years before in the *Southern Literary Messenger.*

These snippets of evidence suggest that the Romantic sensibility cultivated by the antebellum poets of death flickered in the imagination of wartime America like light dancing on the retina after one's eyes are closed. It says much about the tenacious hold of this sensibility on Americans that it survived until the closing moments of the war. The fundamental assumptions that death, the corpse itself, and even the destruction of cities could be considered aesthetically pleasing might well have helped Americans to stomach the horrors of war. Although initially it may seem counterintuitive, it is possible to see the popular poets of the antebellum period as makers of a literary world that had much to do with the willingness of Americans to accept death on a scale that seems unfathomable to us today.

The ethereal and dreamy scenes described in the pages of the *Southern Literary Messenger* simultaneously embraced the reality of death even as they encased it in images of violets and halos. Not surprisingly, poets held the hope of the life-everlasting before readers struggling to understand the loss of a loved one. Poems about the loss of mothers played repeatedly with this bittersweet quality, accenting both the pain of earthly separation and the hope that could be found in heaven. The poets thus detected beauty and hope even in the excruciating loss of a parent. The Tennessee author "W. P." in the poem "My Mother's Grave" looked forward to a resurrection in which "The lovely dead in lustrous forms shall rise, / Like perished violets, at the call of Spring!"[42] In his poem "My Mother," A. B. Meek recalled the purity of his mother and guide and, like W. P., yearned to see her again in eternity.[43] In "My Mother Dear," poet E. C. W. imagined a scene in which his/her mother appeared in angelic form, "with thy bright and sunny hair / Halo-like around thy brow."[44] In some sense, those who died in the death poems never really died; they were simply translated into a new state of existence.

The lure of heaven evident in death poetry verifies that popular interest in eternal life extended well beyond the debates that embroiled theologians and philosophers. Unlike America's loftier thinkers— men such as George Bush or Rufus Clark whom we have considered in chapter 2—the poets of death did not spend much time debating the nature of the resurrection body itself or whether the cycles of day and night would endure in heaven. While they certainly accepted and championed a staunchly materialistic vision of the heaven, the poets stressed repeatedly that heaven and earth were separated by a mere sliver of time. The living and the dead, they insisted, lived almost side by side. While it would be a mistake to cast our death poets as Spiritualists in the narrow sense of the word, it is possible to see them as offering their readers an imaginative vision of heaven that placed it close at hand. A hefty number of poems take on an epistolary formula, one in which the author addresses lines "To an Angel in Heaven" or "To Friends in Heaven" or "To One in Heaven" or to "My Mother in Heaven" as if poetry itself was the medium most appropriate to bridge the narrow divide between life and death. The poems insisted that those in heaven continued to be tied to the earth by the bonds of sentiment and pure affection, and that, in some sense, the dead had never really died at all.

Those who composed odes to departed friends in heaven yearned for some form of continuing contact beyond the grave. Jane Tayloe Worthington sought assurance that she would not be separated from the child that she had lost. She looked forward to the day when she might join her child in heaven, praying "that the restless-hearted / May soon come home."[45] In her poem "To One in Heaven," the poet Amie declared that she carried the memory of the lost one in her heart. "But my soul with thine keeps talking," she wrote, "in thought's mystic hush profound." Beyond this, Amie sought the comfort of her friend's embrace. "Tho' our pathways seem divergent," she conceded, "thou where raptured seraphs stand, / While I hear no strain celestial for the dropping of time's sand, / Yet we oft are gliding closely for the warm claspings of the hand."[46] Like Amie, other writers held out the possibility that the physical presence of the departed might yet be felt on earth. In a poem entitled "To Friends in Heaven," the author E. P. C. began each stanza with the words "Hover around me" as if her verses were an invocation that would make departed loved ones appear.[47] While the saints in heaven were generally regarded to be singing in angelic choirs, the faint echo of their speaking voices might sometimes be detected on earth. Mrs. Maria G. Buchanan could thus write in her poem "To My Mother in Heaven":

> Thou hast *not* left me—I am *not* alone—
> I see thy smile—thy voice murmurs low
> As in *old times,* now steals upon my ear.[48]

A whispering voice, a hovering presence, perhaps even the warm touch of a hand—these were the tokens of assurance that poets sought from the departed. Such poetic reveries would not have been considered strange in the decades before the Civil War. This was an age, after all, in which the dramas of Shakespeare enjoyed renewed and enormous popularity. Like young Prince Hamlet, antebellum Americans were sometimes sure that they could see the shades of departed family and friends walking in the night.

Writers gave free reign to their thoughts in imagining visions of loved ones now in heaven. One of the most striking examples of this is the poem "A Vision of the Blessed. Affectionately Inscribed to Her Sister" by Mrs. E. H. Evans of Paineville, Virginia. Evans first described the realm of beauties of heaven, including "trees of strange mysterious bloom, / And lofty palaces, of splendor rare." She noted "angel-tended flowers, too pure to fade" and "crystal streams where forms celestial glide." From these idyllic scenes proceeded the figures of her mother, a transcendently beautiful group of her friends, and the image of small twin boys who "with small clasping hands, did our shore leave." These small "angelic ones" now lived on eternally in heaven.[49] An anonymous poem entitled "The Mother's Vision. The Birthday in Heaven of Mary Ann. Her Second Year Among the Angels" also took readers into eternity. Here, the mother caught a glimpse of a young child that she had lost two years before. Devastated by the tears of grief, the mother sought some consolation in seeing the "cherub form" of her daughter. She discovers this peace of mind in the figure of "an angel mother" who now stands ready to care for the child—this "in glad exchange for loved ones left behind."[50] Taking up a similar theme, the poet T. V. M. composed "Emily. Her Second Birth-Day Among the Angels." This time the author writes from the perspective of a grieving sister who comes to terms with the reality of infant death and the promise of life-everlasting:

> But we know that they were summoned
> To a better home on high;
> To a joy that never darkens
> In the bright enduring sky.[51]

For all of these poets, the glories of heaven helped to mitigate the pain of separation felt upon the death of family members or friends.

Of all of the poets published in the *Southern Literary Messenger*, no one explored the beauty of heaven with more élan than did the poet Susan whom we have already met. In her three poems, "The Spirit Land" (1846), "The Silent Land" (1846), and "The Land of Dreams" (1848), she conjured landscapes of rich, luminous appeal. Theologians may have nailed down the details of heavenly life by means of a careful exegesis of the scriptures, but their writings appear drab and pedantic when set along side Susan's imaginative palate. In her "visions" Susan found heaven to be a place of unparalleled beauty. In "The Spirit Land," she accented its Edenic and pastoral quality. Here could be found "balmy groves and fadeless flowers" and "clear waters in their sparkling play." The "silvery tones" of angelic hosts wafted through the woods "in one perpetual anthem pealing high." Untouched by grief, free from fear, liberated from decay, the saints passed by in brightness. "Beautiful, beautiful land," Susan exclaimed, "How doth my lonely spirit yearn to roam / Amid thy loveliness, sweet spirit home!"[52] Life on earth pales in comparison to the glories of Susan's heavenly visions. "The Silent Land" built on this foundation and added to this landscape the internal glories that the saints would possess. Thus heaven emerged as a place where "a voice from the spirit-shore" called to earth with the sweet invitation, "Come to the land of peace, / Come to that happy strand." The calmness and stillness of heaven in this poem stood in sharp contrast to the tumult and chaos of earth. "Oh! My spirit doth rejoice to flee / To that far and peaceful strand," she concludes.[53] More ethereal yet was the final poem in Susan's trilogy, "The Land of Dreams." In verses that border on the macabre, she wrote of "strange and shadowy phantoms" as well as of "an angel sweet and mild." The "mystic Land of Dreams" imagined by Susan made earth some dull and "dreary." She sang "How our weary spirits yearn / For the sweet familiar faces!" of all those who had passed before us into death.[54] In "The Land of Dreams," Susan assured her readers, all would be made fair, lovely, and whole again.

Given the evident superiority of heavenly life over earthly existence, it is little wonder that some poets extended a forthright invitation to meet there. In 1859, the poet Claude from South Carolina contributed a poem entitled, "Willie—Meet Me in Heaven" that described such a scene. Here, on a bright spring morning rested a young woman on the verge of eternity: "A young disciple lay / With arms folded upon her dying bed." After praying, she turned to her "chief mourner" and urged him to "Meet me in that bright land." The final stanza of the poem concluded by insisting that "My Saviour calls me home—I cannot stay / Willie! Meet Me in Heaven!"[55] Given the glorious afterlife that the poets knew awaited them, it would have been difficult to resist this declaration.

Such highly idealized scenarios of deathbed invitations to heavenly life surface in accounts of Civil War soldiers dying on the field of battle. Consider for a moment the dozens of Civil War death scenes reported by Rev. J. William Jones in his monumental work, *Christ in the Camp or Religion in the Confederate Army*. Compiled in the 1880s, Jones's book included not only his personal reminiscences as a chaplain in Robert E. Lee's Army of Northern Virginia, but drew on other sources that he had collected over time.[56] Jones's insistence on the legions of Christian converts who populated the Confederate Army must be tempered by the recognition that his text emerged in a period in which the "Lost Cause" mythology began to coalesce in the postwar South.[57] In short, Jones had something to prove in writing an account that pitted the South's holy warriors against swarms of godless Yankees. Still, we know that the Confederate Army did indeed experience waves of revivalism, especially in the years 1863 and 1864 as hopes for Southern victory dimmed. As historian Drew Gilpin Faust has argued, these religious impulses probably served a complex variety of human needs—they helped Southern troops find identity as members of an army that required discipline and that infringed on their sense of independence; they gave solace to survivors after brutal battles. We know, for example, that interest in religious topics spiked after bitter Confederate defeats. The language of these revivals, writes Faust, "invited soldiers to relive the emotions of the battlefield, to express the resulting tensions, then to resolve them in the promise of eternal life—the only real assurance of safety from war and the more general inevitability of death."[58] Viewed from this perspective, Confederate ideas about heaven might be seen as military resource in the fight for Southern independence.

Jones's collection of the death scenes of Confederate soldiers traded on popular ideas about heaven that could have been pulled from the pages of the *Southern Literary Messenger.* Like Claude's poem "Willie—Meet Me in Heaven," Jones reported dozens of deaths in which dying soldiers expressed a perfect willingness to die because heavenly bliss and a sure reunion with friends awaited them. Cut down at the battle of Chancellorsville, one Major Augustus M. Gordon pronounced his last words: "Lay me down now, captain, for I am dying. I am not afraid to die, for I *know* I am going to be with Jesus."[59] One Georgia chaplain described the death of his son at the battle of Sharpsburg: "I asked him if he was going to heaven; he said: 'I hope so;' and wanted all of us to meet him in heaven."[60] Another dying man at Second Manassas exclaimed "I hope to meet you in heaven."[61] Jones recounted the case of one Francis M. Bobo of Spartanburg, South Carolina, who proclaimed when dying "I would not take ten thousand worlds for my prospect in heaven!"[62] Yet another "stalwart warrior" left his troops with the words "Tell me wife farewell—all is right—to meet me in heaven."[63] In the bleak and blasted trenches of Petersburg, Virginia, during closing days of the war, Lieutenant J. P. Duncan's "last noble act was to distribute a package of tracts to his men on the subject of heaven."[64] Again and again, Jones packaged death scenes in which noble, brave, and earnest Confederates bid adieu to comrades and loved ones braced by the sure prospects of heaven.

The formulaic death scenes that J. William Jones provided in *Christ in the Camp* themselves might be seen as a literary genre that owed much to the sentimental poetry of the prewar years. Indeed, Jones laced his account of faithful Southern troops with plenty of actual poetic verse. In one instance he noted a young soldier who, knowing he was about to die, began to sing a hymn about heaven.[65] He pointed to another example in which a young "lady friend" of a dead soldier composed lines to be placed on his coffin during burial.[66] At another juncture, Jones recounted the death story of Willie Abell of the Fifth Virginia Cavalry along with a poem about his demise attributed to the regimental chaplain.[67] Thus did the antebellum poets of death shape the ways in which survivors constructed the meaning of death on the battlefield. That such sentimental forms "so full of childlike simplicity" survived the horrors of war speaks to how powerfully engrained they were in the hearts and minds of those who confronted death on a mass scale.[68]

The poets of the *Southern Literary Messenger* were not content merely to dazzle their readers with the glories of heaven or the beauties of the corpse. The work that they produced also displayed a profound appreciation for history. The poets of death took their readers to places in the past and revealed how those living in previous times had navigated their passage from this world. In executing this didactic mission, the poets ranged freely across the years—exploring both scenes that they hoped readers would avoid and those moments that they hoped readers would emulate. The historical works they composed revealed a fascination with the theme of martyrdom and the deaths of heroic men who died in the service of a greater cause. They also discovered examples of less seemly deaths that they encouraged their readers to shun.

As the poets scoured the generations for models, they found the deaths of some great men to be less laudable than others. According to Margaret Junkin's 1852 poem, "The Death-bed of William the Conqueror. An Historic Ballad." things could not have turned out more horribly for this Norman hero.[69] Junkin, a woman keenly interested in politics, became a literary force during the Civil War "as one of the Confederacy's foremost poets."[70] From her perspective, William the Conqueror's brutal invasion of England—an unjust war if ever there were one—backfired on him at the moment of his death. With "no loving, loyal subjects pressed around the lonely bier" the great king died without the affection of his people. Repaying William's cruelty in life with the neglect of him in death, the citizens of England left him in "ghastly solitude" as he passed from this earth. The message of Junkin's "historical ballad" was clear: A life of ruthlessness and greed would circle around to damn one at the moment of death.

Lydia Sigourney, one of antebellum America's most prolific poets, would have agreed with Junkin's assessment. Her 1848 reflection on the "Death of Cardinal Mazarin" showed readers a miserable death, albeit one enriched with a hearty dose of anti-Catholicism.[71] With a scant two months to live, the Cardinal is entreated by a "spectral form" to "Make restitution!" to those whom he has wronged, largely by usurping their power and stealing their fortunes. But Mazarin is deaf to such pleas and dies still clutching his ill-gotten gains. His fortune cannot save him as death tracks him down:

> But on, the King of Terrors came,
> With strong, relentless hold,
> And shook the shuddering miser loose
> From all is idol gold,
> And poorer than the peasant hind
> That humbly ploughs the sod,
> Went forth that disembodied mind
> To stand before its God.

Several important ideas spring from this last stanza. Unprepared, defiant, and unrepentant, Mazarin dies among the worst of all deaths. Sigourney will not even give Mazarin a soul or a body, referring to his "disembodied mind" at the moment of death. Death comes here not simply as the "great equalizer," but in some sense as the great reducer—for in death the once mighty Mazarin is rated less worthy than a humble peasant. Avaricious to the end, Mazarin receives no mercy in death. Compounding his pathetic demise, Sigourney assures her readers that his grim death will live on in poetic memory.

In contrast to the self-interested figures of William the Conqueror or Cardinal Mazarin, the poets held up for emulation the examples of pure patriots and Christian missionaries. Matilda F. Dana's 1849 offering on the "The Grave of Byron" celebrated the life of the poet and freedom-fighter for Greek independence, praising his sacrifice in choosing to accept "a grave in foreign climes / Where only strangers wept for thee."[72] Choosing certain death while in service of the cause of freedom also emerged as a key theme in the 1858 poem "Martyrdom of the Patriots. Italy 1830."[73] Here the poet known as "Carador" celebrated the agonies of those who met their end for liberty's sake: "We mourn not for the Patriots! They have perished, / As the good perish, for a deathless faith!" For Carador, the best death was one in which the immortality of the cause conferred a species of immortality on those who had died for it.

In 1848, Paul Hamilton Hayne of Charleston, South Carolina, joined the chorus of those who sang the praises of martyrs. Hayne's poetry has not been welcomed into the modern canon of American letters, but his work was widely known in the early nineteenth century. He stood second only to William Gilmore Simms in the minds of his Southern contemporaries. "More than any other southern author of his time," writes Rayburn S. Moore, "save perhaps Simms, Hayne was a professional writer and man of letters."[74] In addition to his literary reputation, Hayne also possessed intimate connections to the state's political elite. His uncle, South Carolina Senator Robert Hayne, had crossed swords with Daniel Webster of Massachusetts in the midst of the debate surrounding the "nullification" crisis of the early 1830s. As befit a man of letters in antebellum America, Hayne frequently chose the theme of death for his work. One such contribution for the *Southern Literary Messenger* was entitled "The Christian Martyr."[75] Writing from the perspective of a deceased martyr ascending to heaven, Hayne chartered the glories that the faithful would glimpse on their entrance to eternal life. Here they would discover "soft-toned voices sacred anthems singing," followed by a triumphant passage into the "Port of Peace." There to welcome the martyr would be "a white-robed, glitt'ring throng" and "the loved ones, whom I lost in sadness." All would be light and good and fine, with "No clouds of gloom t' obscure the eternal day." Hayne's celebration of the glories of Christian martyrdom reinforced the idea that the sweetness of heaven would be enriched beyond measure for those who had died while clutching the promise of the Gospel.

Beyond celebrating martyrs to the faith, the death poets also carried their readers to the field of battle. Once again, Hayne illustrated this trend with his "Lines, on the Death of Col. Pierce M. Butler, of the Palmetto Regiment, who fell in the Battle of Churubusco, August 20th, 1847."[76]

Dedicating the poem to Butler's daughters, Hayne imagined for them heroic images of their father's last moments fighting in Mexico:

> His gallant sword is firmly grasped: hold! Let it linger
>   there—
> The spotless blade that BUTLER bore, *another* must not
>   bear—
> He kept his honor like the steel—the bright steel by his
>   side,
> And clasped the treasure close—still *closer* when he
>   died.

With its forthright references to Butler's honor and to his valiant sword, Hayne's death scene brims with the chivalric code that scholars, such as Bertram Wyatt-Brown, have identified as being central to the antebellum Southern ethos.[77] Significantly, Hayne's scene avoids any direct description of Butler's corpse or the means of his physical death. Instead, he encases the death in paeans to Butler's valor, honor, and "warrior spirit." Hayne thus venerates Butler's heroic death, but does so at a level of abstraction that relieves the reader from coming to grips with the horror and messiness of death on the battlefield. Moreover, Hayne assures readers that even death far from home will not tarnish Butler's enduring fame. He concludes his memorial poem with an appropriate burial ritual and with words that validate that Butler's heroic deeds will long survive his remains:

> Cover the pale face of the dead: ere long the flowers will
>   bloom,
> And scatter o'er his honored grave their glory and perfume:
> Ere long they too will withering lie, like the cold dust
>   beneath—
> But round his name *the flowers of fame will form a fadeless
>   wreath.*

In such ways did the death poets confirm what the rural cemetery reformers also understood—that the virtue of fame was immortality.

A whole range of poems in the *Southern Literary Messenger* hammered home the conviction that martial glory was imperishable. In a "Dirge for the Funeral Solemnities of Zachary Taylor," an anonymous author thus celebrated the deceased president and hero of the Mexican War: "The cord is loosed, but lives he yet, / His star in glory's azure set, / His name embalmed in freedom's songs / His fame upon then thousand tongues."[78] Ingeniously playing with the idea that enduring fame is the equivalent of the embalming of memory, the poet thus implicitly evokes Taylor's corpse but does not have to deal with the corruption of his mortal remains. A very different poem—one that takes for its subject the sinking of a British ship of war in the 1850s—also insists that fame is the portion of those who die gloriously. Although all aboard the "Frigate Birkenhead" were lost at sea, this does not mean that the crew will be forgotten.[79] To the contrary, the poem concludes:

> There's room in Heaven—there's fame on earth
> For him who nobly dies;
> And those beneath that sea have won
> Two immortalities.

It would be difficult to find a more succinct statement of the antebellum American conviction that two happy outcomes—glory in heaven and fame on earth—greet all those "who nobly die."

Martial glory attained against frightening odds seemed to interest poets and readers alike. A spectacular example of this trend is exemplified in the 1859 poem entitled "On the Massacre of Dade's Detachment."[80] Another anonymous contribution, this poem recounts the brutal end of a battalion of white soldiers during the bloody war waged against the Seminole Indians in Florida. As a mixed group of Indians and African-Americans descend on the hapless contingent, "the sable fiends rush in with loud hurrah; / they wound, they tear their unresisting prey, / And add new horrors to the dreadful day." Despite the horrors of the massacre—and perhaps *because* of the massacre—the lost men of Dade's detachment seem to have a special claim on the memory of the living. As the poem concludes, those who follow in the aftermath of this disaster will always retell "How gallantly you fought—how nobly fell." There appears to have been something particularly compelling to the Romantic imagination in lingering over the fate of groups who died en masse, overwhelmed by fate or by circumstance, or by the sheer number of their adversaries.

In the case of the poem "Lines to a Mound on the Banks of the Mississippi," the poet Estelle deploys the literary trope of the "vanishing Indian" to valorize the valiant struggle for freedom waged by the last members of "a fallen race."[81] While in "On the Massacre of Dade's Detachment" the Indians are the "sable fiends" who swoop in upon the cut-off American troops, in Estelle's poem it is the Indians themselves who are fighting for freedom against impossible odds—and must therefore be celebrated. Refusing to be driven from their lands, a young Indian war chief decides to rally his men to make a final stand, "his native wilds to save; / And yield them!—sooner would he die." Collecting his men, they go forward to the doomed, yet gloriously contest: "His youthful braves will with him go: / They die—and scorn the captor's chain." The only monument to this hopeless struggle is the "verdant mound" upon which the poet ponders as she composes her verse. The demise of the "Natcheze" Indians provides the occasion for a poetic reflection that considers the annihilation of a group—in this case, an entire race of people.

That poets of the antebellum years were fascinated with the glory that accrued to those who undertook the longest struggles, faced overwhelming opposition, and confronted hopeless odds is a matter of prime importance. If the poetry in the *Southern Literary Messenger* is any indication of wider national trends, then it is the case that those men and women who fought the Civil War had grown up on a steady literary diet that valorized death in its most terrible prospect. If massacres and slaughters captured the imaginations of Americans in the 1840s and 1850s, might not this have had an impact on the willingness of Americans to tolerate, and perhaps even to celebrate, the mass casualties that they would inflict on each other in the 1860s? Indeed, from start to finish, the history of the Civil War might be told as an inventory of hopeless charges and assaults—from Malvern Hill to Fredericksburg, from Fort Wagner to Pickett's Charge, from Cold Harbor to Franklin. These desperate efforts were precisely the kind of heroic gestures celebrated by the antebellum poets of death. To survey the body of literature in the *Southern Literary Messenger* is to glimpse a dreadful vision of what would confront Americans in the crucible of war.

Even as the Civil War took a terrible physical and emotional toll on America, the traditions of sentimental poetry provided citizens with a way of comprehending the conflict—simultaneously embracing the suffering that surrounded them while wrapping that suffering in the language of heavenly redemption and the prospect of earthly fame. Two literary examples are indicative of the staying power of the antebellum poetic imagination—the wartime poetry of Paul Hamilton Hayne of South Carolina and the literary memorial published by the family of Robert Gould Shaw after his death on the assault at Battery Wagner, near Charleston, South Carolina, in 1863. Both South and North, the spirit of the death poets survived the worst carnage of the war. This spirit may also have helped to facilitate that carnage by continuing to frame death in laudatory and heroic terms.

As a native of South Carolina, Hayne experienced the whipsaw emotions of those who had witnessed the beginning of the conflict at Fort Sumter. As South Carolina left the Union, Hayne wrote giddily to his wife that, "I've just finished reading the Charleston papers. How gloriously everything is progressing!"[82] As troops began to muster, though, the "delicate" state of Hayne's health prevented him from taking on a role in field service. Instead he "became an aid on Governor Picken's staff."[83] From then on, things went downhill. As Union troops prepared to take Charleston in the closing months of the war, Hayne's home crumbled under the weight of Yankee artillery shells—"his beautiful home was burned to the ground, and his large, handsome library utterly lost." Escaping toward Columbia, South Carolina, proved a bad move as well. For here family valuables were lost in the wake of William T. Sherman's famous "March to the Sea." Virtually destitute, Hayne retreated to the "Pine Barrens" of Georgia and began to rebuild his literary career from the small cottage that was now his home. If anyone had title to harbor bitterness, resentment, and cynicism about South Carolina's role in all of this suffering, it would have been Hayne.

When Hayne looked back on the Civil War, though, he saw it through the lenses that he had worn before the conflict began. In a series of works gathered together under the rubric "Poems of the War. 1861–1865." he continued to praise those who had died in heroic circumstances.[84] A hymn

of praise to his native state contained lines that would not have been out
of place in his ode to Col. Butler composed during the Mexican War:

> Death! What of death?—
> Can he who once drew honorable breath
>   In liberty's pure sphere,
>   Foster a sensual fear,
> When death and slavery meet him face
>   To face
> Saying: "Choose then between us; here,
>   The grace
> Which follows patriot martyrdom, and
>   There,
> Black degradation, haunted by despair.[85]

To be sure, these lines trade on the venerable traditions of Southern
honor. Yet there is more. Perhaps without intending to, Hayne drew a
conclusion (as we shall see in chapter 5) to which many African Americans would have given their assent: that it was preferable to die as a free
man than it was to suffer the sting of slavery.

Again and again, Hayne returned to the theme of martyrdom—
something in which he had been keenly interested even before the war
began. One tribute to the Confederate war dead was entitled simply
"Our Martyrs."[86] Hayne's war poems also included memorials to Confederate generals J. E. B. Stuart and "Stonewall" Jackson, both of whom
were fast becoming iconic figures in the rhetoric of the Lost Cause. An
ode "in honor of the bravery and sacrifices of the soldiers of the South"
referred to the sleeping "martyrs" who were now laid to rest in "those
lonely desolated graves!"[87] Without some acquaintance with Hayne's antebellum poetry, these songs to dead Southern patriots might appear to
spring solely from the suffering borne of war. And to some degree they
did. At the same time, though, it is important to see these verses standing in continuity with a long train of antebellum poetry that had been
obsessed with the deaths of heroic martyrs fighting for a vaunted cause.

Hayne's poetry on his native city of Charleston, South Carolina, also
smacks of the "Voice from the Ruins" tradition that had been a sta-
ple in the pages of the *Southern Literary Messenger.* His collection of

war poetry contained three poems on the Union attacks on Charleston: "Charleston," "Battle of Charleston Harbor, April 7, 1863," and "Charleston at the Close of 1863."[88] In the first of these poems, perhaps drawing on an image from classical antiquity (the sack of Troy or the scene of Dido's funeral pyre from Virgil's *Aeneid*), Hayne anticipated the destruction of his town:

> If strength, and will, and courage fail
> To cope with ruthless numbers,
> And thou must bend, despairing, pale,
> Where thy last hero slumbers,
> Lift the red torch, and light the fire
> Amid those corpses gory,
> And on thy self-made funeral pyre,
> Pass from the world to glory.[89]

For Hayne there was clearly something beautiful in the defiance of a city that refused to bend to the enemy and that chose the glories of the funeral pyre rather than allowing the dead to fall into the hands of the attacker.

When Charleston did eventually succumb to the legions of the Union, it was in part due to the much-celebrated efforts of Col. Robert Gould Shaw and the 54th Massachusetts Colored Infantry. Now celebrated in modern memory by Edward Zwick's feature film *Glory*, the attack on Battery Wagner—a key fortification in the defense of Charleston's Harbor—brought a showcase regiment composed of free black troops into a bitter contest with well-entrenched Confederate troops. On July 18, 1863, taking part in an assault that included other Union regiments, the 54th breached Wagner's walls for a moment before being driven back in a hail of shot and shell. Of the 600 men the 54th had brought into the fray, the regiment lost 256, including 14 officers—among them Col. Shaw.[90] Judged strictly by tactical terms, the assault on Fort Wagner was a bungled mess—Union troops advancing behind the 54th had actually discharged their weapons into the backs of their charging comrades. In a wider sense, though, the reputation for courage that the 54th earned as a result of the attack was a decisive turning point in convincing whites that black troops were worthy comrades. Shortly after the assault on Wagner,

George E. Stephens, black veteran and correspondent with the regiment, wrote that "on the whole, this is considered to be a brilliant feat of the 54th. It is another evidence that cannot now be denied, that colored soldiers will dare go to where any brave men will lead them. Col. Shaw, our noble and lamented commander, was the bravest of the brave. He did not take his thirty paces to the rear, but led the column up to the fort, and was the first man to stand on the parapet of the fort."[91] Within moments of the failed attack, Stephens's comments suggest, Col. Shaw was well on the way to achieving status as a martyred hero.

Francis George Shaw and Sarah Shaw, Robert's parents, played a decisive role in launching the publicity efforts that would enshrine their son in Union memory. Massachusetts reformers with great energy and a wide array of influential friends, the Shaws were eager to promote Robert's death in ways that would ensure that the Union war effort could not be divorced from the abolitionist aim of dealing a death blow to the institution of slavery. Ironically, the actions of the Confederate defenders of Fort Wagner played directly into the hands of the Shaw family. When the Shaws learned that Confederate commander General Johnson Hagood had tossed their son's corpse into a burial trench—along with the bodies of his men—they turned this intended disgrace into a badge of virtue. Rather than decrying the promiscuous burial as an outrage, Shaw's family deemed that no more appropriate honor could have been bestowed on their son than to have been buried with his men. They politely refused offers to help them recover Robert's body for a proper burial at home. "We can imagine no holier place than that in which he lies," wrote Frank Shaw, "among his brave and devoted followers, nor wish for him better company—what a body-guard he has!"[92] The dead body of Shaw thus emerged as a powerful symbol of racial reconciliation in the Union Army.[93]

The absence of a burial for their son in Massachusetts did not stop Frank and Sarah Shaw from memorializing their son. Indeed, Sarah Shaw took up the task of memorializing her son's legacy with incredible resolve and energy, publishing three literary works devoted to the task: (1) *Letters: RGS;* (2) *Memorial: RGS;* and (3) "Robert Gould Shaw," an essay for *Harvard Memorial Biographies.*[94] The *Memorial: RGS* volume, in particular, warrants special attention. Published in 1864, the Shaw

Memorial volume bristles with letters, military orders and correspondence, press clippings, and literary reflections on Robert's brief career with the 54th Massachusetts Colored Infantry. Weighing in at almost two hundred pages, the volume presents an almost encyclopedic, if fundamentally heroic, account of Shaw's military service.[95] Well before 1897, when the famous Augustus St. Gaudens bronze relief sculpture was unveiled on the Boston Common, Shaw had already achieved mythic status.

The poetry of death played a critical role in shaping the ways in which Shaw was memorialized in the *Memorial: RGS*. In the months following his death, anonymous admirers and friends of the family composed "countless poems" that celebrated the young man's role in the war for freedom.[96] In response to this deluge of verse, the Shaws included a dozen of these poems in the *Memorial: RGS*, including works by Elizabeth B. Sedgwick, Ralph Waldo Emerson, and James Russell Lowell. Taken together, the poems served as a literary memorial to the legacy of Col. Shaw, one that the poets claimed would render obsolete the need for a more traditional monument of stone. As the poet "A. N." wrote in the poem "One Grave" (which also appeared in *Harper's Weekly*) "Monuments rock-sculptured fade away, / But there are deeds whose praise shall live through heaven's unclosing day."[97]

Not surprisingly, more than half of the poems took as their subject the circumstances of Shaw's burial. From Lenox, Massachusetts, Elizabeth B. Sedgwick invoked Shakespeare's play *Henry V* when she began her poem with the lines:

> Buried with a band of brothers
> Who for him would fain have died;
> Buried with the gallant fellows
> Who fell fighting by his side.[98]

For the poets of the *Memorial: RGS* the fact that Shaw had been buried with his own troops was emblematic of the unity between the races that he had fought to achieve in the first place. Furthermore, the poets saw Shaw's efforts as all the more laudable because he had been a child of privilege and could have avoided death on the battlefield. Instead of shirking his responsibilities, the young colonel had stepped forward and forthrightly embraced his own death. In the hands of one poet who had written for the *Northern Christian Advocate,* Colonel Shaw stood forth as nothing short of "The Martyr of Freedom." Thus the opening stanza of the poem:

> Fair in his manhood, an offering he made;
>> Youthful ambition and talent so high,
> All on his country's red altar he laid,
>> Battling for freedom, for freedom to die.[99]

The rhetoric of martyrdom that organized the *Memorial: RGS* shared much of the same sensibility that surfaced in the poems of Hayne when he wrote about the valiant Southern troops who had died defending the cause of freedom. It also shared much with the sensibility of the romantic poetry that had appeared in journals such as the *Southern Literary Messenger* in the years leading up to the Civil War. Tales of fiery patriots, doomed sailors, Mexican War heroes, and vanishing Indians provided the American psyche with a well-stocked library of images on which they could draw in time of war. In short, to die in war was a beautiful thing.

Americans had been well schooled to see the beauty inherent in death, to see the world that waited on a distant shore beyond this one, and to celebrate the deaths of those who had fallen in a noble cause. Like Robert Gould Shaw, hundreds of thousands of Americans were willing to make the "offering" that made the Civil War the bloodiest conflict in our history.

⋅⋅⋅⬦⋅⋅⋅

"Better to Die Free, Than to Live Slaves"

George E. Stephens was one of the men who followed Col. Robert Gould Shaw in the 54th Massachusetts Colored Infantry's 1863 assault on Fort Wagner, South Carolina. A resident of Philadelphia's free black community, Stephens's family had moved to Pennsylvania from Virginia in the wake of Nat Turner's rebellion. In 1831, his parents—both free and of mixed blood—had headed north fearing the tightening pressure of white retaliation in the months following Turner's revolutionary activities. Nat Turner's spontaneous and ferocious uprising had resulted in the deaths of more than sixty white Virginians and had terrified the state legislature to the point where plans for gradual abolition were once again dusted off and debated. White Virginians came face-to-face with the worst horrors they could have imagined, and they concluded that clamping down on their slaves rather than freeing them was the safest course. Although young George was born in Philadelphia in 1832, the legacy of Turner's violent resistance to slavery was never far from his mind.[1]

By 1863, when it became clear that the Union would employ black troops in the cause of war, Stephens jumped at the chance. During the spring of 1863 he joined Frederick Douglass and a host of other black luminaries in recruiting troops for the newly forming 54th Massachu-setts regiment. Stephens argued energetically, both in print and before crowds, that black men could and would be able adversaries in the fight against the Confederacy. On April 2, 1863, writing to New York's *Weekly Anglo-African* newspaper, he sought to steel the resolve of potential recruits for the bloody work that lay ahead. Deploying lines from Henry Highland Garnet's fiery 1843 speech before a convention of African American leaders in Buffalo, New York, Stephens blasted those who resisted the mustering of black regiments: They "do not tell you that it were 'better to die free, than to live slaves'—that your wronged and out-raged sisters and brothers are calling on you to take up arms and place your interests and lives in the balance against their oppressors—that 'your dead fathers speak to you from their graves.'"[2] From Stephens's perspective it was better to die in the cause of freedom than it was to live in the state of slavery.

In resurrecting Garnet's speech, Stephens yoked his recruiting efforts to an oration that had displayed an intricate latticing of the themes of slavery and death.[3] Addressing directly the slave population of America, Garnet argued that even those free Northern blacks who were not "par-takers with you" in slavery could still never be utterly free themselves until slavery had been dealt a death blow.[4] Garnet traced the rise of slavery in America in terse and moving lines. The first slaves brought to American shores did not "come flying upon the wings of Liberty, to a land of free-dom." Rather, they came as doomed men. "Nor," said Garnet, "did the evil of bondage end at their emancipation by death."[5] For generation after generation of American people now endured the curse of perpet-ual human bondage. Here Garnet cast the institution of slavery itself in deathly terms when he intoned that "slavery had stretched its dark wings of death over the land."[6] At one level in Garnet's thinking, then, there worked the idea that slavery equaled death. Conversely, freedom equaled life. Thus when the founders of America issued their famous declaration and when the Virginia patriot Patrick Henry had pronounced the lines "Liberty or Death," he had said more than he knew.[7]

As a remedy to the curse of slavery, Garnet reminded his audience that "no oppressed people have ever secured their Liberty without resis-tance."[8] Anticipating by two decades what tens of thousands of African

Americans would do when the Civil War began, Garnet urged the slaves of the South to stop working for their masters. But there would, he imagined, be hell to pay for what W. E. B. Du Bois would come to call "the General Strike" of black workers against the slave system.[9] If the slaveholders were to "commence the work of death, they, and not you, will be responsible for the consequences. You had far better all die—*die immediately,* than live slaves, and entail your wretchedness upon your posterity."[10] Garnet's argument here seems to be that if the current generation of slaves were to "*die immediately*" in resisting this great evil, it could not be perpetuated. Slavery itself would die in the wake of the death of slaves. Garnet held that hope for emancipation resided in the willingness of slaves to accept the risk, if not the reality, of death in the quest for freedom. "Let it no longer be a debatable question," he cried, "whether it is better to choose LIBERTY or DEATH."[11] But even this declaration was more complex than it seemed—for to grasp fully the fruits of liberty, enslaved people would need to make friends with the prospect of death.

To drive home the point that it was worth risking death to achieve freedom, Garnet concluded his speech with a historical genealogy of those African American heroes who had died in the cause of liberty. Here he pointed to Denmark Vesey of South Carolina who had "died a martyr to freedom" as a result of his effort to free blacks and spirit them away to Haiti. He pointed to "the patriotic Nathaniel Turner" who had landed the terrible blow for freedom in Virginia. "By Despotism," Garnet speculated, "his name has been recorded on the list of infamy, but future generations will number him upon the noble and the brave." He pointed to the heroic Joseph Cinque of *Amistad* fame. He pointed to Madison Washington of the brig *Creole* who had led nineteen who had "struck for Liberty or Death." Although all of Garnet's heroes had deployed the sword in the pursuit of freedom, he urged massive labor action as the best and most practical way to defeat slavery on its own turf. "From this moment," he urged, "cease to labor for tyrants who will not remunerate you." It was within the reach of the enslaved people of the South to end slavery. Calling on African traditions which held that the spirits of departed ancestors were available for inspiration and consolation, Garnet urged his listeners to action: "Your dead fathers speak to you from their graves, Heaven, as with a voice of thunder, calls on you to arise from the dust."[12] In these closing lines—which reference a rising from the dust—Garnet sees the liberation from chattel slavery as a form of social and political resurrection.

Garnet's speech articulated an intricate understanding of the interplay between slavery and death. On the one hand, he suggested that to suffer at the hands of slavery was to suffer a form of living death. Anticipating the work of contemporary sociologist Orlando Patterson, Garnet believed that enslaved people experienced a form of "social death."[13] At the same time, however, Garnet's speech suggested that death itself offered a pathway to freedom. Indeed, he said that death presented a means of "emancipation." But here he did not mean only that physical death on earth opened up the way to a life of freedom in heaven (although, as we shall see, this idea was certainly a potent one in antebellum America) but also emphasized that it was better to die in the act of resisting slavery than it was to live under the death imposed by the slave masters. In some sense, Garnet was offering to his audience a distinctively African American understanding of the "Bad Death" and the "Good Death." The "Bad Death" was the death experienced under the crushing weight of slavery. The "Good Death" was the death experienced by free men battling to end evil in the world.

This chapter explores more closely the complicated relationship of slavery and death in antebellum America. First, it explores the ways in which slavery and death were inextricably bound together for the enslaved people of the early Republic. Next, it examines the ways in which a willingness to risk death or to embrace death provided a way to freedom. In so doing, it suggests that the willingness of thousands of African Americans to rise up in such numbers during the Civil War may have owed much to their understandings of the relationship between slavery and death. Like Henry Highland Garnet and George Stephens, they resolved that it was indeed better "to die freemen, than to live slaves."

The institution of slavery may be seen as complicating and intensifying the culture of death for antebellum African Americans. On the one hand, they participated with many free people in an evangelical Christianity that stressed calm resignation and acceptance in the face of death. Recall, on this point, the deathbed narratives of James Forten and James Jackson (considered in chapter 1). Enslaved people, too, shared a robust vision of the glories of heaven and the conviction that sin would be punished and faith would be rewarded in a life beyond the grave. But slavery—perhaps even more than disease, more than epidemics, more than the sheer vicissitudes of life—placed African Americans on a level of intimacy with death that many whites could not comprehend. The forthright discussion of reported slave suicides in the African American press, which we will consider in this chapter, is evidence that for some enslaved people death (and the freedom it promised) offered a means of escape. And the willingness of African Americans to risk death in seeking their temporal freedom may well have proved to be the decisive turning point in the military outcome of the Civil War. In all of these ways, enslaved people participated in and shaped the wider antebellum engagement with death, but did so in ways that also reflected the economic and political realities of the peculiar institution of slavery.

From the beginning, slavery in the Americas was overshadowed by what Garnet had so chillingly called the "dark wings of death." Olaudah Equiano's famous eighteenth-century narrative describes the prospect of death that loomed over enslaved people at virtually every moment during the torturous "Middle Passage" from Africa to the New World. From the outset, Equiano gave voice to the apparently pervasive fear that whites had taken up slaves in Africa with designs on consuming them as a source of food. One of the first things he asked once on board a slaver was "if we were not to be eaten by those white men with horrible looks, red faces, and long hair."[14] Even if the fear of outright cannibalism proved to be unfounded, there is a sense in which Equiano and his fellow slaves were devoured by the transatlantic slave system. Equiano reported an incident in which the crew beat a slave to death and then "tossed him over the side as they would have done a brute."[15] So horrid were the conditions below decks that some slaves determined that only death could bring them relief. Breaking through the obstacles of chains, nets, and riggings, they jumped overboard. Having successfully made it over the side of the ship, Equiano wrote that "many more very soon would have done the same, if they had not been prevented by the ship's crew."[16] Equiano detailed the perverse spectacle of one man who had been pulled from the surf for attempting to commit suicide. The man was then scourged "unmercifully, for thus attempting to prefer death to slavery."[17] What may have been an act of desperation on the part of this tortured slave was perceived as an act of rebellion by the crew of Equiano's ship.

When they controlled the fate of their property, slavers had no qualms about throwing their human cargo overboard when economic calculation dictated such a move. In his role as a free man and antislavery spokesman, Equiano "helped to break the story of the massacre on the slave ship *Zong*"—an incident in 1781 in which the ship's captain ordered that 132 slaves be hurled to their deaths in order for him to collect the insurance payments due on them as cargo.[18] While the case of the *Zong* might have revealed an act of exceptional cruelty, the omnipresence of death during the "Middle Passage" can hardly be exaggerated. Historian Philip D. Morgan estimates that "on average, about a sixth of a slaver's complement failed to survive the transatlantic crossing, although this figure varied tremendously depending upon the coastal region of origin, the date of departure, and the duration of the voyage."[19] If we accept the current judgment of historians that "a total of 10 to 11 million living slaves crossed the Atlantic Ocean from the sixteenth to the nineteenth century," we can gain some grim appreciation of the sheer scale of death that accompanied this brutal species of commerce.[20]

Once in America, death continued to haunt enslaved people. Take, for example, the case of slavery in the late eighteenth-century North. As a commitment to urban slavery grew in places like Philadelphia and New York, newly arriving slaves from Africa encountered a world rife with European filth and disease. "The crude death rate of black people in Boston and Philadelphia during the 1750s and 1760s," writes historian Ira Berlin, "was well over 60 per thousand, nearly one-third to one-half more than the death rate of white people."[21] Even as the American Revolution crippled the endurance of slavery in the North, black fertility rates there declined as a result of high death rates and the attendant disruptions of family life.[22] On the rice plantations of South Carolina and Georgia, too, slaves faced a grim existence. In the late colonial era, notes historian Philip D. Morgan, low country planters might anticipate losing "perhaps a third of arrivals within the first year."[23] As late as 1807, municipal officials in Charleston, South Carolina, continued to worry about the profusion of dead slave bodies dumped into the harbor by owners anxious "to avoid paying burial fees."[24] Well into the nineteenth century, slaves in the rice fields faced much higher death rates than those of slaves elsewhere in the United States. On the Manigault family plantations of South Carolina, for instance, "slaves could expect to live only nineteen years from their date of birth—seventeen years less than their counterparts across the entire South."[25] Clinging to their emerging paternalistic ideology, the planters "never acknowledged that they were killing their slaves by forcing them to labor in the swamp," preferring instead to hold the slaves themselves responsible for the appalling death rates.[26] North and South, evidence indicates American slaves continued to see death close at hand.

Beyond demographics and the measurement of crude death rates, it may not be too much to say that the genre of the slave narrative in North America was born in death.[27] Some of the earliest first-person narratives of African Americans are essentially gallows confessions of men reciting their crimes before the moment of execution. Published predominantly in the late eighteenth- and early nineteenth-century North, these narratives owed much to the residue of Puritan religious practice in colonial New England whereby condemned criminals testified to their heinous crimes before the assembled community. These rituals made the death of criminals instructive to the faithful while simultaneously cementing acceptable norms of behavior. The narratives of early African American criminals also reflected the growing scrutiny under which blacks came to live in the postrevolutionary North.[28] In this increasingly hostile racial climate, white calls for the policing of black life became shrill. And African American political and religious leaders—men such as Philadelphia's Richard Allen—became dedicated to the idea that their communicants must lead lives of sterling conduct and unimpeachable virtue.

The confessions attributed to these African American men sometimes follow a rhythm in which the articulation of the most deviant of behaviors is followed by heartfelt Christian repentance and submission. In 1768, the young Massachusetts runaway known as Arthur admitted to a litany of the most "notorious Crimes" including the rape of one Deborah Metcalfe. Before his execution, however, Arthur thanked a local clergyman for his ministrations and then delivered a warning to other potentially wayward men. "I would solemnly warn those of my

Colour," he said, "as they regard their own souls, to avoid Desertion from their Masters, Drunkenness and Lewdness; which three Crimes was the Source from which have flowed the many Evils and Miseries of my short Life."[29] Now converted and sorrowful, Arthur was resigned to his fate. In 1795, Edmund Fortis, another runaway slave, owned his dreadful work in committing both rape and murder. Fortis had been born and raised in Virginia before he escaped slavery. He then began his trek North and his downward spiral of crime. Standing before a court in Dresden, Massachusetts, Fortis freely admitted his crimes and accepted death while feeling "perfectly resigned and thankful to the court."[30] Stephen Smith, like Fortis a runaway slave from Virginia, also recited an inventory of crimes he had committed, culminating in arson and theft. In 1797, from Boston, Smith prepared to meet his end, saying that "I die in peace with all mankind, and beg that all people will take warning by my Awful END."[31] In 1808, writing from Philadelphia, John Joyce, another former Maryland slave who had broken out of the service of his mistress, Sarah Saunders, also confessed to a life of crime, eventually resulting in the horrific murder of Mrs. Sarah Cross. The details of Joyce's trial, published "For the Benefit of Bethel Church" in Philadelphia under the watchful eye of Rev. Richard Allen, was meant to send a clear message about the necessity of sound Christian instruction.[32] But it may also have unintentionally contributed to another trend that can be glimpsed in these sources: These narratives suggested that lives of criminality and death awaited those slaves who escaped from slavery—that freedom, not slavery, brought about death.

As the debate over the future of slavery in America intensified, abolitionists and former slaves forged a rhetoric that cast the institution of slavery itself as a form of death. Gone were the intimations—evident in some of the late eighteenth- and early nineteenth-century narratives— that freedom itself might be implicated in bringing about death for African Americans. To be sure, such ideas endured in antebellum America, but they came largely from the mouths of proslavery ideologues. Abolitionists sang a different tune. When, for example, William Lloyd Garrison denounced the U.S. Constitution as a "covenant with death, an agreement with hell" he was not dabbling in hyperbole.[33] Rather Garrison put his finger on what would become an important theme in the

THE DESPERATION OF A MOTHER.

Fig. 9. *The Desperation of a Mother,* from *The Anti-Slavery Record,* September 1835. This illustration follows a line of argument familiar in abolitionist circles—that death might well be preferable to a life in bondage. Courtesy of the Library Company of Philadelphia.

literature of the abolitionist movement—that to live under slavery was to live under what Henry Highland Garnet had termed the "dark wings of death." In her harrowing autobiography, *Incidents in the Life of a Slave Girl, Written By Herself,* Harriet Jacobs wrestled with the relationship of slavery and death as she worried over the fate of her sick, young son. "Alas, what mockery it is for a slave mother to pray back her dying child to life!" she wrote. "Death is better than slavery."[34] In Jacobs' mind, the living death her child might experience under slavery was by far more dreadful than the death that would take him beyond this world of suffering. The runaway slave, author, and abolitionist William Wells Brown made a similar point in reflecting on his flight from bondage. "The thought of death," he wrote, "was nothing frightful to me, compared with that of being caught, and again carried back into slavery."[35] Even free blacks living in the North could experience the crushing force of slavery as a form of death. Thus the abolitionist David Walker of Boston could write in his incendiary 1829 *Appeal to the Colored Citizens of the World*, these extraordinary lines: "If any wish to plunge me into the wretched incapacity of a slave, murder me for the truth, know ye, that I am in the hand of God, and at your disposal. I count my life not dear to me, but I am ready to be offered at any moment. For what is the use of living when in fact I am dead."[36] From Walker's perspective, even the prospect of slavery could bring death to those who contemplated it.

An 1850 lithograph depicting the liberation of the former slave Henry Box Brown also equated the institution of slavery with death (fig. 10). Brown's celebrated tale of how he liberated himself by being shipped in a small crate from Richmond, Virginia, to Philadelphia, Pennsylvania, made him a celebrated figure in abolitionist circles. The 1850 illustration depicts him emerging from a box, surrounded by a cluster of abolitionists. The full title of the lithograph—"The resurrection of Henry Box Brown at Philadelphia, who escaped from Richmond Va."—indicated that freedom resurrected him from the living death he had experienced under slavery. Indeed, the box itself might be seen as a coffin—symbolizing the horrid suffocation of the slave system. In the evangelical hothouse of antebellum America, to speak of the "resurrection" of freedom was simultaneously to speak of the death that held slavery's victims.

Perhaps no abolitionist or former slave developed the relationship of slavery and death as richly as did Frederick Douglass in his 1855 narrative, *My Bondage and My Freedom*. Composed ten years after his initial *Narrative of the Life of Frederick Douglass*, this volume was not a mere updating of the first autobiography.[37] It was instead "a different and much more penetrating look into the heart of slavery."[38] It was the product of a man looking back on his experiences as a slave with ten more years of life under his belt. Douglass explored in greater detail the psychology of slavery—with an eye toward excavating the emotional and spiritual landscapes of master and slave alike. The book also signaled the

Fig. 10. *The Resurrection of Henry Box Brown at Philadelphia, who escaped from Richmond, Virginia in a box 3 feet long 2½ ft. deep and 2 ft. wide,* 1850. Courtesy of the American Antiquarian Society, Worcester, Mass.

maturation of Douglass as an abolitionist in his own right, breaking with his former mentor and friend William Lloyd Garrison—particularly on the question of whether it was morally justifiable to strike violently at slavery. Whereas Garrison still clung to his pacifist proclivities, Douglass' personal reckoning with the brutalities of slavery had led him to believe that only force would pry slave property from the hands of the master class. Over time, Douglass' militancy in the cause of freedom would only deepen. With the Civil War in full swing, he threw himself into helping to muster troops for the 54th Massachusetts Colored Infantry. In March 1863, in a famously quoted recruiting speech, he announced that it was now time to "smite with death the power that would bury the Government and your liberty in the same hopeless grave."[39]

The rhetoric of death that Douglass deployed in this 1863 recruiting oration had deep roots in *My Bondage and My Freedom*. If one revisits this narrative with the issue of death in mind, a whole new dimension of the narrative opens up. In the early pages, Douglass reflected on the separation from his mother that he endured when he was taken to the plantations of Col. Lloyd. As a boy on the Lloyd lands, Douglass could only learn secondhand about his mother's life and death. Indeed, Douglass' recounting of the death of his mother emphasizes the alienating force of slavery in breaking apart slave families. He wrote that he had not been allowed off the plantation to visit her even when her illness grew more serious. He learned of her death only after the fact. "The heartless and ghastly form of *slavery*," he wrote, "rises between mother and child, even at the bed of death." It was largely for the free to enjoy "scenes of sacred tenderness, around the death-bed never to be forgotten."[40] Enslaved people rarely, if ever, had such a rich experience. Given the prime importance of the deathbed scene in the early nineteenth-century narrative framings of death, Douglass' critique of the slave system would have hit the mark. Harriet Beecher Stowe's novel *Uncle Tom's Cabin*, with its famous deathbed scene of Little Eva, had been freshly published only three years before *My Bondage and My Freedom* appeared. Readers familiar with Little Eva's dying moments would have known exactly what Douglass had missed in learning secondhand of his own mother's death. This was not only a brilliant treatment of the psychology of slavery, but a deft stroke of propagandistic genius.

Douglass was also concerned, of course, with what he had called "the mere physical cruelties" of plantation life. Among other scenes of violence in the early pages of the text—which seem to build in their intensity throughout the narrative—is the execution of the slave Denby by Col. Lloyd's overseer Austin Gore. As Douglass described it, Denby, "a powerful young man, full of animal spirits," had offended Gore in some way. Rather than suffer a brutal whipping at Gore's hands, Denby jumped into a creek and refused to come out. Gore gave Denby three chances to come out of the water and receive his whipping. Denby refused. Gore then "took deadly aim at his standing victim, and, in an instant, poor

Denby was numbered with the dead. His mangled body sank out of sight, and only his warm, red blood marked the place where he had stood."[41] Relating this scene of outright murder, Douglass challenged directly the ideology of proslavery thinkers who had argued that both the dictates of economy and Christianity militated against the slaughter of slave property. After all, they asked, what decent master in his right mind would kill an investment and a righteous soul with the same shot? Indeed, the "slave codes" passed by state legislatures in the 1840s and 1850s, had made a point of reminding slave owners to treat their property with "humanity."[42] They also held masters accountable for the murder of their slaves. As legal scholars of the Old South have demonstrated, some masters did receive a modicum of correction in courts of law—penalized "typically with ten-year jail sentences—for murdering slaves."[43] But given the relative isolation of most of the South's plantations and the political realities of planter power, it is likely that "most crimes committed against slaves went unpunished."[44] This is the point that Douglass drove home. Although he insulated Col. Lloyd from direct responsibility for the murder of Denby by putting the gun in the hands of the overseer Austin Gore, Douglass nevertheless made a larger argument: Slavery killed not only souls and spirits; it killed bodies too.

The pivotal moment in Douglass' life as a slave was his own battle with an overseer—a brutal figure known as "Covey, the Negro Breaker." Having lived for a period of years as a slave in Baltimore, when Douglass returned to the eastern shore of Maryland he came back as an educated, powerful, and willful young man. Verging on the incorrigible, he was sent to Covey to be instilled with the discipline required of adult, male field hands. The plan failed miserably. Taking on Covey in a physical confrontation that lasted the better part of a day, Douglass outlasted the overseer. The epic struggle against Covey marked the turning point in Douglass' life as a slave and set him on the irrevocable path to liberty. "After resisting him, I felt as I had never felt before," Douglass wrote, "It was a resurrection from the dark and pestiferous tomb of slavery, to the heaven of comparative freedom."[45] Open defiance of his status as a slave had brought Douglass back from the dead. His commitment to the violent overthrow of slavery may have had its genesis in the midst of his fight with Covey. He came to understand that the only way to avoid the penalty of the lash was to defy it. "From this time, until that of my escape from slavery," he boasted, "I was never fairly whipped."[46] Exploding the myth that compliant slaves might receive softer treatment at the hands of their masters than would rebellious ones, Douglass' life provided ample evidence of his dictum that "he is whipped oftenest, who is whipped easiest."[47]

Armed with this resolve to escape the bonds of slavery, Douglass made concrete plans to leave Maryland's eastern shore. On the verge of his attempt to run to freedom, he reflected in *My Bondage and My Freedom* on the "intense agony which is felt by the slave, when wavering on the point of making his escape."[48] At this point in the narrative—in accord with Garnet and Stephens—he recalled the words of Virginia patriot Patrick Henry. He drew steel from them. For Douglass, the phrase "Give Me Liberty or Give Me Death" had particular resonance for American slaves. The stakes for them were higher than it was for white folk, with the odds stacked against them. "With us it was a *doubtful* liberty, at best, that we sought," he wrote, "and a certain, lingering death in the rice swamps and sugar fields if we failed." Still, even after weighing his long chances for a successful escape, Douglass determined to try—even if it meant death to him. "I believe there was not one among us," he recalled of those with whom he conspired, "who would not rather have been shot down, than pass away in hopeless bondage."[49]

As the escape attempt unfolded, Douglass' worst fears materialized. Betrayed by one of the members of his own party, Douglass and a small band of his followers were apprehended and brought before "Master Thomas" for an informal hearing at his small store. Douglass and his group denied that they were truly intent on stealing away to the North. Thomas Auld rejected their arguments in bone-chilling terms, saying (according to Douglass) "that the evidence he had of our intention to run away, was strong enough to hang us, in a case of murder."[50] Languishing in a jail cell in Easton, Maryland, Douglass imagined being sold off to the hard labor regimes on the plantations of Georgia, Louisiana, or Alabama—places in the deep South from which escape would have been doubly difficult. Again, he fell back on the language of death to describe his plight. "A life of living death," he wrote, "beset with the innumerable horrors of the cotton field, and the sugar plantation, seemed to be my doom."[51] But a miracle saved him from that fate. Thomas Auld, as he had done on two occasions before, intervened on behalf of the young slave who may, indeed, have been his own son. Sending Douglass back to his brother Hugh in Baltimore, Maryland, virtually ensured that the young and headstrong slave would bolt to freedom. In the spring of 1838 that is exactly what he did.

Throughout *My Bondage and My Freedom,* Douglass explored the intricate interrelationship between death and slavery. From his perspective, the institution of slavery brought with it at least two species of death: spiritual and physical. The first form was the "living death" that slaves experienced by virtue of their status as human property. This was the "soul-crushing and death-dealing" dimension of slavery that Douglass described at every step in his narrative. This was the social death that even impeded slaves from enjoying the consolations of the pious deathbed. In addition to the death of the soul and the spirit, Douglass also identified the ways in which slavery destroyed the bodies of slaves. For him, the death brought by slavery was as real as the bullet that killed the slave Denby as he cowered in the creek bed. As rich as Douglass' narrative is in its exposé of the psychological punishment inflicted by slavery, it is clear that he also wanted his readers to understand that slavery killed slaves.

As the national debate over the extension of slavery into the West came to a boil in the 1850s, the African American press—especially the *Frederick Douglass Paper*—continued to insist on the lethal character of chattel slavery. Given the overall level of violence that attended the slavery issue in that decade, such charges would have seemed of a piece with the times. In the wake of the passage of the Kansas-Nebraska Act in 1854, a virtual border war broke out in the Kansas Territory as free state settlers and the so-called border ruffians of Missouri sought to gain political power. In 1856, Massachusetts Senator Charles Sumner fell bloody on the Senate floor under the blows of South Carolina Representative Preston Brooks for a speech he had given on "The Crime Against Kansas." Back on the plains, the radical abolitionist John Brown led a raiding party of grimly determined free-staters in the butchering of five proslavery settlers at Pottawatomie Creek, Kansas. The violence that the *Frederick Douglass Paper* pointed to, however, existed not on the lawless prairies of Kansas but on the refined plantations of the American South. We must be quick to acknowledge that in objective terms it would be a gross error in historical judgment to say that the outright murder of slaves was the order of the day on average Southern plantations. No sane and sensible scholar of the Old South would make such a claim. At the same time, however, we must examine seriously the rhetoric of death in these accounts and observe how it framed abolitionist understandings of the evils of slavery.

Some accounts of slave deaths in the *Frederick Douglass Paper* drew directly on the literary type of the demonic slaveholder—Simon Legree— that novelist Harriet Beecher Stowe had popularized in her book *Uncle Tom's Cabin*. An item reported on April 15, 1853, directed readers to the doings of "Another Legree" who operated near Warrenton, Georgia. The brief article claimed that a local slaveholder was now on trial for the murder of his fourth slave. "The last one he whipped to death," the story declared, "another he burnt to death literally roasting him alive, tied to a tree. He will probably be let off with a small fine."[52] An account from the August 26, 1853, issue identified "a Legree" from Louisiana who had killed a slave of ninety years of age, in part because of his "revolutionary reminiscences." As a result, the slaveholder had "deliberately whipped, stamped, and kicked him to death." Those who had seen the body of the deceased slave said "that the sight was sickening—his whole back cut and bruised into a jelly, and the lower part of his body nearly kicked to pieces."[53]

Lurid and detailed descriptions of badly damaged slave bodies bring to mind historian William S. McFeely's point "that accounts of floggings were one of the most sought-after forms of nineteenth-century pornography (disguised in the plain wrapper of a call to virtuous antislavery action.)"[54] Even if we readily concede this observation, it is difficult to get around the conclusion that such accounts did contain a grain of truth about the terrible violence of the slave system. An item from the February 24, 1854, issue of the *Frederick Douglass Paper* reported the case of a Mississippi slave who was burned to death for striking a white man. Local planters may have wanted to make an example of him, as illustrated by the report that "nearly four thousand slaves were collected from plantations in the neighborhood to witness the scene."[55] On April 26, 1856, the *Provincial Freeman* (an African American newspaper published in Canada), also decried an instance of "Burning a Negro"—and wondered aloud if this were the type of system that slaveholders wanted "established on the free soil of Kansas and Nebraska."[56] Another press account identified the death of a slave boy, aged about fourteen years, due to savage violence that revealed "his back dreadfully excoriated, the wrists cut deeply with cords, one or two ribs broken, and an abcess in the right side."[57] Another pointed to the example of a Virginia slave who was whipped to death by his master Henry Birdsong.[58] Still another narrative described the "Execution of a Negro in Louisiana" for the crime of murdering his former master.[59] Whether related in the language of gothic horror or in the rhetoric of pornographic violence, it is clear that antislavery advocates saw death at work on the plantations of the American South.

Ironically, death itself offered an avenue of escape from the dehumanizing force of slavery. The *Frederick Douglass Paper* made this point clearly in a poem entitled "The Dying Slave." Published on July 6, 1855, it presented earthly death as a means to open the way to heavenly freedom:

> The glorious light of Freedom beams around me,
> O'er death's advancing gloom her star I see;
> The chains are riven, which have rankling bound me,
> From life's captivity the slave to free.[60]

That death offered relief from the searing pain of slavery became axiomatic in Harriet Jacob's formulation that "death is better than slavery." But this observation could be read in several ways. On the one hand, as we shall see shortly, the willingness to accept the risk of death could emerge as a wellspring of strength in the battle to achieve freedom on this earth. Thus, W. E. B. Du Bois in *The Souls of Black Folk* could relate the words of the old hymn:

> O Freedom, O Freedom, O Freedom over me!
> Before I'll be a slave
> I'll be buried in my grave,
> And go home to my Lord
> And be free.[61]

Such language raised a battle cry to achieve freedom here and now. Resistance was the message. But there was another path to freedom—the path by which slaves could take their own lives. If death were indeed to be preferred to slavery, then suicide offered a means of escape.

Accounts of slave suicide surface with surprising frequency in the antislavery literature of antebellum America. An 1850 article from the *National Era* responded to a query about the maltreatment of slaves by concluding that "if our anonymous friend be a reader of the newspapers, he must know that suicide among slaves is not infrequent."[62] Another article from Frederick Douglass's first newspaper the *North Star* urged slaves to seek their freedom on earth rather than in heaven. "Do not abandon yourselves, as have many thousands of American slaves, to the crime of suicide," the article exhorted, "Live! Live to escape from slavery. Live to serve God!"[63] *The North Star*'s claim that "many thousands of American slaves" had ended their own lives seems to stretch credulity. Careful students of slavery in the American South have not found evidence to sustain this assertion. Still, we might at least entertain the possibility that slaves may have chosen the option of suicide more frequently than previously assumed. At the very least, the dramatic and irrevocable nature of the act of suicide drew the attention of the African American press.

We need to think carefully about how to interpret accounts of slave suicide. It may be tempting to conclude immediately that to take one's own life is to commit an act of utter hopelessness. At a fundamental human level this makes sense. And critics of slavery certainly held that it was in the nature of the slave system to produce a soul-killing anomie. But there was more at work in accounts of slave suicide than deep despair. In case after case, descriptions of suicidal slaves identified specific features of the slave system that critics found reprehensible— particularly the inhumanity of the domestic slave trade. As portrayed in antislavery literature, then, accounts of slave suicides were highly charged political sermons that conveyed specific lessons. They took aim at particular social problems. We need to see these acts of suicide not only as individual attempts to gain a freedom beyond life but also as acts of rebellion against the slave system as a whole.

Early nineteenth century accounts of slave suicide targeted directly the kidnapping of slaves and the barbaric cruelty of the slave trade. Take the harrowing description offered in the 1803 Philadelphia antislavery tract entitled *Reflections on Slavery; with Recent Evidence of its*

Inhumanity. Occasioned by the Melancholy Death of Romain, A French Negro.[64] Composed by the "Humanitas," the tract related the tale of the slave Romain and his family. Romain's owner had retreated from the West Indies to the relative safety of Philadelphia with his slave property "to avoid the troubles in St. Domingo"—that is, the massive slave revolt underway in the French Caribbean.[65] After a time, Romain's owner resolved to return to his plantations and gathered up Romain and his family for the trip home. This proved a thorny task. Romain's wife and child slipped away, and he was left alone to contemplate the return to a life of bondage. Humanitas indicated that Romain had already felt the driver's lash, writing that "he knew well the cruelties inflicted on slaves in the West Indies, of which he probably bore visible marks."[66] Rather than face transport back to the stern world of Caribbean slavery, Romain ended his life in Philadelphia. Rendered almost mad by the decision he had to make, Romain "still determined to be free." He "took a pruning knife from his pocket, and dreading a spark of life should remain, whereby he might be restored, he three times cut his throat across and fell dead on the pavement, thereby emancipating himself from the grasp of avarice and inhumanity."[67] The public nature of Romain's suicide— indicated in graphic form in an illustration in the text (fig. 11)—made it a political statement. "Many of those who witnessed the lifeless monument of oppression," according to Humanitas, recalled with some shame their own recent struggle for liberty against the British crown.[68] They had rejected monarchy in 1776, but had retained another form of "domestic despotism" under the name of slavery. Romain's suicide emphasized the hypocrisy of the American political order, one that claimed to cherish liberty while still holding thousands in bondage.

Even cautious critiques of American slavery held up suicide as a form of ultimate rebellion against the system. Consider, for example, the arguments made by the Philadelphia physician Jesse Torrey in his 1817 pamphlet *A Portraiture of Domestic Slavery in the United States.*[69] Torrey was no radical. While he considered the institution of slavery undemocratic in that it set up slaveholders as virtual lords of their own little fiefdoms, he did not wish to sweep it away with one violent stroke. Slaves, he thought, had been debilitated by the mind-numbing labors to which they had been set and were not ready to enjoy the fruits of liberty. To turn them

Fig. 11. From *Reflections on Slavery; with Recent Evidence of its Inhumanity. Occasioned by the Melancholy Death of Romain, A French Negro,* by Humanitas (Philadelphia: R. Cochran, 1803). Courtesy of the Library Company of Philadelphia.

loose without "intellectual and moral improvement" would be a recipe for disaster.[70] Rather than immediate and unconditional emancipation, Torrey proposed a gradual approach in which slaves would slowly be educated and then turned into docile freeholders. Such a gentle transformation would work to the benefit of both slaves and masters alike.

To bolster his gradualist arguments, Torrey illuminated for his readers "some facts and remarks on the interior traffic in slaves, and on the practice of kidnapping coloured persons legally free."[71] These, he reasoned, were unassailable examples of the savage workings of the peculiar institution. He pointed particularly to the shocking case of a woman in Washington, D.C., who had been taken up and was awaiting shipment to a plantation in Georgia. Rather than being passively swept along with the others in her group, she "attempted to escape, by jumping out of the window of the garret of a three story brick tavern in F. Street, about day break in the morning; and that in the fall she had her back and both arms broken."[72] Torrey included in his pamphlet an illustration of the escape attempt, showing the woman in midair hurtling toward the pavement below (fig. 12). Miraculously, the woman survived these shattering injuries. She lived long enough to explain her desperate measure, noting that "her family was dispersed from north to south, and herself nearly torn in pieces, without the shadow of a hope of ever seeing or hearing from her *children* again!"[73] As in the case of the slave Romain, this Philadelphian sought death at the moment that she realized she would be forever cut off from her immediate family.

Torrey continued in *A Portraiture of Domestic Slavery* to detail a handful of other slave suicides, all precipitated by the nefarious "trade in the souls and bodies of men."[74] Here "a woman who been sold in Georgetown, for the southern slave market, cut her own throat" repeatedly until she finally ended her life. Another young mother, Torrey reported, who "had been sold in Maryland, with her child, on the way from Bladensburgh to Washington, heroically cut the throats of both her child and herself, with mortal effect." Another case involved "an African youth in the city of Philadelphia" who had "lately cut his throat almost mortally, merely from the apprehension, he said, of being sold."[75] Again and again, Torrey linked the reality of individual slave suicides to the larger political issue of the domestic trade in slaves.

Evidence gleaned from the African American and abolitionist press confirms that the slave trade was a critical precipitating factor in leading slaves to take their own lives. As early as January 16, 1829, an article in *Freedom's Journal* excoriated the federal government for allowing slave trading in its very seat of government. "Instances of maiming and suicide, executed or attempted," the article maintained, "have been exhibited, as growing out of this traffic within the District."[76] In November, 1848, the *National Era* wove together accounts of three different slave suicides under the heading of an article on "The Slave Trade."[77] In 1855, from Chatham, Canada—a community that boasted a robust population of runaway American slaves—there came the blunt report from the *Provincial Freeman* that "a negro committed suicide at Memphis last week, by shooting himself because his master had sold him to go to Arkansas."[78]

A. Rider del.

"— but I did not want to go, and
I jump'd out of the window.— "

Designed and Published by J. Torrey Jun. Philad. 1817.

Fig. 12. From Jesse Torrey, Jun., Physician, *Portraiture of Domestic Slavery, in the United States: With Reflections on the Practicability of Restoring the Moral Rights of the Slave, without Impairing the Legal Privileges of the Possessor* (Philadelphia: John Bioren, 1817). This image may have served as the inspiration for the illustration in William Wells Brown's work, *Clotel; or, the President's Daughter: A Narrative of Slave Life in the United States* (1853). Courtesy of the Library Company of Philadelphia.

These clipped accounts of suicide do not give us access to the private thoughts and complex motives that may have driven individual slaves to such fatal action, but they do connect the destruction of life with the evil of the domestic trade in slaves.

In his 1853 novel, *Clotel; or, the President's Daughter: A Narrative of Slave Life in the United States,* the runaway slave and abolitionist author William Wells Brown, presented one of the most popular images of slave suicide in antebellum America.[79] Brown's novel dealt forthrightly with the issue that had dogged Thomas Jefferson from the days of his first presidential run in 1800; namely, that he had fathered a substantial number of slave children. In ways that Jefferson's contemporary Federalist adversaries could not have fathomed, Brown tore into the hypocrisy that allowed the avatar of American liberty to exploit his own female property. In one of the book's most dramatic scenes, Clotel is sent by her masters to a "negro pen" in Washington, D.C, to await shipment to New Orleans and then to the harsh regime of plantation life.[80] By locating this final drama in the nation's capital, Brown tapped into a major abolitionist demand of the day—that Congress take steps to eradicate the slave trade in Washington, D.C., a place where even ardent states' rights advocates had to admit that federal authority held sway.

Rather than accept the fate of being sold down the river, Clotel made a break for freedom. Fleeing on foot from her pursuers, she soon discovered that her routes of escape had been blocked. Trapped on a bridge over the "deep foamy waters of the Potomac" Clotel determined to take her own life. Brown's description of her final moments is worth quoting at some length: "Her resolution was taken. She clasped her *hands* convulsively, and raised *them,* as she at the same time raised her eyes toward heaven, and begged for that mercy and compassion *there,* which had been denied her on earth; and then, with a single bound, she vaulted over the railings of the bridge, and sunk forever beneath the waves of the river!"[81] Had Clotel not been a slave, Brown insisted, her decisive action would have been considered an act of high moral courage. "No honour within the gift of the American people," he wrote, "would have been too good to have been heaped upon this heroic woman."[82] Here Brown insisted that Clotel's act was an act of heroic rebellion against slavery even as it signaled her own ultimate despair. Capturing this ambiguity,

Fig. 13. From William Wells Brown, *Clotel; or, the President's Daughter: A Narrative of Slave Life in the United States (1853)*. Used with the permission of Documenting the American South, University of North Carolina at Chapel Hill Libraries.

Brown entitled his chapter "Death Is Freedom" and included an illustration of Clotel—airborne with hands outstretched as if she might just fly away—leaping to her own death (fig. 13). Like the illustration in Torrey's abolitionist work, a suicidal slave is pictured in liminal terrain—between earth and heaven, life and death, slavery and freedom.

It may seem a desperate politics that declares that "death is freedom." As contemporary critic Russ Castronovo has suggested, "legitimate citizens of the state, white propertied males, reap tremendous benefit from this gruesome metaphor," for it seems to imply that death offers the only remedy for the ills of the oppressed.[83] By offering death as the means of freedom, Brown and others may have unintentionally bought into a political shadowland in which true freedom is not something to be manifest in the historical realities of the present world but must be deferred to some abstract and indeterminate world in the beyond. What is unaccounted for in such an interpretation is the degree to which accounts of slave suicide—whether historical or fictional—implied a devastating critique of the social arrangements of slavery. Clotel's leap to the freedom of death is prompted by the monstrous political fact that the domestic slave trade was alive and well in Washington, D.C. There was, for Brown, a giant chasm between the realities of slavery and the ideals upon which the nation was founded. This is the fundamental message he articulates when he observes that "thus died Clotel, the daughter of Thomas Jefferson, a president of the United States; a man distinguished as the author of the Declaration of American Independence."[84] The freedom that Brown and his colleagues ultimately sought was a freedom for the here and now.

In characterizing Clotel's leap to death as "heroic," Brown grounded her suicide in a neoclassical frame of reference, one that likened suicidal slaves to admirable figures in the ancient world. This is the same frame of reference deployed in some accounts of slave suicide. Take, for example, an account offered by the Washington, D.C., newspaper the *National Era* in June 1848. In an article entitled, not surprisingly, "Liberty of Death," the author began with the words of a "Roman heroine, as she drew the dagger from her bosom, and handed it to her husband, to perform upon himself the same fearful office of suicide."[85] Invoking this act—the sacrifice of Virginia—the author connected it to an outrage in the world of nineteenth-century slavery. "An event has just occurred in our own country," the piece continued, "which transcends in tragic interest these passages from the history of the heroic age of Rome." The case involved a Kentucky slaveholder who had sold off a husband and wife to a trader wanting merchandise "for the market of New Orleans." The trader, however, did not want their child. Jailed for safekeeping, the couple determined that their family would not be torn apart. "In the calmness of their great despair," said the article, "they deliberately resolved to die together. The mother cut the throat of the child, and then gave the knife to her husband, who killed her, and then attempted to complete the sacrifice by cutting his own throat. He was found alive, but it was thought he could not recover." The actions of this slave family, however desperate, were framed with clear reference to the prized values of ancient Rome. Indeed, narratives of slave suicides contain elements of the heroic and themes of martyrdom that resonate with the death poetry discussed in chapter 4.

One celebrated case from Nashville, Tennessee, reported the death of an unnamed "negro girl" owned by one Mr. L. C. Lisby. According to the account issued by the *North Star,* the young girl's mother had run away and now the daughter was being threatened with punishment if she did not yield up information about the escape.[86] Rather than endure this torturous ordeal, she hanged herself. "Had the two persons referred to above (the mother and daughter) been white slaves in Constantinople or some other place," the article insisted, "the conduct of this self-sacrificing daughter would have been thought most heroic, even by those who make merchandise of human flesh and blood." But because those in question were slaves, their actions would be seen only as "another indication of the natural obstinacy and stupidity of the African race." An account from North Carolina, reported in New York's newspaper the *Colored American,* praised a different form of female heroism.[87] In September 1837, Lucy, a young runaway slave, had been captured and confined to prison. Before she could be returned to her master, she committed suicide by hanging herself. "We have never known an instance where so much firmness was exhibited by any person," insisted the article, "as was by this negro." Again, it was her resolve and heroic determination that the paper celebrated. Continuing in the vein of steely determination, still another female runaway refused to be apprehended. According to an 1853 account in the *Frederick Douglass Paper,* a Tennessee woman "belonging to Dempsey Weaver, Esq., jumped into the river, night before last, with a child in each arm, and all three were drowned."[88] Because she had displeased her master, he had threatened to sell her away, and this she refused to accept.

Suicides that sprang from the open defiance of the slave system were given sympathetic if not admiring treatment in the African American press. Take the case of Stephen Redden of Maryland. A free black man, Redden had nevertheless been convicted under the terms of an 1835 state law that prohibited citizens from possessing and circulating antislavery literature. Convicted of owning the forbidden tracts, Redden was sent to prison. There he ended his own life rather than serving the ten-year sentence that had been handed down by the court. The account of Redden's suicide in the *North Star* acknowledged that it had been an act consonant with "the spirit of Roman chivalry."[89] The reporter acknowledged that "I have never been able to justify the act of suicide," but nevertheless admitted "that exception is furnished in a case such as this." He continued: "If there was meaning, beyond the mere sound of a rhetorical imprecation, in the exclamation of Patrick Henry, 'Give me Liberty, or give me Death!' then this was it." As it was framed by the *North Star*, the case of Stephen Redden was the story of a heroic martyr to African American freedom.

The narrative of a Tennessee runaway slave known as Levi fits the same mold. A man of yellow complexion, Levi's escape attempt was facilitated by his ability to pass as a white man wearing a "fine suit of clothes." Sporting his fancy attire, Levi boarded a train bound for Chattanooga and from there hoped to travel north to freedom. By a terrible stroke of luck, however, a merchant traveling on the same train sniffed out Levi's true identity and sought to apprehend him. Although he was traveling with a gun, Levi turned the weapon on himself when all hope of escape seemed futile. Passengers scampered out of the car when they heard the discharge of the weapon, thinking "he was firing at them." When they returned to the car they discovered that "he had drawn a bowie-knife and cut his throat, and was a corpse." Piecing together reporting from the *Nashville Banner* and the *Frederick Douglass Paper*, the *Provincial Freeman* insisted that "he could not have died in a better cause. He died struggling to be free! 'BETTER, as our own eloquent GARNET says, 'DIE FREEMEN, THAN LIVE AS SLAVES.' Would that the whole slave population would adopt the motto!"[90] In this telling of the tale, Levi's suicide emerges simultaneously as an act of despair and as a bold assault on the institution of slavery. As Henry Highland Garnet had urged, Levi had refused to labor for tyrants and died while seeking the higher ground of freedom.

What is striking about this brief sounding into the narratives of slave suicide is the degree to which an act of ultimate desperation is transformed into a heroic gesture that seeks freedom. Rather then viewing these accounts of slave suicide as evidences of pathological behavior or as acts of utter defeat, we might instead see them as evidence of the degree to which slaves detested their enslavement and would stop at virtually nothing to be free. This willingness to court death in the pursuit of freedom was certainly a feature of antebellum slave life and may also have steeled African Americans during the conflict of the Civil War. If Garnet's dictum—that it was better to die freemen than to live as slaves—had achieved wide currency, then this may help us to better understand the willingness of African American troops and their families to risk all for the cause of freedom.

Scholars have long known that slaves risked their lives in the cause of violent resistance against the regime that shackled them. This is not to say, of course, that the history of the antebellum era is studded with large-scale slave revolts of the sort led by Toussaint L'Overture in Haiti. With a handful of exceptions that scholars can name in their sleep—Gabriel's Rebellion in 1800; a march on New Orleans in 1811; the Denmark Vesey plot of 1822, and Nat Turner's rebellion in 1831—American slaves did not challenge their masters in pitched battle. Still they resisted with vigor and in ways that put their own lives at hazard. "It was not the sort of rebellion that slaveholders had customarily feared and that historians customarily chronicle," historian Steven Hahn argues, "—the sudden, massive, and direct violence against the white population. It was rather a rebellion that proved more difficult to detect and even more difficult to staunch, a rebellion many months in duration."[91] Scholars have now detailed with great care how slaves navigated the terms of their bondage: how they forged underground economies, fashioned a religious culture that sustained them, engaged in forms of subtle resistance, worked the edges of the slave system to find better treatment, shaped a nascent political agenda, and ran away from their plantations by the thousands.[92] At the same time, though, to the extent that the Civil War put guns into the hands of nearly 180,000 African American men, it was exactly the kind of major conflict that had long kept planters awake at night. The uprising of African Americans, South and North, during the Civil War comes like a bolt from the blue unless we comprehend it as an extension of these powerful patterns of resistance. Long before the first shot was fired at Fort Sumter, South Carolina, American slaves had been dying in the cause of freedom.

Slaves understood that resistance to the peculiar institution could get them killed. The history of slavery in North America would have offered them plenty of grisly reminders. In 1712, in New York City, some twenty-three slaves rose up and killed nine whites before "they were overwhelmed by a superior force." In fierce retaliation, whites executed twenty-one African Americans—some by burning, others by hanging, and one broken on the wheel.[93] In 1741, another New York plot (which never came to fruition) resulted in even wider reprisals: thirteen African Americans were burned alive, eighteen hanged, and more than eighty transported from the city.[94] In 1739, in South Carolina, a band of slaves determined to set off to reach the promise of freedom in Spanish Florida. In what became known as the Stono Rebellion, white militiamen subdued the rebels—and later spitted their heads on pikes as a warning to other restless bondspeople.[95]

The mutilation of the corpses of slave rebels, argues historian Douglas Egerton, served a number of ends that planters found useful. On the one hand, this practice demonstrated in savage fashion the mastery of whites over the bodies of their slave property, not only in life but also in death. Moreover, because "Africans, and many African Americans, believed that an unnatural death, or failure to observe proper burial rites, doomed the soul to wander forever in the desolate waste of the damned," wanton destruction of the corpse constituted a punishment that could haunt a rebellious slave well into eternity.[96] We know, too, that the mutilation of black bodies continued into the antebellum era. Historian Kenneth S. Greenburg argues that the notorious rebel Nat Turner and many of his comrades "suffered mutilation." He observes as well that "there is strong evidence that his body was dissected."[97] Like others criminals who fell astride of antebellum law, Turner continued to pay for his crimes even after he had died. The atrocities suffered by African American soldiers during the Civil War at the hands of their Confederate captors—at places like Fort Pillow, Tennessee, and Poison Spring, Arkansas—are of a piece with the punishments doled out to rebellious slaves in the eighteenth and nineteenth centuries.[98]

American slaves continued to risk death as they pursued freedom in the era of the American Revolution. Despite historian Gary B. Nash's trenchant point that "in reality, the American Revolution represents the largest slave uprising in our history," this conflict is typically not recognized as part of the canonical inventory of instances of slave resistance in early America.[99] Yet we know that African Americans across North America seized the chaos of war as an opportunity to desert their masters in mass numbers, to enlist as soldiers in the fledgling Continental Army (where states would accept them), and to attach themselves to

British military units—such as Lord Dunmore's Regiment in Virginia. Exploiting the opportunities in what historian Sylvia R. Frey calls "the triagonal war," African Americans forged a sophisticated politics that put the interest of their freedom front and center.[100] Adumbrating the flight of fugitive slaves to General William Tecumseh Sherman's force in South Carolina during 1864–1865, thousands of southern slaves fled to Lord Cornwallis's British columns in South Carolina during 1780–1781. "In defiance of staggering odds," writes Sylvia Frey, "they militantly rejected slavery by running to the British."[101] In ways that historians may still need to investigate, the American Revolution itself may have served as a political dress rehearsal for African Americans as they approached the Civil War.

As we have already observed, African Americans of the antebellum era had latched upon Patrick Henry's impassioned ultimatum, "Give Me Liberty, or Give Me Death." In plotting his 1800 insurrection in Richmond, Virginia, the blacksmith Gabriel intended to hoist a banner inscribed with the words "Death or Liberty." As historian Douglas Egerton argues, Gabriel's allusion to Henry's words cast this potential rebellion in the language of urban, artisan republicanism rather than in the idiom of evangelical Christianity that rebels such as Nat Turner would use.[102] Gabriel was, indeed, an American incarnation of a "black Jacobin." But Gabriel's inversion of the terms in Patrick Henry's slogan is puzzling. While we can never know what was on his mind, perhaps his flip-flopping of the terms *death* and *liberty*—placing death in the leading position—indicated an appreciation of what political action would cost him. By the time it was all over, the state of Virginia would eventually execute twenty-seven men for their role in the plot.

As the Civil War approached, American slaves continued to contest slavery in dramatic and violent ways. Perhaps the most celebrated of all instances of African American resistance to slavery were Denmark Vesey's 1822 alleged conspiracy in Charleston, South Carolina, and Nat Turner's all too real 1831 rampage in Southampton County, Virginia. As Henry Highland Garnet's 1843 address suggests, antebellum blacks quickly incorporated both of these two men as exemplars in a larger narrative that traced their struggle for freedom. Denmark Vesey, a free black carpenter living in an urban area, and Nat Turner, an enslaved field hand living in the relative isolation of a plantation in rural Virginia, both put their lives on the line in the quest for freedom. Although they drew inspiration from evangelical Christianity, religion informed their actions in divergent ways. Vesey had deep roots in a specific "African Church" in Charleston and hatched his conspiracy in the context of community. Turner received unmediated visions from God that drove him to action. Both Vesey and Turner paid with their lives for their rebelliousness, becoming African American martyrs in the cause of freedom.[103]

Although Nat Turner's body had been dismembered some twenty years before, the memory of his rebellion may have traveled with slaves who moved west with their masters. Virginians settled with particular density in places like Callaway County, Missouri, where in 1850 armed rebellion again surfaced when a company of "some thirty slaves in western Missouri had armed themselves with knives, clubs, and three guns and attempted to escape."[104] It was also in this region that, during the summer of 1855, a young slave woman, Celia, rose up and killed Robert Newsom, the slave-owner by whom she had been systematically molested and abused. Although given ample opportunity to implicate other slaves in the crime, Celia claimed the murder as her own. Found guilty and condemned to death, Celia confessed on the eve of her execution that initially she had not meant to kill Newsom only to injure him. But she then explained that "as soon as I struck him the Devil got into me, and I struck him with the stick until he was dead, and then rolled him in the fire and burnt him up."[105]

While Celia's case had been a matter of wide public interest and debate in Missouri—particularly as the border wars raged in neighboring Kansas—planters in Adams County, Mississippi, took pains to conceal the dangerous "plan" they had discovered in their midst.[106] According to the painstaking research assembled by historian Winthrop Jordan, Adams County slaves had evidently timed their act of rebellion to mesh with the onset of the Civil War. Throughout the year 1860–1861, Mississippi slaves had picked up on the fact that serious political fissures existed among the white people who governed them. "What happened was that a certain group of slaves heard of fighting between groups of white people," writes Jordan, "and learned about political and ideological differences between the antagonists that seemed to them very pertinent to their own situations as slaves."[107] More particularly, as one plantation mistress noted in her diary, slaves "had been talking a great deal about Lincoln freeing the servants."[108] Just how many slaves had absorbed this idea or exactly why they decided to participate in what became known as "The Plan" remains murky. To be sure, Jordan's book is as much about the silences in the historical record as it as about what little we can know with certainty. What is plain, however, is that as Confederate troops mustered for battle against the Union, at least twenty-seven slaves (and perhaps as many as forty, maybe more) were hanged for their role in planning an insurrection.[109] For the slaves of the Natchez area, the Civil War began well before anyone glimpsed federal troops setting foot in Mississippi.

American slaves forthrightly risked death in challenging those who would hold them in bondage. Free blacks, like George Stephens, could also carry the legacy of slave rebellion in their hearts. One need not subscribe to overly romanticized notions of slave resistance—such as the ones sometimes attributed to historians such as Harvey Wish or Herbert Aptheker—to draw this conclusion. But to the extent that we recognize that to live under slavery was to live under "the dark wings of death," we may gain some deeper appreciation of the willingness of African Americans to risk death for the cause of freedom. As the case of the slave Celia indicates, to possess the terms of one's own death and to face that fate directly is a species of freedom in itself. If slaves were already living under a system that killed their souls and their bodies, it may help us to understand why they risked so much in the era of the Civil War.

Black soldiers faced daunting problems during the war: They received less pay than their white counterparts; they endured the condescension of their white officers; they risked being executed if taken prisoner; they were sometimes brutally impressed into service; they put up with being placed on grueling labor detail; they fought without the certainty that the federal government even considered them citizens of the Republic for which they were asked to die. This much we know. But as the war unfolded, hopes for black citizenship leaned heavily on the willingness of men to be killed on the field of battle. Of course, the ideal of the citizen–soldier ran deep in the traditions of republicanism that Americans had embraced during the Revolutionary War. By the time of the Civil

War, the stakes, especially for African American men, had been raised. It was necessary for black soldiers not only to prove their competence to master the drill, to shoot straight, and to take orders but also to show their willingness to die. When contemporaries wondered if black troops would fight, what they really wanted to know was whether black men would be willing to kill and be killed in combat. Competence, in some sense, was beside the point. As W. E. B. Du Bois recognized, black citizenship was predicated on the willingness of black men to kill and to risk death just as willingly (and often as recklessly) as whites. Indeed, he noted that those blacks who labored "quietly and faithfully" for the Union cause often displayed courage and moral purpose superior to that displayed by troops on the field of battle. Yet, he observed, these workers were often reviled by those whom they served. But when a black man "rose and fought and killed, the whole nation proclaimed him a man and a brother."[110] Paradoxically, death figured prominently in defining the nature of slavery and in setting the terms that had to be fulfilled for African Americans to gain freedom.

Evidence from the battlefield indicates how important it was for black men to be killed in order for them to lay claim to the rights of citizenship. Key battles that earned black soldiers the respect of the nation—the attack on Port Hudson, Louisiana, in 1863; the assault on Fort Wagner, South Carolina, in 1863; and the "Battle of the Crater" during the siege of Petersburg, Virginia, in 1864—were notable largely for the sheer death toll that they exacted. None of these battles could be categorized as victories for the Union troops or as memorable displays of martial competence. Both tactically and strategically, they were characterized by incompetence and shoddy planning. What made these conflicts praiseworthy in Union quarters was the willingness of black men to participate in the same kind of suicidal charges that white troops had been executing since the opening days of the war.

The siege of Port Hudson, Louisiana, marked a critical juncture in the attempt of Union forces to wrest control of the Mississippi River from the Confederacy. Along with the stronghold of Vicksburg, Mississippi, Port Hudson served as an anchor point in the system of Confederate defenses. Located just north of Baton Rouge along the banks of the river, it was defended by a determined Confederate garrison of about 6,000 men under General Franklin Gardner. Union forces from the Army of the Gulf numbered about 25,000 to 30,000 by the time they worked their way to the fort. Among these Union forces were a sizable contingent of African American forces—members of the Corps d'Afrique, including the First and Third Louisiana Native Guards. Their task was to capture the fort.[111]

On May 27, 1863, Union General Nathaniel Banks orchestrated a major attack on Port Hudson that called for the use of troops from both black and white units. It was an unmitigated disaster. Union troops slogged through swampy marshes receiving murderous fire from the fort's defenders. Captain Andre Cailloux, of the First Louisiana Native Guards—a unit that included some of the elite free blacks of New Orleans—was cut down in what one scholar calls "a hopeless charge."[112] Even by Civil War standards, the casualties suffered the Louisiana Native Guards were extreme; so severe, in fact, that Union General Banks endured accusations that he doctored the numbers to mask the extent of the carnage. According to historian Lawrence Lee Hewitt's account of the attack, the Native Guards constituted "less that one twenty-fifth of the Union soldiers present and suffered at least 20 percent of the casualties." Of some 1,080 Native Guards in the attack, Hewitt estimates that some 371 were killed and 150 wounded, "and these figures are reasonable only if those killed included the mortally wounded and the missing."[113] The Louisiana Native Guards incurred a virtual 50 percent casualty rate during their attack—a figure that exceeds significantly battlefield losses in some of the Civil War's most horrific encounters.[114] Nor did the collapse of the charge end their miseries. At first, Confederate troops "refused to let the Union troops retrieve the bodies of black soldiers." Captain Cailloux's corpse was finally recovered on July 8, 1863, only after Port Hudson had finally surrendered.[115] One can only imagine the condition of his body. Moreover, evidence suggests that black troops taken prisoner, probably during the ensuing siege rather than the May 27 attack, were summarily executed. One Confederate officer wrote to his Union counterpart bragging that he had used his "Six Shooter" in cutting down black troops he said were trying to escape. "There was not any Federal prisoners with the Negroes," he explained.[116] From start to finish, it would be difficult to imagine a more grisly military debacle.

Yet some cheered the assault of African American troops on Fort Hudson as validation that they would make excellent soldiers. One Union officer wrote that "valiantly did the heroic decedents of Africa move forward cool as if Marshaled for dress parade, under a murderous fire from enemy guns, until we reached the main ditch that surrounds the Fort."[117] The *New York Times* crowed that the splendid behavior of the black soldiers ought to silence those who thought they could not pass muster. "It is no longer possible to doubt the bravery and steadiness of the colored race," it opined, "when rightly led."[118] When Captain Cailloux's body was finally recovered, it received a magnificent funeral in New Orleans, attended by troops of both races, with the "band of the 42nd Massachusetts (white)" providing the music.[119] As scholars have noted, the praise lavished on these African American troops may well have been exaggerated.[120] But the fact remains that only in death did the men of the Louisiana Native Guard achieve heroic status as Americans.

The assault of the 54th Massachusetts Colored Infantry on Fort Wagner, South Carolina, marked another futile assault that was deemed glorious. The account of George Stephens of that attack, the climax of the popular Edward Zwick film *Glory,* details what in military terms was a tragic defeat. After battling their way through a "hellish storm" of shot, shell, and rifle fire, the men plunged through a moat, struggled up the parapets, and found the interior of the rebel lines. Close on their heels, the men of the 3rd New Hampshire regiment climbed up from behind and "emptied their rifles into us. Thus we lost nearly as many men by bullets of our presumed friends as by those of our known enemies."[121] Pinned between deadly fire from both sides, the men of the 54th had no hope of holding their position. Corporal James Henry Gooding, another member of the regiment, put it this way: "Mortal men could not stand such a fire, and the assault on Wagner was a failure."[122] The aftermath of the fighting proved Gooding to be correct. In his report of the battle to superior officers, Colonel E. N. Hallowell stated that out of a force of about six hundred men, the 54th Massachusetts suffered a total of 256 casualties—including dead, wounded, and missing.[123] And, as was the case with Fort Hudson, Confederate troops remained in control of the military objective. Yet, despite the bungled attack and the fact that Union troops had opened fire on their own men, George Stephens reported the assault to be a "brilliant feat" that demonstrated that "colored soldiers will dare go where any brave men will lead them."[124]

As the Union forces of Ulysses S. Grant put the final stranglehold on Robert E. Lee's Army of Northern Virginia, African American troops were again called on to demonstrate their willingness to die. The summer of 1864 in Virginia marked the most continuous and savage fighting of the Civil War, with Grant's forces applying unremitting pressure against Lee's dwindling numbers. The result was stalemate in a line of trenches stretching across the blasted countryside. In an effort to break the deadlock, Union General Ambrose Burnside set Pennsylvania miners to work on the task of tunneling under the Confederate defensive positions. The plan would be to set gigantic mines and then blow a gap in the lines through which Union troops could pore. This assault (included in the recent Civil War film *Cold Mountain*), too, could not have been handled with greater incompetence. On July 30, 1864, when Union troops detonated the massive charge, confusion reigned over the order of battle. General Edward Ferrero's all-black Fourth Division played a major role in the chaotic assault and charged into the pit created by the explosion. According to historian William Glenn Robertson, Confederate forces were "enraged to find that they were fighting African Americans" and "refused to permit the surrender of beaten foes, black or white. Evidence from both sides is overwhelming that racial hatred turned an already brutal struggle into heinous atrocities as the Federal perimeter inexorably contracted."[125] The results were predictable. Ferrero's Fourth Division suffered the loss of 1,327 men, "38 percent of the corps total and more than the losses of the First and Third Divisions combined."[126] Again, black men were required to lay down their lives in great numbers to demonstrate their worthiness.

Judged in strictly military terms, the engagements at Fort Hudson, Fort Wagner, and the "Battle of the Crater" at Petersburg, were utter disasters for the Union forces. None of these battles achieved their military objectives. What was necessary here was not victory or even a show of competence, but rather a demonstration by "colored soldiers" of their willingness to be blown to pieces. This was the cost of citizenship. In throwing themselves at immovable defenses, black and white soldiers could meet each other as equals.

For many African Americans, the Civil War tested the resolve that it was "better to die free, than to live slaves." From his pulpit at New York City's Shiloh Presbyterian Church, Henry Highland Garnet sustained the war effort by "serving on Riker's Island as chaplain to the Twentieth, Twenty-Sixth, and Thirty-first regiments of the United States Colored Troops."[127] In 1864, at a convention of African American leaders in Syracuse, New York, he praised "the brave deeds of the colored soldiers" and urged their ultimate success.[128] At the same time, there was some irony in Garnet's advocacy of a broader form of "Negro nationality" that would transcend Union victory and the freedom of former slaves in America. But there was more irony still in the words that he had uttered in Buffalo, New York, over twenty years before. For in the era of the Civil War, death defined simultaneously the nature and character of slavery and the cost to be paid for citizenship in the American Republic.

❖

"The Court of Death"

Sometime during the middle of the 1840s, the firm of James Baillie, head-quartered in New York City, published a memorial lithograph (fig. 14). In a variety of ways, this small scene offers a "thick description" of the culture of death in antebellum America.[1] The image depicts a trio of figures— a man, a woman, and a young girl—standing to the right side of a large monument topped by a decorative urn. This family of mourners is attired in formal mourning wear, a gesture toward the elaborate rituals pre-scribed for middle-class, city dwellers as they grieved for the dead. On the monument are handwritten lines that recorded the deaths of three members of the Derby family, the deceased ranging in age from seven years to fifty-two years. Here the lithograph identified directly the ubiq-uity of death in the experience of early nineteenth-century Americans. As was the custom in this genre, lithographers left open the faces of their monuments so that purchasers would be free to customize their artwork with the names of their own family members. Memorial lithography emerged as an interactive and democratic medium in which purchasers could have a hand in shaping their own works of art. The scene, too, makes unmistakable reference to the cultural currents of Romanticism

Fig. 14. James Baillie, *In Memory of...* Lithograph (ca. 1845–1847). Courtesy of the American Antiquarian Society, Worcester, Mass.

in American life: Weeping willows surround the image on the left and the right, thus framing it in bucolic and sentimental terms. Between the boughs of the willows, a church peaks out from the background, suggesting the profoundly religious context within which death and mourning was understood for many antebellum Americans. Evident as well is an homage to the Greek revival—the urn atop the monument resonates not so much with Christian iconography as with classical antiquity. Read from these varying angles, Baillie's image renders in concise fashion some of the major forces that shaped the culture of death in the early nineteenth century.[2]

As highlighted in Baillie's lithograph, death was a central subject in the visual arts in antebellum America. This chapter explores three media in which mourning and death were portrayed in the visual culture of antebellum America: memorial lithography, postmortem photography, and painting. It examines first the rise of memorial lithography, especially the highly stylized scenes of mourners by gravestones that flowed from the studios of lithographers such as Nathaniel Currier, James Baillie, and the Kellogg brothers. Although other works by Currier and his partner James Merritt Ives have been studied by historians, scholars have largely sidestepped the outpouring of memorial lithography that appeared in tandem with other forms of art, such as family registers recording births and deaths, which were meant for domestic consumption. The chapter turns next to consider the genre of postmortem photography. Indeed, one of the first wide-scale uses of the medium of photography in America was to record the likenesses of the recently deceased. As part of an emerging mass market for art in antebellum America, the postmortem photograph played a key role.[3] We turn, finally, to painting. Part of the ordinary American's encounter with the visualization of death included the genre of the traveling exhibition painting. And no exhibition painting in the decades before the Civil War garnered more attention than did Rembrandt Peale's magnificent work, *The Court of Death* (1820). In each case—memorial lithography, postmortem photography, and in *The Court of Death*—we can observe that antebellum visualizations of death continued to frame the understandings of death evinced by wartime Americans. In affording Americans a way to understand, absorb, and frame death, these visual representations of death proved a durable source of consolation for Americans even in time of war.

The lithographs produced by men like James Baille stood on the cutting edge of efforts by American artists to market their works to a mass audience. Because lithographs were printed images lifted from the impressions made on a stone, they could be reproduced in huge quantities. As early as the 1820s, "a printer employed by Nathaniel Currier could print 1,000 impressions from a lithograph stone each day."[4] In his work on the firm of Currier and Ives, historian Bryan F. Le Beau argues that the mass production of lithographs proceeded in "assembly-line fashion," with all of the processes of production housed under a single roof.[5] Currier and Ives was also "the first American lithographic firm to establish a national and international print market."[6] It is safe to say, then, that even in the antebellum era, American consumers snapped up literally hundreds of thousands of lithographic prints. Charting precisely who these consumers were is difficult. Because most of the major lithographic firms were established in the North—James Baille and Currier and Ives in New York City and the Kellogg brothers in Hartford, Connecticut—we might assume that the majority of their customers were relatively affluent Northeastern families. But there is tantalizing evidence that suggests that some of their work spread to the West and to the South. An 1848 business receipt from a Pittsburgh, Pennsylvania, merchant house indicates that it served as an "agent for the sale of N. Currier's prints, sold wholesale at New York Prices."[7] A memorial lithograph produced during the 1830s by Daniel Wright Kellogg in Hartford, Connecticut, records the death of one Artemas Wood who died at Fort Gibson, Arkansas, on August, 19, 1836.[8] If these prints had made their way west of the Mississippi River by the 1830s, we should not be too quick to posit an exclusively Northeastern audience for them. It might well be the case that Northern lithographers were beginning to tap into a national market as early as the 1830s or 1840s.

One interpretation for the popularity of these lithographs suggests that they served an American need to create "a usable past" for a new nation in the throes of rapid growth. The public gobbled up historical scenes of Pilgrims, Indians, Revolutionary heroes, and epic battles to give themselves a kind of national grounding in the midst of a country undergoing

the vicissitudes of the Market Revolution. Picturesque scenes of stable
domestic life could thus create an illusion of permanence when none was
to be had. "America's usable—and largely fictional—past flourished in the
nineteenth century," writes Le Beau, "despite the widespread availability
of factual information that contradicted it."[9] In this rendering, the lithographic tradition created a kind of false consciousness for Americans—
they could salve themselves with images of a golden past to stave off the
anxieties of the turbulent present. But Le Beau's concept of a "usable
past" might also be employed, albeit from a slightly different perspective,
to explain the popularity of lithographs depicting scenes of mourning.
These private scenes of mourning were aimed at preserving and idealizing
individuals and their families, rather than glorifying the new nation. The
memory that they sought to cultivate was an individual one, not a collective one. Memorial lithography in the antebellum era served to create a
"usable past"—but one dedicated largely to the preservation of individuals and their families rather than to the nation-state.

The genre of memorial lithography flourished in an era in which the
practice of mourning carried profound social significance. Mourning
"was held sacred by sentimentalists as the purest, the most transparent,
and thus the most genteel of all sentiments. In mourning, a middle-class
man or woman was believed to establish very clearly the legitimacy of his
or her claims to genteel social status."[10] Because mourning was yoked
to the making of a new, urban, and genteel class, it is not surprising
that it involved a whole range of new merchandise. Antebellum Americans could purchase a vast array of products designed to aid them in the
process of proper mourning, including memorial portraits, platters and
dinnerware, sheet music, and jewelry of various sorts (sometimes made
of ringlets of human hair.)[11] A rich material culture thus grew apace with
the cultivation of mourning. Memorial lithographs might well be interpreted in the context of other items that Americans used to relish and to
refine what jurist Joseph Story had called "melancholy pleasure."

What is, perhaps, most striking about the memorial lithographs is
their relentless consistency. It almost seems as if lithographers had devised
a checklist of standard features for these illustrations and were determined
to incorporate them into every image that they produced. There is some
irony in the observation that a genre of art that invited the participation

of individual mourners was so standardized. But the uniformity of the lithographs may have provided mourners with some level of comfort and consolation by assuring them that the eyes of other grieving Americans were lingering over the same sorts of images. The art of mourning was thus intensely private and necessarily public.

Virtually all of the memorial lithographs featured a blank memorial stone or monument upon which the name, or names, of deceased family members could be written. In most cases, the faces of these stones were blank except for a phrase at the top of the stone that contained the words "To the Memory of" or "In Memory of"—or some other phrase to that effect. The lithographers thus gave their customers maximum latitude in writing in the name, or names, of the individuals whom they sought to commemorate. The monuments themselves typically stand in the center of the lithograph, emphasizing that the focus of the observer should be on the memory of the departed one. The size of the monuments, too, is impressive; they command the attention of the scene serving almost as another character in the tableau.

The centrality of the monuments in these scenes implies a narrative that might be seen to bolster the arguments of those who championed the rural cemetery. For example, in an 1830 image produced by James Baille's firm (fig. 15), a woman leans against a large stone monument that records the deaths of five children of the Dunn family. At the bottom of the image, one can see the crumbling headstones and burial markers from previous days, suggesting that without proper care the memory of the dead could easily be lost. A similar scene appears in a Nathaniel Currier lithograph (fig. 16). Here, another woman laments the deaths of a host of family members whose names appear on the new and ornately decorated monument. But in the foreground, one can see smaller headstones that are leaning precariously toward the ground and other markers that seem scattered willy-nilly over the landscape. The features of the lithograph suggest that it is up to the current generation to create more durable monuments to the dead and not let them slip into obscurity. In the background of this Currier image, one can detect two tiny figures on the path that leads to the church. One of the figures—a man with a top hat—is pointing into the distance, presumably at a monument. Here again is a gesture to the rural cemetery

Fig. 15. James Baillie, *To the Memory of...* Lithograph. Courtesy of the American Antiquarian Society, Worcester, Mass.

movement and its deep conviction that memorials served a didactic and public purpose. Another image produced by the Brown firm of Boston pictures a young woman, nestled in a forested landscape, who regards a monument that "resembles a tomb in the Pere Lachaise Cemetery in Paris"—a model that American cemetery boosters sought to emulate.[12] In this way, the memorial lithographs might be seen as visual sermons that sustained the claims made by rural cemetery advocates regarding the importance of protecting the memory of the dead.

Mourners interact with the memorial stone in a number of ways, all suggesting the proper dispositions that might constitute the experience of authentic grief. In the Baille lithograph with which we began this chapter, a family of mourners—including a child—is shown to be regarding the memorial stone. The woman and the man link arms. A child holding flowers looks on, almost facing outward from the scene. This lithograph

Fig. 16. Nathaniel Currier, *In Memory of . . .* Lithograph. Courtesy of the American Antiquarian Society, Worcester, Mass.

insists that grief is a family affair, one from which the young and tender should not be shielded. The linked arms of the parents—a common feature in family scenes—suggest that proper reverence for the dead can bring together the living in a climate of support and solidarity. While this family looks on their monument with stoic resolve, other mourners are shown in tears. With amazing consistency the lithographs picture female mourners, with handkerchiefs in hand, leaning against the monuments of the dead. This pose indicates that tears—particularly those of women— were appropriate emblems of mourning. This posture, too, indicates the intimate contact the living could have with the memory of the dead. The physical contact between mourner and memorial stone is a small, but significant, marker of the thin line that divided the living and the dead in antebellum America. As Georgia Brady Barnhill writes, "memorial prints were a means to connect the living and the dead, much in the same way that Spiritualists did in their séances in the second half of the nineteenth

Fig. 17. Benjamin F. Nutting, *To the Memory of...* Lithograph. (1837). Courtesy of the American Antiquarian Society, Worcester, Mass.

century."[13] The living could, quite literally, lean on the memory of the dead for strength and support even as they wrestled with their own sadness.

The inheritance of the Greek revival also surfaced in the memorial lithographs. The placement of urns atop the memorial stones is an obvious gesture toward classical antiquity. But some prints went even further in acknowledging the Greek tradition. An 1837 lithograph produced by Benjamin Nutting of Boston also depicts a woman in classical dress leaning against a massive memorial shaded by two large trees (fig. 17). These classically attired female mourners reveal how women were folded into the tradition of the Greek revival, which, as we have observed earlier, was framed largely in masculine terms in the antebellum era. If it was the job of male heroes to die gloriously on the field of battle or in service to the state, it was the job of women to mourn them and to remember their accomplishments. While this connection was not made explicitly in the rhetoric of the rural cemetery movement, it could be seen at play in the context of memorial lithography.

The memorial lithographers gave Christian themes an understated presence in their works. Churches appear in many of the lithographs, but they typically occupy a niche in the background and are glimpsed through the limbs of trees or at the end of a path. In architectural terms, the churches depicted in these scenes are a motley collection without any real sense of architectural continuity. In one of the Nathaniel Currier images we have already seen, a gothic chapel stands in the back right-hand corner of the image (fig. 16). In another print by Charles Currier, a church with a tall spire—perhaps a gesture toward the fine Congregational churches of urban, New England—appears in the background. In a Nathaniel Currier image dated from 1845, the massive walls of a brick church appear just behind a family of mourners. In this case, the church is moved toward the front of the image, so much so that one cannot detect a spire or a steeple. Unlike the presentation of the monuments themselves, the depiction of churches in the memorial prints lacks any sense of stylistic consistency. Perhaps this hodge-podge of styles instantiates the wide range of religious experiences and denominational affiliations open to antebellum Americans.[14] Lithographers may have had their eyes on a wide market and did not wish to limit their customers by playing theological favorites. Clearly the artists took pains to avoid giving their religious institutions a sense of uniformity. They also avoided forthrightly any symbols of the resurrection or the heavenly life beyond the grave. No doves, no beams of glorious light, no hosts of angels appear in the memorial prints. Given the paramount importance of heaven in the religious discourse of antebellum America, these omissions are striking and curious. The kind of immortality offered in the prints is that conferred by human memory rather than that assured by the resurrection. The lithographs disclose a kind of secular immortality that is available to human beings if they choose to cultivate the proper dispositions.

Women held an exalted station in the vital tasks of weeping for and remembering the dead. Whether appearing in traditional nineteenth-century mourning garb or in robes that recalled ancient Greece, women emerge almost universally in memorial lithography. It is true that lithographers created some scenes in which women are to be mourned rather than to serve as the one in mourning. James Baille's 1848 print "The Mother's Grave" is a prime example of this genre (fig. 18). It pictures a trio of figures—a dog, a kneeling girl, and a young boy—standing before a memorial of their mother. The young boy appears to comfort the young girl. Their eyes are downcast. A cherub, as if singing in harmony with the youthful mourners, tops the monument behind them. Nathaniel Currier produced a print that features a single, young man resting one elbow on a memorial (fig. 19). Unlike most of the other memorial prints, the mourner in this scene gazes out at the viewer—tending neither to the message of the monument nor to the work of grief. The expression on his face is very nearly a sly smile. Rather than clutching a handkerchief with his free hand—as a mourning woman no doubt would—the young man holds a top hat. This scene marries emerging bourgeois symbols of prosperity and self-consciousness with the work of mourning. Both in the scene of "The Mother's Grave" and in the case of our young man, overt symbols of grief—the handkerchief, for example—are missing. Even when men and children are pictured in the memorial lithographs, they appear not to be crumpled by grief. Viewed from this perspective, we might conclude that the male artists who created these lithographs assigned women to the cultural work of mourning.

The established visual pattern of women mourning their families—and their men in particular—translated easily into the memorial lithographs produced in the North during the Civil War. Currier and Ives produced a series of images during the war—in 1862, in 1863, and in 1865—that depicted scenes of women in mourning for fallen soldiers. The 1862 print entitled "The Soldier's Grave" illustrates how the idioms of antebellum memorial lithography could be used and modified to serve the purposes of war. It reveals how prewar American practices and ideas about death simultaneously endured and were transformed by the exigencies of the Civil War.[15]

In many respects, "The Soldier's Grave" reflects familiar elements of the memorial prints produced before the war. The memorial monument stands squarely in the center of the image. Weeping willows droop from

Fig. 18. James Baillie, *The Mother's Grave*, 1848. Lithograph. Courtesy of the American Antiquarian Society, Worcester, Mass.

Fig. 19. Nathaniel Currier, *To the Memory of . . .* Lithograph. Courtesy of the American Antiquarian Society, Worcester, Mass.

the top of the print, enveloping it in a romantic and sentimental land-scape. Flowers sprout and bloom in the foreground. Dotting the terrain around the monument are the leaning headstones marking the graves of those who had passed before. A woman kneels next to the memorial, pressing a handkerchief to her face. In all of these ways, "The Soldier's Grave" of 1862 situates itself in a particular genre with which antebellum Americans were well acquainted. It offered a comfortingly predictable set of visual tropes that prospective purchasers would have recognized instantly.

But in other respects Currier and Ives' "The Soldier's Grave" works a revolution in the prewar genre from which it sprang. Let us begin with the monument itself. It displays clearly the "In Memory of" formula that graced virtually all antebellum memorial lithographs. But here the

Fig. 20. Currier & Ives, *The Soldier's Grave*, 1862. Lithograph. Courtesy of the American Antiquarian Society, Worcester, Mass.

familiarity ends. Instead of Greek urns or cherubs, it is the national symbol of the eagle that adorns the top of the monument. Below the memorial phrase are images of American flags, muskets, and a single soldier's cap. The imagery of the nation-state has replaced the older symbols of the Greek revival or gestures toward celestial beings. The abstract image of national identity and memory has replaced the familiar universe of images that were at once more idiosyncratic and oriented to the memory of individual family members.[16]

"The Soldier's Grave" brought restrictions to what purchasers might be free to inscribe in the memorial space provided for them. As we have seen, in the years before the war lithographers left the faces of their memorials blank—purchasers were invited to include whatever type of information they wished to customize their image. Of course, those who customized their memorials followed widely held cultural assumptions about what kind of information should be recorded—name, birth and death dates, etc. What is important to note, however, is that the antebellum lithograph itself did not proscribe the freedom of the purchaser other than in limiting the size of the space available for writing. The wartime image is different. It requires that the purchaser inscribe, first, the name of the fallen soldier, and it provides a space for the dead man's military unit affiliation. One imagines here a regiment, brigade, division, or corps designation—the familiar markers of identity in Civil War era armies. It demands, too, that the name of the battle where the soldier died be included. It follows antebellum convention only in providing a space for the date of the death of the fallen soldier. But even here there is a slight modification in the wartime image, as the date designating the decade of the 1860s is clearly evident as the time of death. The customer need add only a single digit. Ironically, at the very moment that Union war aims began to shift toward the ideal of freedom, this Currier and Ives image curtailed the liberty of mourners who lamented those lost in the struggle.

In another departure from antebellum precedent, the words at the foot of the monument offer a uniform judgment about the character of the deceased soldier. It declares that he was "a brave and gallant soldier and a true patriot" and concludes with a little death poem that ensures the eternal rest of the man, presumably in heaven. By definition, then,

Currier and Ives refused the existence of soldiers in the Union Army who were anything other than brave, gallant, and true. Such pronouncements would have been foreign to the antebellum memorial lithograph. While it is true that prewar lithographs celebrated the heroics of Mexican War soldiers and Indian-fighters on the frontier, they did so in a way that celebrated the individual identity of these men. Recall, for example, the image of Henry Clay Jr. from the Mexican War (discussed in chapter 1) that includes his own distinctive last words. Those sorts of gestures toward the character and ideas of specific soldiers is not a part of "The Soldier's Grave." Rather it celebrates a universal and abstract notion of martial glory in which all soldiers perform their duty. All of those who die in war, the image insists, are perforce valiant warriors and therefore worthy of remembrance. Such a pronouncement may well have been comforting to those who lost soldiers under unknown or even shadowy circumstances. It may have provided a kind of validation for families on the homefront who could often not trust the rumors that drifted back to them via the gossip of neighbors or in the notoriously unreliable casualty lists that were published in the newspapers.

The female mourner in "The Soldier's Grave" is crumpled by grief. Her kneeling posture is actually closer to that of the young girl in James Baille's "The Mother's Grave" than it is to mature women in the other memorial lithographs. With her eyes covered by her handkerchief, the mourner of "The Soldier's Grave" is in greater distress than were her antebellum sisters. One can imagine easily Currier and Ives producing this image in recognition of the crippling grief that could come with the death of a son or a husband on the field of battle. The woman also mourns alone. No family members comfort her. The family is conspicuously not part of this memorial scene—no children, no parents. Presumably the image captures a spouse (or perhaps a mother?) in the agony of grief. Although it trades on the traditional image of female mourning inherited from the antebellum era, the single mourner in this scene appears more forlorn, more disconnected from her community, and more crushed by her loss than the women of prewar decades.

Although removed from the solace of family and friends, the female mourner in "The Soldier's Grave" is not entirely alone. A column of Union troops marches out of the frame into the background. Why are they present at all? We might speculate that the memory of the fallen soldier will live on in the bodies of his comrades as well as those he left behind at home. Indeed, the memory of the individual soldier in this image is inextricably linked to the endurance of the nation—evident both in the design of the monument and in the presence of the marching soldiers. The context for the preservation of memory, then, has shifted toward the Union itself. Eternal life is to be found not merely in the memories cherished by family and friends, but in the endurance of the nation-state. There is nothing in the image to remind us of the religious context of death, which was a feature in many of the antebellum lithographs. No church can be seen. No religious imagery of any kind is present. Instead we are left with an image that connects the "rest" of the fallen soldier to the active participation of his fellow soldiers in the ongoing war effort. "The Soldier's Grave" begins to take us into an ideological terrain in which the national government has taken the place of the church. The antebellum precedents of memorial lithography now serve the war for the Union.

Remember that Currier and Ives ran a commercial industry and were not the puppets of or the paid propagandists for the federal war effort; this may make their work even more remarkable and historically significant. The prints that they produced were designed with customers in mind; customers who looked for solace and comfort to the prints they sold. Currier and Ives created imaginary soldier's graves for those tens of thousands of Union troops who died many miles from their homes. "Although memorial prints could not replace the comfort of an appropriate funeral and proper monument," writes Georgia Brady Barnhill, "they provide an object to venerate."[17] In creating funerals for the mind and for the spirit, wartime memorial lithographs such as "The Soldier's Grave" sustained Americans as they confronted loss of life on a mass scale. Some measure of their effectiveness might be glimpsed from the fact that "the publication and use of mourning prints declined precipitously after the Civil War."[18] Having served their purpose, perhaps, the public's need for them evaporated when the conflict ended.

Like the older medium of memorial prints, the new technology of photography also helped Americans to understand and to frame the trauma of war. The genre of the postmortem portrait—already well established in the decades before the Civil War—set the stage for portraits of the battlefield dead. When photographers such as Mathew Brady, Alexander Gardner, George N. Barnard, and Thomas C. Roche took to the fields with their cumbersome equipment, they carried as well ideas about how dead bodies ought to be portrayed for public viewing. Although the war transformed in important ways the art of photographing the dead, it is crucial to understand how antebellum precedent shaped presentations of the carnage of war. Even under the demands of imagining death on a mass scale, the conventions of antebellum memorial portraiture contin- ued to guide how photographers approached their grim subjects. Pho- tographers thus presented to the public highly stylized and carefully constructed images of death on the battlefield rather than unvarnished scenes of martial horror. In this way, they helped the public to come to terms with the unimaginable by giving them images that could be com- prehended.

From our contemporary vantage point, it is difficult to re-create the sense of wonder that accompanied the emergence of the photographic image. In 1839, the Frenchmen Louis Jacques Mande Daguerre intro- duced the world to a new technology by which an image was transmit- ted to a silver-coated side of a copper plate after it had been placed in a camera and exposed to the light. The "daguerreotype" that emerged from the process was heralded as an advance for both art and science. Commentators held that these "sun-paintings" (as they were sometimes called) held not merely an approximation of reality, but caught the per- fect essence of a moment in a way that had always eluded the painter. The daguerreotype captured an image that was entirely complete and true. As Daguerre himself announced "the DAGUERREOTYPE is not merely an instrument which serves to draw Nature; on the contrary it is a chemical and physical process which gives her the power to reproduce herself."[19] From America, Edgar Allen Poe sang that the medium of the daguerre- otype "is *infinitely* more accurate in its representation than any painting by human hands."[20] In 1855, photographer Nathan G. Burgess argued that the power of the daguerreotype, in its ability to capture reality, was virtually miraculous. Writing on the "Value of Daguerreotype Like- nesses," he exclaimed that it "possesses the sublime power to transmit the almost living image of our loved ones." He went on to say that "true indeed has this art been termed magic, as it works with such unerring precision, and with such wonderful celerity, that it only requires the spells and incantations of the device itself to complete the task."[21] The daguerreotype promised nothing less than a vision of pure truth.

As the Civil War neared, technological innovation enlarged the potential market for photography. The development of the glass-plate negative had made it possible for the same image to be reproduced many times over, a vast improvement over the singular character of the daguerreotype—which could be reproduced only by taking another daguerreotype. Moreover, the invention of the stereoscope made it possible for viewers to inspect images in their own homes that offered a three-dimensional look at reality. "The importance of this small hand-held wooden device cannot be stressed enough," writes scholar Alan Trachtenberg, "for it not only made possible portable and private panoramas, but facilitated a decisive moment in the evolution of bourgeois domestic life: the transformation of the living room into a microcosmic world unto itself."[22] In a series of important essays on photography that appeared in the *Atlantic Monthly*, Oliver Wendell Holmes heralded the glories of these advances. In his 1859 piece "The Stereoscope and Stereograph," he insisted that "it has become such an everyday matter with us, that we forget its miraculous nature, as we forget that of the sun itself, by which we owe the creations of our new art."[23] Indeed, Holmes claimed that since it was the sun itself that produced this new art form, its ability to capture reality was limitless, democratic, and all inclusive. "The sun is no respecter of persons or things," he said.[24] The outbreak of the American Civil War coincided with a wave of technological innovation in the nation's most exciting art form.

Even before bodies began falling on the battlefield, American photographers had made the corpse a subject for artistic representation. They frequently advertised their willingness to take images of the recently deceased for grieving family members. As anthropologist Jay Ruby has observed, "postmortem photography was socially acceptable and publicly acknowledged in nineteenth-century America." These images served as "a normal part of the inventory of many families—displayed in wall frames and albums along with other family pictures."[25] These images could also be placed into tiny lockets in jewelry to be treasured by future generations of family members. While we moderns may profess embarrassment at the ghoulishness of our ancestors in surrounding themselves with photographs of dead bodies, scholars remind us that this practice has endured even in contemporary America. What is more important to bear in mind, however, is that the generation of Americans that fought the Civil War had become accustomed to viewing the corpse as an appropriate subject for reflection and artistic representation. So when battlefield photographers such as Alexander Gardner and Thomas C. Roche brought forth their images of dead soldiers, these would have been viewed in the context of antebellum precedent. They would not have been seen as shocking, but rather as an extension of an art form that had already been well established in the 1840s and 1850s.

Antebellum daguerreotypists shrewdly promoted their skills in a number of ways. First, rather than aiming to supplant the work of the painters, photographers promised to be trusty colleagues in the important work of memorialization. In his 1855 essay, "Taking Portraits After Death," Nathan G. Burgess argued that the "the only object of a portrait of the deceased can be to retain a fac-simile of the outline of the face to assist the painter in the delineation of the portrait, and in this particular it has been found of essential service."[26] Early photographers thus saw themselves in the tradition of painters who had sought to capture the image of a loved one near the moment of death. They also sought to comfort the living with their realistic images of the deceased. Because photographs were held to capture a glimpse of reality, it seems that the public hungered for postmortem photographs as a way to assure themselves of the peacefulness of their loved ones after death. Blissful, restful scenes of "the last sleep" of the dead would assure the bereaved that the process of death had been an easy one.[27] In this way, early photographers perpetrated something of a legerdemain—while claiming to represent reality with crystalline clarity, they also sold the lie that the dead body was merely asleep.

The most common forms of antebellum memorial photography pictured living family members in frames that also held the dead. The archetypal image captured a living mother with her dead child. A photograph from the collections of the Historical Society of Pennsylvania—one Elizabeth Louisa Foust posing with her dead child on her lap—is emblematic of this genre (fig. 21).[28] Images such as this one drive home the reality

Fig. 21. Elizabeth Louisa Foust with her dead child on her lap, ca. 1853. Courtesy of the Historical Society of Pennsylvania, Philadelphia, Pa.

of the death of infants and children in antebellum America (discussed in chapter 1). This scene also trades on a well-established convention of memorial painting that includes both mother and child. Here the bedrock image for American artists may well have been Charles Willson Peale's classic painting "Rachel Weeping."[29] The photograph reveals, too, what historian Philippe Ariès has called the "promiscuity" of the dead and the living that characterized Western attitudes toward death in medieval Europe.[30] Like their ancestors, antebellum Americans did not recoil in fear or in horror from the touch of a dead body. Moreover, as both the subjects and observers of these photographs knew, these were carefully staged productions. In his essay "Taking Portraits After Death," Nathan G. Burgess provided detailed guidelines for commercial photographers who engaged in this kind of work, explaining how to pose corpses, adjust lighting, and arrange furniture accordingly.

Civil War battlefield photography drew on the conventions of post-mortem photography.[31] First, and most obviously, the images of dead soldiers taken by wartime photographers were carefully staged. Historian William Frassanito's pioneering work on these photographs reveals them to be anything but untouched depictions of warfare.[32] Even the most grisly depictions of battlefield carnage reflect the studied eye and deliberate hand of the photographer.

Take, for example, Alexander Gardner's arresting photograph "A Burial Party, Cold Harbor, VA., April, 1865" from his *Photographic Sketchbook of the Civil War*. A former associate of Mathew Brady, Gardner tramped along with Union troops throughout long stretches of the conflict. Gardner's famous *Photographic Sketchbook* appeared in 1866, immediately after the conclusion of combat, and contained a handful of some of the most gripping scenes of battlefield death produced by the war.[33] Among these images was his depiction of the "Burial Party" at Cold Harbor. As his audience surely knew, the 1864 battle of Cold Harbor was one of the Civil War's most horrific encounters. As part of his campaign to crush Robert E. Lee's Army of Northern Virginia white during that long summer, Union General Ulysses S. Grant hurled three full corps of troops at Lee's entrenched men—resulting in some seven thousand Union casualties in a single afternoon. In Union minds at least, the name Cold Harbor spelled slaughter.

Fig. 22. Alexander Gardner, "A Burial Party, Cold Harbor, VA., April, 1865."
Gardner's Photographic Sketchbook of the Civil War (1866). Courtesy of the Library of Congress.

Alexander Gardner's rendering of the "Burial Party" takes the worst that the Civil War had to offer and packages it into a highly stylized composition. African American gravediggers frame the scene—one man seated in line with a row of skulls, while four more men work in the background. In the center is a stretcher that contains the row of skulls set atop an array of rags and other bones. A single, booted foot hangs below the stretcher and a canteen has been propped up on one end. One can almost imagine a whole person being assembled out of the wreckage of body parts that Gardner has given the viewer. The row of skulls draws the eye of the viewer along—and it either starts or ends with the living face of a gravedigger seated on the ground. He is posed immediately adjacent to a skull that has been propped up to gaze directly at the camera. Every detail in this photograph has been considered. The image casts before the viewer an array of issues—the role of race in the disposal of the Union dead, the problems attending the burial of battlefield dead, and the destruction of bodies that was the inevitable portion of warfare. But Gardner takes the dismemberment of the corpse and renders it meaningful in another way. The line of skulls in the midst of a group of gravediggers calls to mind William Shakespeare's "gravedigger's scene" in the play *Hamlet,* complete with the specific visual representation of the skull of poor Yorick.[34] In an age in which familiarity with Shakespeare's plays was a cultural given for many Americans, this connection could hardly have been missed. Gardner repackaged the destruction of war in a familiar and comfortable idiom that his audience could identify with and comprehend.

Alexander Gardner also arranged battlefield corpses in such a way as to recall the antebellum photographic convention of death as "the last sleep." Two of his images from the *Photographic Sketchbook* make this connection explicitly—"A Sharpshooter's Last Sleep, Gettysburg, July, 1863" (fig. 23) and "The Home of a Rebel Sharpshooter" (fig. 24).[35] Again, both bodies have been meticulously posed. The photograph of the "Rebel Sharpshooter" boasts a rifle artfully propped against his stone fortifications and a blanket propped up under the dead man's head, rendering him literally in the posture of sleep. Although Gardner's accompanying text narrative for this image claims that the Confederate soldier had been "wounded in the head by a fragment of a shell which had exploded over him" we see no visible damage to his body. Even some of the photographs take by Thomas C. Roche of the Confederate Army's last stand around Petersburg, in 1865, trade on the trope of "the last sleep."[36] The fighting around Fort Mahone, Virginia, was some of the fiercest of the war, yet the photographer's hand was able to transform that suffering into an artful scene that suggested the peaceful repose of the dead.

Civil War era photographers gestured toward antebellum tradition by showing (with a few prominent exceptions) dead bodies that retained their integrity and wholeness. Given the kinds of weapons that Civil War troops used—exploding ordnance, grapeshot, canister, the rifled musket—mutilated and dismembered corpses were commonplace on battlefields.

Fig. 23. Alexander Gardner, "A Sharpshooter's Last Sleep, Gettysburg, July, 1863."
Gardner's Photographic Sketchbook of the Civil War (1866). Courtesy of the Library of Congress.

But mangled corpses are not evident in the work of Civil War battlefield
photographers. "The bodies of the dead soldiers," writes scholar Timothy
Sweet, "are nearly always shown intact. Few photographs exist of amputees, and none were published in Gardner's or Barnard's albums."[37]
Rather than showing the grim realities of the battlefield, Sweet suggests,
Civil War photographers were keen to imitate the work of nineteenth-
century landscape painters with their visions of the "pastoral" in American life. Thus middle-range photos dominate battlefield photography
(there are relatively few close-ups), and the artists attempted to capture
the effects of war on the landscape rather than draw attention to the
deaths suffered by soldiers.

Fig. 24. Alexander Gardner, "The Home of a Rebel Sharpshooter, Gettysburg, July, 1863." *Gardner's Photographic Sketchbook of the Civil War (1866).* Courtesy of the Library of Congress.

George N. Barnard's *Photographic Views of Sherman's Campaign* (1866) is a prime example of the emphasis on landscape among American Civil War photographers.[38] Barnard followed William Tecumseh Sherman's Union men in their epic campaigns—from the capture of Atlanta, Georgia, to the "March to the Sea," to the capture of Savannah, to the destruction of Columbia and Charleston, South Carolina. Yet not a single dead soldier appears in Barnard's book. The closest he comes to acknowledging the death of a Union man is plate 35, titled, "Scene of Gen. McPherson's Death" (fig. 25). McPherson died during the fighting around Atlanta, and the place of his death is indicated by the bleaching skull of a horse. Another scene of the "Battlefield of New Hope Church,

Fig. 25. George N. Barnard, "Scene of Gen. McPherson's Death." *Photographic Views of Sherman's Campaign (1866).* Courtesy of the Library Company of Pennsylvania.

No. 2" (fig. 26) shows a view of blasted trees, a trench, and clothing scattered along the top of some fortifications. But no bodies can be seen. Rather than a focus on bodies, Barnard draws the viewer's attention toward the ruins of neoclassical buildings in Savannah, Columbia, and Charleston. In Savannah, Barnard includes a view of the Buen-Ventura cemetery (plate 48), complete with a memorial topped by a classical urn (fig. 27). There is a romantic sensibility in these depictions of ruins that casts them as interesting and melancholy places. In their own way, Barnard seems to suggest, the burned landscapes and devastated cities of the South were really quite captivating. In the same way that ancient ruins might be profitably contemplated, the Southern landscape might teach lessons to its viewers.

Fig. 26. George N. Barnard, "Battle of New Hope Church, Georgia, No. 2." *Photographic Views of Sherman's Campaign (1866).* Courtesy of the Library Company of Pennsylvania.

In broad terms, it may not be too much to suggest that Civil War battlefield photographers found beauty in their subjects. Just as antebellum daguerreotypists created "beautiful deaths" for their audiences, battlefield photographers crafted their works in aesthetically pleasing ways. It may seem a reach to think about Gardner's Gettysburg sequence or Mathew Brady's 1862 exhibition "The Dead of Antietam" as beautiful. However, it is clear that these men carefully arranged each of their portraits, dragging dead bodies over the fields, propping up muskets, laying out canteens, and bleaching bones. "That a gory battlefield could be beautiful—in the sublime or awesome or tragic register of the beautiful—is a commonplace about images of war made by artists," writes critic Susan Sontag. "The idea does not sit well when applied to images made by

Fig. 27. George N. Barnard, "Buen-Ventura, Savannah, Ga." *Photographic Views of Sherman's Campaign (1866).* Courtesy of Hargrett Rare Book & Manuscript Library/ University of Georgia Libraries.

cameras: to find beauty in war photographs seems heartless," she continues, "but the landscape of devastation is still a landscape. There is beauty in ruins."[39] Sontag's contemporary analysis might well be applied to the work of men like Alexander Gardner, George N. Barnard, and Thomas C. Roche.

While Civil War battlefield photographers built on the traditions they inherited from antebellum daguerreotypists, they also modified them in the face of war. In some ways, as Franny Nudelman's keen work points out, battlefield photographs diverge sharply from prewar postmortem portraiture.[40] Before the Civil War, pictures of corpses were designed for consumption within families and in private. Battlefield photography portrayed images of strangers and was designed for a wider public audience. The individuals in postmortem photographs were well known to their families; the bodies in Civil War photographs were anonymous. The distance between these two genres of photography was acknowledged by an 1862 *New York Times* review of Brady's famous "Dead of Antietam" exhibition in his New York gallery. At one point, the reviewer imagined the journey of a woman through the exhibit who might "recognize a husband, a son, or a brother in the still lifeless lines of the bodies that lie ready for the gaping trenches."[41] Unlike postmortem daguerreotypes, the reviewer implied, battlefield photographs had the potential to terrorize those who encountered them.

Yet we have little evidence that those who attended Brady's exhibition were traumatized. Audiences responded to the photographs of the corpses with great curiosity and sustained interest. The battlefield contained "a terrible fascination about it that draws one near these pictures, and makes him loath to leave them."[42] Indeed, both the curious and the bereaved streamed into Brady's exhibit and did not run away in horror. As another *New York Times* essay, "Photographic Phases," put the matter: "The enterprise which begets these battle pictures is worthy of support as well as praise. Appealing as they do to the popular heart, they can scarcely fail of success."[43] That photographs of battlefield dead inspired rapt attention from "the popular heart" speaks to the distance that separates nineteenth-century attitudes about death from those in contemporary America, where photographing even the draped caskets of dead soldiers from Iraq has created a national controversy.

The corpses depicted on Civil War battlefields were clearly dedicated to the purposes of the nation-state in ways that postmortem images were not. If postmortem portraiture was designed to help families in the midst of grief, battlefield photography served more explicitly political ends. As we have already seen in the case of memorial lithography, the war heightened the ways in which the memorialization of the dead contributed to the power of the federal government. The sacrifices of soldiers for the Union cause, commentators insisted, made them "martyrs" for the nation. Like the death poets considered in chapter 4, those who wrote about the Civil War dead cast them in heroic terms. The dead of Antietam, averred the *New York Times,* served "to teach the world that there are truths dearer than life, wrongs and shames more to be dreaded than death."[44] Oliver Wendell Holmes, too, looked to the dead for patriotic inspiration. The sacrifices of the Union troops, he believed, would be vindicated in the end. "Yet through such martyrdom," he insisted, "must come our redemption. War is the surgery of crime."[45] The carnage of war was necessary to amputate the diseased limb of secession and to preserve the sacred cause of the Union.

Alexander Gardner's *Photographic Sketchbook of the Civil War* framed the dead within a rigorously pro-Union ideology. Each of the one hundred plates in his book was accompanied by a text that supplied a narrative for viewers as they encountered the photograph. Throughout these texts, Gardner made plain his unabashed admiration for the Federal cause. His "The Home of a Rebel Sharpshooter, Gettysburg," for example, charged the Confederate soldier with hiding among the rocks where he "in comparative security, picked off our officers." His "Burial Party" at Cold Harbor charged the residents of Virginia with failing to offer proper burial for the Union dead. The final plate in his volume shows the "Dedication of Monuments on Bull Run Battle-field" that celebrated the heroism of Union troops. Moreover, many of Gardner's photographs reveal and celebrate the power of the massive federal war machine—they show siege guns, mortars, fortifications, and set "corporation" views of groups of formally dressed Union officers. Gardner nestled his battlefield views in a political rhetoric that justified the horrific cost of war.

In other places in the *Photographic Sketchbook,* however, Gardner supplied words that obscured the suffering in the scenes he showed. As Alan Trachtenberg has noted, Gardner's texts often seem strangely disconnected from the photographs themselves, "indeed in almost all instances the picture might be turned against the text."[46] Take, for example, plate 37 from the battle of Gettysburg titled "Field Where General Reynolds Fell. Battlefield of Gettysburg" (fig. 28). Here we see a cluster of five corpses in the foreground, lying close to the camera in a large field. The men are on their backs with their faces open to the sky. Another body is set in the background to the left. A fence runs through the back of the frame, bracketed by trees, suggesting the edge of the photograph. Given the prominence of the corpses in this view, it might be reckoned

Fig. 28. Alexander Gardner, "Field Where Gen. Reynolds Fell. Battle-Field of Gettysburg." *Gardner's Photographic Sketchbook of the Civil War (1866)*. Courtesy of the Library of Congress.

among the most arresting and disturbing of Gardner's offerings. Yet, the text that accompanies the photograph seems to mute the horror of the scene. First, half the description in Gardner's text deals with General Reynolds' actions on the field at Gettysburg and describes how his "remains were brought off the field under a withering fire," thus assuring Union viewers that his corpse would receive its proper honor. Gardner then described the corpses he encountered on the field. Many of those who had died, he said, "wore a calm and resigned expression, as though they had been in the act of prayer." Some looked as if they "were in the act of speaking." Others looked nearly alive. "The faces of all were pale," he wrote, "as though cut in marble, and as the wind swept across the battle-field it waved the hair, and gave the bodies such an appearance of life that a spectator could hardly help thinking that they were about to rise and continue the fight."

Gardner's descriptive text on "Field Where General Reynolds Fell" is fascinating in a number of respects. First, one can only imagine the fatal wounding of General Reynolds (the hero of the narrative) because his body is not present in the scene. Moreover, Gardner's assurance that the Union troops had fallen with "a calm and resigned expression" is surely not evidenced by the bloated bodies and faces in the photograph. Gardner, however, was anxious to attribute to these men the proper disposition they should have held in the face of death: As good nineteenth-century Americans, they faced their end with the reflective resignation that we have already witnessed in antebellum narratives of death. Gardner also supplied his men with faith. They died, he said, as though they had been praying. Again, Gardner gave his men the religious conviction that they would need on the deathbed as they faced eternity. In this way he recognized the broadly religious framework within which antebellum Americans faced death. Finally, and most amazingly, Gardner's text suggests that the corpses lying dead on the field might actually rise up and walk away. Here was a tantalizing suggestion of life beyond the grave married to the powerful idea that dead heroes never really die. Gardner's evocation of the pale, "marble" countenances of these men evokes the idea that his photographs are monuments to the fallen troops that will keep them alive in memory. Here a kind of neoclassicism (the wind-swept fields of Gettysburg meeting the wind-swept plains of Troy) works with Gardner in his effort to memorialize the dead. Gardner's text transforms what might have been a hard-hitting look at the carnage of the battlefield into a scene that conjures up important elements in the antebellum culture of death.

The notion that photographs presented direct glimpses of reality served to mask the extent of suffering on Civil War battlefields. Oliver Wendell Holmes's writing on Brady's "Dead of Antietam" illustrates how this might happen. Commenting on the "the series of photographs showing us the field of Antietam," he acknowledged the horrible scenes "which the truthful sunbeam has delineated in all their dread reality."[47] Holmes insisted that "the honest sunshine" gave viewers an entirely realistic sense of what the battlefield had been like. However, his insistence on the reality of what the photographer's camera had captured masked the degree to which Brady and his associates had arranged bodies for artistic effect. When Holmes told his readers that the images showed fields "strewed with rags and wrecks," he spun a narrative that the photographic evidence did not sustain.[48] If critics like Holmes said that these photographs revealed the worst damage that the war could produce, then he muted for the public the impact of the war. Viewers could stroll home confident in the conviction that "the honest sunshine" had shown them the worst of the war.

Civil War photographers helped the American public, particularly in the North, to come to terms with slaughter. Trading on the conventions of antebellum postmortem photography, they carefully manicured their battlefield scenes for public consumption. They assured citizens that men fell as whole beings even in the midst of horrific combat. They touted the fact that such suffering and death was necessary to give new life to the Union. They wrapped battlefield death in the familiar tropes of the antebellum culture of death, insisting that men died on the field with resignation in their hearts and with peace in their souls. Like the memorial lithographers, Civil War photographers were not paid propagandists for the Union cause. They did, however, understand their audience and shaped their artistic productions to meet the demands of what the *New York Times* had called "the popular heart."

No visual representation of death had achieved greater acclaim among antebellum Americans than Rembrandt Peale's magnificent exhibition painting, *The Court of Death* (1820)(fig. 29). Taking in a canvas surface measuring 11 feet 6 inches by 23 feet 5 inches, it represented a major contribution to the genre of exhibition painting in America. Between 1820 and 1823, more than thirty thousand Americans flocked to see the painting as it made its way down the eastern U.S. seaboard, making stops from Boston, Massachusetts, to Savannah, Georgia. In 1845, after a substantial sabbatical, *The Court of Death* hit the road again, this time visiting not only the eastern establishment but also making forays into the hinterland of America in cities such as Cleveland, Cincinnati, Louisville, Detroit, and St. Louis before snaking down the Mississippi River to New Orleans and Mobile. Literally hundreds of thousands of people paid twenty-five cents each to imagine themselves into the massive work—perhaps as one of the twenty-three figures Peale had painted

Fig. 29. G. Q. Colton's 1859 lithograph of Rembrandt Peale's 1820 painting *The Court of Death*. Courtesy American Antiquarian Society, Worcester, Mass.

to virtual life-size. In 1858, when Peale sold the painting, it went for a whopping twenty thousand dollars. In 1859 its new owner, the promoter G. Q. Colton, offered 100,000 lithographic prints of *The Court of Death* for sale at one dollar a piece, although larger orders were encouraged by his promotional literature. By any sensible measure, *The Court of Death* must be reckoned among the great cultural icons of the early American Republic.[49]

In painting *The Court of Death*, Peale aimed to create an artistic sensation that would seal his reputation as one of America's premiere painters and produce enough revenue to rescue his museum in Baltimore. In the wake of the economic panic of 1819 and a yellow fever epidemic in the city, Peale faced hard times. He refused to accept these reversals without battling against them. Like his father, the artist Charles Willson Peale, Rembrandt possessed a flair for self-promotion and a brimming confidence in his own talent. Inspired by larger-than-life exhibition paintings he had seen in both Europe and America, he set to work on *The Court of Death*. Taking his keynote from "Death: A Poetical Essay" by Anglican Bishop Beilby Porteus, Peale sought to develop a work that would work a moral reformation in all who saw it. His vision was a lofty one. "Painting is the universal language of man," he wrote as *The Court of Death* was unveiled for the first time, "but a language still in its infancy—yet capable of being cultivated to perfection, as the noblest vehicle of moral sentiment."[50] In such ways did Rembrandt Peale self-consciously produce *The Court of Death* with the largest possible audience in mind.

That Peale seized the topic of death as the vehicle for his "pursuit of fame" tells us much about the cultural universe of antebellum America.[51] It indicates plainly how powerfully interesting the subject of death was to Americans in the decades immediately prior to the Civil War. We have already observed how a pervasive fascination with death found its way into American slave narratives, sentimental poetry, the rural cemetery movement, theological discourses, and personal correspondence, diaries, and autobiographies. Peale's *The Court of Death* may, therefore, be viewed as one more piece of evidence that validates the importance of death in the antebellum American imagination. In taking death as its central subject, *The Court of Death* tapped into deep currents of American concern.

Peale's promotional literature stressed that *The Court of Death* could be most profitably experienced in the company of others. As the painting traveled around the country, he offered his own exciting anecdotes designed to create interest in the work. He told, one suspects with some pride in the painting's magic, that when *The Court of Death* was shown in Albany, New York, "a Senator fell dead as he entered the door to see it." Perhaps anticipating that this striking event might dissuade future visitors, Peale added that "it was not the painting that terrified him, as was generally supposed, for he had not seen it—the circumstance was a mere coincidence." Peale also noted the more intentional, impromptu sermon delivered by the Methodist itinerant preacher Lorenzo Dow when he viewed the painting in Alexandria, Virginia. In New York, Peale reported that *The Court of Death* "was recommended from several

Pulpits, as a Great Moral Painting; and the City Corporation, although uninvited, went in a body to see it." Peale also explained the visit of a group of "Deaf and Dumb pupils" to the painting—an event requiring the teacher to "explain" the painting to them by the use of signs. Above all, it was the figure of the corpse that drew the attention of the students. "The dead body sensibly affected them," Peale explained, "as one of their number had recently been drowned."[52] To visit *The Court of Death*, then, was to be both a participant and an observer in a public drama in which people confronted directly the specter of their own mortality.

These dynamic encounters with death, in Peale's mind, were designed to lead viewers to still waters. Rather than leaving visitors standing in fear, he hoped that the moral message of the work would be, finally, a comforting one. He related the story of "an old friend" who had been resisting the invitation to see the painting, perhaps fearing his own mortality. After Peale "fairly *pushed* him into the room" to see it, the friend changed his tune. Meditating on the picture for an hour, he emerged as a man transfigured. He thanked Peale for "the good I had done him, acknowledging a dread of death, which he always disavowed, but which this painting had entirely removed."[53] This anecdote may contain Peale's own ideal template for audience response to his work. Despite his own rationalistic, Unitarian leanings, what Peale yearned to achieve in painting *The Court of Death* was some form of transcendent transformation in those who experienced it. As he wrote in December 1845, "Death has no terror in the eyes of virtuous old age, innocence, faith and hope—the philosophic Christian must agree."[54] Whatever fear or awe the painting might initially inspire in viewers, these emotions were to prompt the emotional and spiritual transformation that would lead them to peace. If one were to lead a moral life, a life of authentic virtue, then one might face death without fear.

That morality might inoculate one from the terror of death was a potent message to a country on the verge of war. The kind of morality that Peale's painting preached was not merely "middle class" but was, rather, widely accessible to evangelical Americans both in the North and in the South.[55] Peale asserted that virtue, faith, temperance, and sure hope in salvation were the best medicine for those who trembled in the face of their own mortality. Buoyed by the assurance that came with a life well-lived, Americans could face death with confidence. If we assume that in time of war, Union and Confederate troops alike believed that their respective causes held the moral high ground, then Peale's painting would have assured them that death held no gloomy prospect.

As viewers entered the imaginative domain of Peale's *Court of Death*, their eyes would have been carried immediately to the cluster of figures at the center of the painting. Here sat the magisterial figure of Death itself, a figure that Peale noted "reminds us of the first inhabitants of Egypt, the original residence of the human race."[56] Peale considered his representation of death to be a revolutionary one. Avoiding the traditional *danse macabre* image of death in mere skeletal form (as in the pamphlet *Emblems of Mortality* discussed in chapter 1), Peale sought to personify death in a way that was simultaneously more solemn and impressive and yet unmistakably human in form. Approaching Death is the figure of "Old Age"—an elderly man whose face had been based on that of Peale's father and "modified by the Antique Bust of Homer."[57] Supporting "Old Age" as he faces Death is a younger, female figure that Peale called "Faith" (or, in some cases, Virtue.) Peale brought together three major traditions that Americans used to comprehend death and to remember those who had died: those of ancient Egypt, the neoclassical tradition of the Greek revival, and evangelical Christianity. The group of figures at the center of Peale's painting furnishes modern viewers a kind of visual syllabus of the major cultural forces that framed the antebellum American encounter with death.

The focal point at the center of the painting is that of a youthful male corpse. With his back gently arched and head and feet dangling, his chest serves as a footrest for the representation of Death. His prostrate body organizes the first cluster of figures to which the viewer's eye is drawn— the embodiment of the "mighty Monarch" Death, the approaching man designated as "Old Age," and the supporting character of "Faith." Peale expected to grab the attention of his audience by placing this strikingly beautiful corpse in the foreground of the work. "The most impressive idea of Death is excited by the appearance of a DEAD BODY," Peale wrote in 1820 when the painting was first shown. He continued: "This receives the strongest ray of light in the picture.—It is the body of a man in the prime of life, by some casualty, to which all are liable, rendered life-less, prostrate as a foot-stool to the mysterious power of death."[58] When *The Court of Death* made its 1845 tour, Peale contributed promotional literature explaining that "the Corpse was the joint result of a study from a subject in the Medical College and the assistance of my brother Franklin, lying prostrate, with inverted head, which was made a likeness of Mr. Smith founder of the Baltimore Hospital."[59] Both the painting itself and Peale's writing about it make it plain that he invested a great deal of care and effort in producing his dead body. If he intended *The Court of Death* to work a moral transformation on its viewers, urging them to lives of faith and virtue, then representing the reality and unpredictability of death would have been the opening line in his visual sermon.

Rather than offering his audience a body ravaged by disease, which he might have done given the recent outbreak of yellow fever in Baltimore, Peale presented them with the dead body of a beautiful young man. The figure of the corpse is one way, among others, that *The Court of Death* partakes of the neoclassicism of the Greek revival. In some places, Peale openly interpreted his work as homage to the ancient Greeks. He wrote that it was "the first attempt, in modern times, to produce moral impressions on the ancient Greek plan, without the aid of mythology, or conventional allegory, being as readily understood by the ignorant as the learned."[60] The cave in which the painting is set is not only an important symbol of the resurrection in the Christian tradition but also serves in Plato's *Republic* as the setting of the famous "cave analogy" that puts students on the path that leads toward "the Good." But perhaps most important, Peale's corpse evokes the ancient Greek concept of the *kalos thanatos,* or "beautiful death."[61]

Peale's corpse—the model of the *kalos thanatos,* the death of the beautiful, young man in the prime of his powers—may have provided a cultural lens through which Civil War battlefield photographers wit-nessed the war. As we have already seen, men such as Alexander Gardner and Mathew Brady tended to avoid representing dead bodies that had been badly fragmented by fearful combat. In presenting corpses in this way, Civil War photographers deployed the conventions of the antebel-lum daguerreotypists. They may also have been following the example of painters. As Timothy Sweet has pointed out, Gardner and Brady were

Fig. 30. Thomas C. Roche, "Dead Confederate Soldier in the Trenches of Fort Mahone, Petersburg, Virginia," 1865. Courtesy of the Library of Congress.

keenly interested in the traditions of American landscape painting.[62] We also know that in the heroic portraits he produced during the 1850s, Brady drew on the work of painters. Mary Panzer, an expert on Brady's work, writes that "Brady consciously modeled his work on the work of painters, who created our images of Washington at Yorktown, or crossing the Delaware."[63] It may therefore not be too much to suggest that as Civil War photographers loaded up their wagons, they carried in their imaginations a catalogue of images that they had seen in famous American paintings, including *The Court of Death*.

Sometimes the correspondence between the dead body in *The Court of Death* and the photograph of a battlefield corpse is striking. Take, for example, an image shot by Thomas C. Roche of one of the dead Confederates who had been engaged in the defense of Fort Mahone at Petersburg, Virginia (fig. 30). The Union assault on Fort Mahone took place on April 3, 1865—just about a week before Lee surrendered the Army of Northern Virginia to Grant at Appomattox Court House. This is an image, then, from the final moments of the Civil War, after Americans had endured four years of horrific carnage. Yet, Roche's photograph of the young Confederate soldier is exquisitely composed. The young man's musket is placed across his body. A single shoe is placed in plain view. Behind the corpse, another musket's muzzle has been balanced to rest upon a small stone. Wooden logs frame the body at the bottom and right side of the image. With his back gently arched, with his head and feet angled downward, the posture of this young Confederate in the trenches of Petersburg, Virginia, bears a stunning resemblance to that of the dead body painted by Peale in *The Court of Death*.

In noting the power of *The Court of Death* to spark moral transformation among its witnesses, Peale acknowledged that "there is nothing terrible in it, but the scene of War."[64] The figure of War (located to the right) is among the largest and most compelling of the characters in the painting—decked out in neoclassical garb, sword and shield in hand, War is veritably racing out of the painting. In size, only the figure of Intemperance ranks with War, yet she does not embody the dynamism of the figure of the warrior. War, too, seems to have the most impact on other characters in the painting. Conflagration seems to have no purpose other than leading the way for War, the woman and child are innocents trampled by the figure of War, and War is leading the way for Pestilence and Famine. In 1820, Peale wrote of this assembly of characters that "the whole group is expressive of War, by which the passions of man produce premature and bloody death."[65] Promotional material for the 1859 lithograph included even more hair-raising prose: "War, in hot and cruel haste," explained a Colton broadside, "strides over the blighted earth, regardless of the bleeding Soldier, the wailing Widow, and the weeping Orphan, beneath his feet. His glittering sword drips with blood, his shield bids defiance to defense, and his eye is a stranger to pity."[66] Peale may have wanted to dissuade his viewers from organized violence by evoking precisely that sense of pity that the figure of War seems to deny. At the same time, however, the size and dynamism of the "War unit" (the cluster of figures to the right) and the florid language that accompanied it ensured that it received exalted treatment.

The emphasis that Peale placed on the "War unit," also suggests that he knew well his audience: Antebellum Americans were fascinated by images of warfare.

With almost eerie coincidence, the reality of war in America entwined itself with the exhibition history of *The Court of Death*. As Peale labored over the painting and as it began its first national tour, General Andrew Jackson chased Seminole Indians across the Florida territory with bloody resolve, earning himself a reputation as one of the most ruthless and hot-headed of all American military leaders. Curiously, at about the same time that Peale was at work on *The Court of Death*, he also produced a portrait of Andrew Jackson that captures with chilling effect the grim visage of a frontier killer. As one critic notes, "Jackson stands erect and looks out sternly, with not even a suggestion of human warmth."[67] When the painting toured again in the mid-1840s, the nation went to war against Mexico. In 1859, when the lithograph became available for sale, Americans—south and north—veered toward civil war. Indeed, November 1859 witnessed both the release of Colton's efforts to promote the sale of the new lithograph and the hanging of the abolitionist John Brown. It is possible to read this last antebellum appearance of *The Court of Death* as a harbinger of things to come. Like the European artists and writers who felt a sense of doom in the years leading up to World War I, Peale may have intuited the carnage ahead.

Peale's manifest intent, however, was not to presage war but to present the case for living a moral life. As one's eye moves across to the left of the picture's frame, Peale presents images that embody the ways in which lives of loose morality can cause death. Like the figures in the "War unit," the characters in the "Pleasure unit" (the figures clustered to the left) of the painting are depicted in a swirl of motion. Here we see Pleasure (dipping her goblet into what may be intoxicating drink), Remorse, and Intemperance. Suicide plunges a knife into his chest. Gout, Dropsy, Apoplexy, and Hypochondria slouch to the left of them. Consumption sits with a hand to the forehead, perhaps lost in contemplation of when the end might come. Fever and Despair frame the scene as the viewer's eye is drawn up toward the opening of the dark cave. Peale's framing of the moral evils in this unit of the painting suggests that they are the result of chronic overindulgence and intemperance. While some scholars have suggested that this portion of the painting owes much to Rembrandt's concern for the profligate ways of his brother Raphaelle, this may be an overly simplistic view. For what Peale was celebrating here were the dispositions of discipline and self-restraint, which were key to his conception of authentic morality. To stray from these virtues was to invite the suffering that he portrayed in the darkness of the tomb of death.

To the extreme left of *The Court of Death* emerges what Peale called "the bright spot of the painting": the opening of the cave, an image of life everlasting and of the resurrection. "Even death has no terrors," he explained in his 1859 descriptive materials, "in any possible form, for the *Christian*."[68] Here Peale conjured for his orthodox Christian viewers the way out of the tomb—perhaps a concession to those who thought Peale's Unitarianism offered little consolation on the deathbed. As we have also observed, the cave stood as a key symbol in the cultural universe of the Greek revival. According to Plato in *The Republic,* as souls leave the darkness of the cave (with its world of illusions), they come into the light of true knowledge and of the Form of the Good. As he had done throughout the painting, Peale deftly wove Christian and classical images together into a coherent whole. He also concluded the moral lesson of the painting on an upbeat note. "The whole painting," he insisted, "conveys a vast, a varied, an instructive, a solemn, cheering lesson, such as cannot fail to benefit mankind." Peale assured his viewers that redemption awaited them beyond the grave.

Rembrandt Peale's *The Court of Death* joined the memorial lithographs and the photographs we have considered in common purpose. These three visual media shared a commitment to abstracting death from its nitty-gritty historical circumstances, beautifying it to suit the needs of consumers, teach moral lessons, or accomplish some combination of these ends. They disguised the horror of death on the battlefield, trading instead on conventional images of whole persons (either mourners or dead bodies) rather than on blasted corpses. They pointed out that corporeal death did not mean the end for human beings. Memorial lithographs suggested that the memory of dead soldiers would live on in the hearts of family members and in the soul of the nation itself. Civil War battlefield photographers presented dead bodies as if taking their "last sleep," waiting only for the last trumpet to recall them to life. Rembrandt Peale's painting pulled hope from the myriad sufferings and snares of this world by concluding with a gesture toward the resurrection. In providing this powerful visual framework, artists contributed to the ability of the American public to sustain the fearful losses and the fragmented bodies that were the inevitable portion of the Civil War.

Epilogue

It is tempting for us to see ourselves as being very much like the generation of people who fought the American Civil War. Part of this impulse may be attributed to the pervasive egotism of contemporary society; of course, we imagine, those who fought in the past must share much with those of us living in the present. We are all Americans. We all believe in the fundamental values of liberty and freedom. We all struggle to earn a living. We all love our families. We all wrestle with questions of morality and ultimate meaning. How different could the Civil War past be from the present? After all, a mere century and a half separates us from those patriotic ancestors who fought at Gettysburg and Vicksburg. We may have letters and scrapbooks tucked away in attics or in safe deposit boxes that serve as direct physical links to those battles. They speak to us in the same language. They are like us. We are like them.

Images of the Civil War in contemporary culture reinforce this merging of past into the present. When we watch Ken Burns' documentary on the Civil War, we are likely to assume—perhaps unconsciously—that Abraham Lincoln actually did speak in the sonorous cadences of actor Sam Waterston. We can be lured into thinking that Frederick Douglass spoke with the gravitas and eloquence of Morgan Freeman. When we view the film *Cold Mountain*, we might imagine that all Charleston belles looked like the elegant Nicole Kidman or that rugged Confederate veterans possessed the good looks of Jude Law. In a different way, we might see the efforts of legions of Civil War re-enactors as enveloping the past in the present. To be sure, many of these modern veterans go to extreme lengths to recapture the texture of Civil War life—cooking their own hardtack from original recipes, sewing their own clothes, scouring the archives for the documentary evidence that will allow them to swing into proper battlefield formation. Yet, however hard core these "historical interpreters" may be, they nevertheless perpetuate the fiction that we can—if only we pay enough attention to the details—make the Civil War breathe again.[1]

The beautiful battlefields maintained by the National Park Service and by state agencies can also add to the impression that we know the Civil War better than we do. When I teach my Civil War and Reconstruction class at Hendrix College, I typically take a group of students to the Shiloh National Battlefield Park in Tennessee. As we stroll around the woods and fields of Shiloh, we can identify easily the archetypal markers of that battle—the famous "Sunken Road," the Peach Orchard, the Bloody Pond. That we can pick out these features of the landscape with such speed tempts us to think that we can know with certainty what happened at Shiloh. A closer look at the field, however, raises a host of confounding issues. The collage of memorial markers to individual units and the descriptive plates that identify the course of the fight are mixed together in what appear to be rather random ways across the battlefield—a problem made especially complex because Confederate and Union troops ranged across much of the same terrain on April 6 and April 7, trading off roles as attacker and defender. Sorting out actual troop movements proves to be a much thornier task than one might at first suppose. Furthermore, as the Civil War's first great bloodbath, the battle of Shiloh was attended by more than the usual amount of chaos and insanity. It was difficult even for those who fought the battle to tease out what happened. As Ulysses S. Grant, commander of the Union forces at Shiloh, put the matter in his *Memoirs*, "the battle of Shiloh, or

Pittsburgh landing, has been less understood, or to state the case more accurately, more persistently misunderstood, than any other engagement between National and Confederate troops during the entire rebellion."[2] What appears to be a neatly laid out historical site, nestled in the dense woods and green fields astride the peaceful Tennessee River turns out, at second glance, to be the location of a furious fight that we still struggle to understand.

Particularly impressive to me and my students are the burial trenches that contain the Confederate dead who fell during the battle. As many as five of these mass graves dot the battlefield—they are long rectangles marked by neatly mowed grass, surrounded by borders of black cannonballs. The remains of as many as seven hundred bodies rest in each trench. The burial trenches of Shiloh give us pause for reflection. In ways that individualized graves cannot, they bring home the barbarity of the war. How could Americans heap other Americans in long trenches as if they were so much wood? (The traditional interpretation is that Grant hastily interred the Confederate corpses because they were rotting in the heat.) Mass graves belong in places like Germany, Poland, the Gulag in Russia, Bosnia, Cambodia, or Rwanda. They don't belong in America. But the testimony of Shiloh is that they do belong in America. The burial trenches do not rate with the Sunken Road, or the Peach Orchard, or the Bloody Pond as tourist attractions because they tell us more than we may want to know about the Civil War.

The burial trenches of Shiloh are symbolic of a sensibility with which we have, for the most part, lost touch. They remind us that in many ways—ways suggested in this book—Americans participated in a culture of death that may seem alien to us. They show that nineteenth-century Americans were well familiar with death on a mass scale. They reveal to us that our ancestors raced off to war with visions of a glorious paradise in their heads. They instantiate the results of a robust belief in the martial ideals of the Greek revival. They suggest that our ancestors believed their deeds would be seen as beautiful and would be memorialized by those who followed in their footsteps. If we participate in the nineteenth-century culture of death today, it is most evident perhaps in our willingness to honor and valorize the past. Like the architects of the rural cemetery movement, we have constructed our battlefield parks as didactic landscapes designed to impart wisdom to the living. But in venerating the past, let us try to approach it with clear eyes; let us take it when we can on its own terms. Let us seek to understand those who fought the American Civil War in such a way that respects both the manner in which they lived and the ways in which they died.

Notes

Introduction

1. On these issues see Mark E. Neely Jr., "Was the Civil War a Total War?" *Civil War History* 37 (1991): 5–28; Charles Royster, *The Destructive War: William Tecumseh Sherman, Stonewall Jackson and the Americans* (New York: Alfred A. Knopf, 1991); Mark Grimsley, *The Hard Hand of War: Union Military Policy toward Southern Civilians, 1861–1865* (Cambridge: Cambridge University Press, 1996); James M. McPherson, "From Limited to Total War 1861–1865," in *Drawn with the Sword: Reflections on the American Civil War* (New York: Oxford University Press, 1996), 66–86.

2. Shelby Foote makes this point in *The Civil War: A Narrative*, vol. 1, *Fort Sumter to Perryville* (New York: Random House, 1958), 350.

3. Some of the long-term demographic effects of the war are assessed by Maris A. Vinovskis, "Have Social Historians Lost the Civil War? Some Preliminary Demographic Speculations," in *Toward a Social History of the American Civil War*, ed. Vinovskis (New York: Cambridge University Press, 1990), 1–30.

4. James M. McPherson argues in *Battle Cry of Freedom: The Civil War Era* (New York: Oxford University Press, 1988) that "the rifle and the trench ruled Civil War battlefields as thoroughly as the machine gun and trench ruled those of World War I" (477).

5. Ibid., 332.

6. Ibid., 484–488. As McPherson rightly notes, this was the age not only of heroic soldiers but the "heroic age" of medicine as well. See 487.

7. James M. McPherson, *What They Fought For 1861–1865* (Baton Rouge: Louisiana State Press, 1994); idem., *For Cause and Comrades: Why Men Fought in the Civil War* (Oxford: Oxford University Press, 1997).

8. McPherson, *For Cause and Comrades*, 168.

9. On "death before dishonor" see McPherson, *For Cause and Comrades,* 77. For the bedrock study of honor, see Bertram Wyatt-Brown, *Southern Honor: Ethics and Behavior in the Old South* (New York: Oxford University Press, 1982).

10. Although historian Edward L. Ayers comes very close to making the point that cultural forces drove Americans into the sectional conflict: "The secret of the Civil War was that many Americans wanted it to come, wanted it to prove their patriotism and demonstrate that they held God's favor." See Ayers, *In the Presence of Mine Enemies: The Civil War in the Heart of America, 1859–1863* (New York: W. W. Norton, 2004), 187.

11. For a recent review of some of the outpouring of literature on the suicide bombers and their motivations, see Christian Caryl, "Why They Do It," *New York Review of Books,* September 22, 2005, 28–32.

12. Edward L. Ayers, "Worrying About the Civil War," in *Moral Problems in American Life: New Perspectives in Cultural History,* ed. Karen Halttunen and Lewis Perry (Ithaca: Cornell University Press, 1998), 148. For a wider engagement of the Ken Burns Civil War documentary, see Robert Brent Toplin, ed., *Ken Burns's The Civil War: Historians Respond* (New York: Oxford University Press, 1996.)

13. David W. Blight, *Race and Reunion: The Civil War in American Memory* (Cambridge, Mass.: The Belknap Press of Harvard University Press, 2001).

14. Ayers, "Worrying About the Civil War," 165.

1. "Emblems of Mortality"

1. See, e.g., Karen Halttunen, *Confidence Men and Painted Women: A Study of Middle-Class Culture in America, 1830–1870* (New Haven: Yale University Press, 1982).

2. *Emblems of Mortality; Representing, By Engravings, Death Seizing All Ranks and Conditions of People. Imitated From a Painting in the Cemetery of the Dominican Church at Basil, in Switerland. With an Apostrophe to Each, Translated from the Latin. To which is now added, for the first time, a particular description of each cut, or engraving* (Charleston & New Haven: Babcock & Co., 1846), 67.

3. Ibid., 35.

4. See Charles Sellers, *The Market Revolution: Jacksonian America, 1815–1846* (New York: Oxford Univeristy Press, 1991).

5. Lewis O. Saum, "Death in the Popular Mind of Pre-Civil War America," *American Quarterly* 26 (December 1974): 479.

6. Philippe Ariès, *Western Attitudes toward Death from the Middle Ages to the Present,* trans. Patricia M. Ranum (Baltimore: Johns Hopkins University Press, 1974), 106.

7. Gary Laderman, *Rest in Peace: A Cultural History of Death and the Funeral Home in Twentieth-Century America* (New York: Oxford University Press, 2003), 206.

8. See Robert V. Wells, *Facing the "King of Terrors": Death and Society in an American Community, 1750–1990* (Cambridge: Cambridge University Press, 2000), 171–235, 291–292.

9. See esp. Nicholas Marshall, "'In the Midst of Life we are in Death': Affliction and Religion in Antebellum New York," in *Mortal Remains: Death in Early America,* ed. Nancy Isenberg and Andrew Burstein (Philadelphia: University of Pennsylvania Press, 2003), 176–186 and the sources in note 4 on 238.

10. Christian Warren, "Northern Chills, Southern Fevers: Race-Specific Mortality in American Cities, 1730–1900," *Journal of Southern History* 63 (February 1997): 38.

11. Charles E. Rosenberg, *The Cholera Years: The United States in 1832, 1849, and 1866 with a New Afterword* (Chicago: University of Chicago Press, 1987), 115.

12. Barbara J. Logue, "In Pursuit of Prosperity: Disease and Death in a Massachusetts Commercial Port, 1660–1850," *Journal of Social History* 25 (1991): 316.

13. Jo Ann Carrigan, "Yellow Fever: The Scourge of the South," *Disease and Distinctiveness in the American South*, ed. Todd L. Savitt and James Harvey Young (Knoxville: University of Tennessee Press, 1988), 60.

14. "Yellow Fever in Charleston," *Southern Quarterly Review* 7 (January 1853): 144.

15. Edward L. Parker, *A Sermon Delivered at Bedford, N. H., March 26, 1822, occasioned by the Sudden Death of James Parker, Esq.* (Amherst: Richard Boylston, 1822), 8.

16. Diary of Mary Edmundson, January 24, 1854, from the Edmundson/Bray/Williams/Stidham Collection, transcribed by Jennifer W. Ford, Department of Archives and Special Collections, J. D. Williams Library, University of Mississippi.

17. Otis Thompson, A.M., *A Sermon, Preached at the House of Dr. Calvin Martin, in Seekonk, February 9th, 1821, on the Occasion of the Death of Three of His Children, viz., Susan, who died January 8th, 1821, aged 25 years; Angelina, who died January 31st, 1821, aged 18 years; and Elisha May, who died February 7th, 1821, aged 11 years* (Providence: Miller & Hutchens, 1821) 13.

18. See broadsides titled *Statement of Deaths, With the Diseases and Ages, in the City and Liberties of Philadelphia, during the year 1834; Statement of Deaths. With the Diseases and Ages, in the City and Liberties of Philadelphia, during the year 1835; Statement of Deaths, with the Diseases and Ages, in the City and Liberties of Philadelphia, during the year 1836; Statement of Deaths, with the Diseases and Ages, in the City and Liberties of Philadelphia, during the year 1837* at the Library Company of Philadelphia.

19. Pickering Dodge, "A Tribute to the Memory of the Infant Dead, 1842," Manuscripts, American Antiquarian Society, Worcester, Mass.

20. *The Tragi-Comic History of the Burial of Cock Robin; with The Lamentation of Jenny Wren; the Sparrow's Apprehension; and the Cuckoo's Punishment. Being a Sequel to the Courtship, Marriage, and Pic-nic Dinner of Robin Red-breast and Jenny Wren* (Philadelphia: Benjamin Warner, 1821), 12.

21. *The Mount Vernon Reader, A Course of Reading Lessons, Selected with Reference to Their Moral Influence on the Hearts of the Young. Designed for Middle Classes* (New York: Collins, Keese & Co., 1837), 114–115.

22. *The Infant's Library. A B C* (New York: Baker, Crane & Day, 1845–1847).

23. *Heaven* (Philadelphia: American Sunday School Union, n.d.), 8.

24. Elizabeth A. Fenn, *Pox Americana: The Great Smallpox Epidemic of 1775–1782* (New York: Hill and Wang, 2001), 275.

25. Laurel Thatcher Ulrich, *A Midwife's Tale: The Life of Martha Ballard, Based on Her Diary, 1785–1812* (New York: Vintage Books, 1990), 36–71.

26. Rosenberg, *Cholera Years.*

27. See *The Epidemic Summer. List of Internments in all the Cemeteries of New Orleans, From the First of May to First of November, 1853* (New Orleans: The True Delta, 1853); see "Statistical Recapitulation" chart.

28. See Elaine Forman Crane, ed. *The Diary of Elizabeth Drinker: The Life Cycle of an Eighteenth-Century Woman* (Boston: Northeastern University Press, 1994), 111–121 for an account of the 1793 outbreak.

29. Ibid., 115.

30. Ibid., 118.

31. Rosenberg, *Cholera Years,* 32.

32. Ibid., 112.

33. "The Plague in the Southwest. The Great Yellow Fever Epidemic in 1853," *Debow's Review, Agricultural, commercial, industrial progress and resources* 15 (December 1853): 595–634, 619.

34. Ibid., 620.

35. Ibid., 624.

36. Ibid., 595.

37. *Epidemic Summer.*

38. James M. McPherson, *Battle Cry of Freedom: The Civil War Era* (New York: Oxford University Press, 1988) gives a total of 28,000 casualties for the Confederates at Gettysburg—including dead, wounded, and missing. In light of what we know of percentages of casualties dispersed in these categories, the number of dead would have been far less than 28,000. Shelby Foote estimates the number of Confederates killed outright at Gettysburg to have been slightly less than 2,600 in *The Civil War: A Narrative,* vol. 2, *Fredericksburg to Meridian* (New York: Random House, 1963), 578.

39. McPherson, *Battle Cry of Freedom,* notes about 2,000 total Confederate casualties and roughly 2,700 total Union losses for a total count of 4,700 at the First Battle of Bull Run. See 147.

40. Sheila M. Rothman, *Living in the Shadow of Death: Tuberculosis and the Social Experience of Illness in American History* (Baltimore: Johns Hopkins University Press, 1995), 13.

41. Todd L. Savitt, *Medicine and Slavery: The Diseases and Health Care of Blacks in Antebellum Virginia* (Chicago: University of Illinois Press, 1978), 142–148.

42. All material on the "invalid" experience is drawn from Rothman's brilliant treatment, *Living in the Shadow of Death,* 13–127.

43. Gary Laderman, *The Sacred Remains: American Attitudes toward Death, 1799–1883* (New Haven: Yale University Press, 1996), 55.

44. Daniel C. Eddy, *Angel Whispers; or the Echo of Spirit Voices Designed to Comfort Those Who Mourn* (Boston: Wentworth & Co., 1857).

45. Ibid., 120.

46. Ibid., 122.

47. Ibid., 125.

48. See Elaine Forman Crane, "'I Have Suffer'd Much Today': The Defining Force of Pain in Early America," *Through a Glass Darkly: Reflections on Personal Identity in Early America,* ed. Ronald Hoffman, Mechal Sobel, and Fredrika J. Tuete (Chapel Hill: University of North Carolina Press, 1997), 370–403. More broadly see Elaine Scarry, *The Body in Pain: The Making and Unmaking of the World* (New York: Oxford University Press, 1985).

49. Eddy, *Angel Whispers,* 128.

50. See Rothman, *Living in the Shadow of Death,* esp. 116–127.

51. Eddy, *Angel Whispers,* 130.

52. These accounts grew up along with new definitions of "horror" in American literature. See Karen Halttunen, *Murder Most Foul: The Killer in the American Gothic Imagination* (Cambridge, Mass.: Harvard University Press, 1998).

53. Michael Sappol, *A Traffic of Dead Bodies: Anatomy and Embodied Social Identity in Nineteenth-Century America* (Princeton: Princeton University Press, 2002).

54. Drew Gilpin Faust, "The Civil War Soldier and the Art of Dying," *Journal of Southern History* 67 (February 2001): 3–38.

55. Laderman, *Sacred Remains,* 136–143.

56. The narratives of death I have included for analysis here are admittedly idiosyncratic. Nevertheless I have tried in this brief compass to include a fair sampling of the diverse narratives of death composed in the years before the Civil War. I've included the narratives of great political leaders as well as those of more obscure figures; some of these narratives were published, others were tucked away in diaries or letters; some contain a single narrative strand, others draw on multiple sources. Indeed, the diversity of approaches manifest in

the death narratives themselves suggests what an elastic form it was for antebellum Americans. I also have attempted to be sensitive to issues of region, gender, and race in selecting sources for analysis. What is all the more striking in light of their variety, then, are the ways in which these narratives of death voice overlapping and interwoven themes.

57. Andrew Burstein, "Immortalizing the Founding Fathers: The Excesses of Public Eulogy," in *Mortal Remains,* 106. A classic account of Jefferson's death remains Merrill D. Peterson, *The Jefferson Image in the American Mind* (Charlottesville, Va.: Thomas Jefferson Memorial Foundation and the University of Virginia Press, 1998), 3–14. See also Andrew Burstein, *Jefferson's Secrets: Death and Desire at Monticello* (New York: Basic Books, 2005), 237–288.

58. Unless otherwise noted, the eulogies cited here are from the anthology *Selection of Eulogies, Pronounced in the Several States, in Honor of Those Illustrious Patriots and Statesmen; John Adams and Thomas Jefferson* (Hartford: Norton & Russell, 1826).

59. *Selection of Eulogies,* 96.

60. Ibid., 195.

61. William Wirt, *A Discourse on the Lives and Characters of Thomas Jefferson and John Adams, who both died on the Fourth of July, 1826. Delivered, at the request of the Citizens of Washington, in the Hall of the House of Representatives, on the Nineteenth of October, 1826* (Washington: Gales & Seaton, 1826), 11.

62. *Selection of Eulogies,* 88.

63. William Staughton, D.D., *Sermon Delivered in the Capitol of the United States; on Lord's Day, July 16, 1826; at the request of the Citizens of Washington, on the Death of Mr. Jefferson and Mr. Adams* (Washington: Published at the Columbian Office, North E. Street, 1826); Stephen R. Rowan, D.D., *An Address, Delivered July 12, 1826, in the Middle Dutch Church, at the Request of the Common Council, on Occasion of the Funeral Obsequies of John Adams and Thomas Jefferson* (New York: Printed by William Davis, June, No. 38, William Street).

64. Rowan, *Address,* 8; *Selection of Eulogies,* 191–192.

65. Wirt, *Discourse,* 7.

66. *Selection of Eulogies,* 88.

67. Staughton, *Sermon,* 4.

68. William Emmons, *Sacred to the Memory of Patriots John Adams and Thomas Jefferson, Who Died July 4, 1826. Eulogy Pronounced at Salem, July 27, 1826, After the Delivery of a Patriotic Address to the Assembled Citizens* (Salem, 1826), 3.

69. *Selection of Eulogies,* 343.

70. Staughton, *Sermon,* 8.

71. Wirt, *Discourse,* 66.

72. Ibid.

73. *Selection of Eulogies,* 163.

74. Ibid., 226.

75. Emmons, *Sacred to the Memory,* 4.

76. Wirt, *Discourse,* 67.

77. Alfred Johnson Jr., *Eulogy Delivered at Belfast, August 10, 1826 on John Adams and Thomas Jefferson. At the Request of the Citizens of Belfast* (Belfast: E. Fellowes, Printer, 1826), 20.

78. *Selection of Eulogies,* 160.

79. Cited in David McCullough, *John Adams* (New York: Simon & Schuster, 2001), 646.

80. *Selection of Eulogies,* 136.

81. Ibid., 52.

82. Rowan, *Address,* 20.

83. *Selection of Eulogies,* 296.

84. Ibid., 92.

85. Ibid., 151.

86. Joseph Story, *An Address Delivered on the Dedication of the Cemetery at Mount Auburn, September 24, 1831* (Boston: Joseph T. & Edwin Buckingham, 1831), 20.

87. Quoted in Gary B. Nash, *Race and Revolution* (Madison, Wis.: Madison House Publishers), 190. More broadly, see also Gary B. Nash, *Forging Freedom: The Formation of Philadelphia's Black Community, 1720–1840* (Cambridge, Mass.: Harvard University Press, 1988).

88. Rev. H. S. Gloucester, *A Discourse Delivered on the Occasion of the Death of Mr. James Forten, Sr., in the Second Presbyterian Church of Colour in the City of Philadelphia, April 17, 1842, Before the Young Men of the Bible Association of Said Church* (Philadelphia: I. Ashmead and Co., 1843). From the Rare Books and Manuscripts Division of the Schomburg Center for Research in Black Culture, New York.

89. Ibid., 18.

90. Ibid., 30–32 for all quotes from the Forten deathbed description.

91. Ibid., 36.

92. Melba Porter Hay, ed., *The Papers of Henry Clay,* vol. 10, *Candidate, Compromiser, Elder Statesman January 1, 1844–June 29, 1852* (Lexington: University of Kentucky Press, 1991), 312.

93. Ibid.

94. Ibid., 314–315.

95. Ibid., 315.

96. Ibid., 322.

97. Ibid.

98. Ibid., 321.

99. Ibid., 320.

100. Ibid., 319.

101. Ibid., 324.

102. Ibid., 338.

103. Ibid., 339.

104. Ibid., 312.

105. Ibid., 341.

106. Ibid., 340–341 on the breast-pin, locket, and coffin.

107. Benjamin B. Wisner, *Memoirs of the late Mrs. Susan Huntington, of Boston, Mass.* (Boston: Crocker and Brewster, 1829.)

108. Ibid., 303.

109. Ibid., 304.

110. Ibid., 307.

111. Rev. Wm. W. Patton, *Freedom's Martyr. A Discourse on the Death of the Rev. Charles T. Torrey* (Hartford: William H. Burleigh, Printer, 1846), 7. From the Rare Books and Manuscripts Division, Schomburg Center for Research in Black Culture, New York.

112. Ibid.

113. Ibid., 9.

114. Clyde N. Wilson and Shirley Bright Cook, eds., *The Papers of John C. Calhoun,* vol. 27, *1849–1850* (Columbia: University of South Carolina Press, 2003), 253.

115. Ibid., 248–251 for all quotes in the Scoville letter.

116. Ibid., 257.

117. Ibid., 262.

118. Ibid., 271 for all quotes.

119. Rev. Moses D. Hoge, *A Sermon Preached at the Funeral of Mrs. Caroline E. Morris in the Second Presbyterian Church, Richmond, Va.* (Richmond: Printed for Private Circulation, December 29, 1856), 17.

120. Ibid., 19 for both quotes.

121. Ibid., 20.

122. Ibid., 23.

123. Ibid., 20.

124. Miss Susan Paul, *Memoir of James Jackson, the Attentive and Obedient Scholar, Who Died in Boston, October 31, 1833, Aged Six Years and Eleven Months* (Boston: James Loring, 1835), 70.

125. Ibid., 71.

126. Ibid., 76.

127. Ibid., 79.

128. Ibid., 82.

129. Bertram Wyatt-Brown, "'A Volcano Beneath a Mountain of Snow': John Brown and the Problem of Interpretation," in *His Soul Goes Marching On: Responses to John Brown and the Harper's Ferry Raid,* ed. Paul Finkelman (Charlottesville: University of Virginia Press, 1995), 13. David S. Reynolds concurs with the judgment that Brown was ready to welcome death if it advanced his abolitionist dreams. Awaiting execution in prison, Brown wrote, "I go joyfully in behalf of Millions that 'have no rights' that this 'great & glorious'; 'this Christian Republic,' is bound to respect." Brown quoted in Reynolds, *John Brown, Abolitionist: The Man Who Killed Slavery, Sparked the Civil War, and Seeded Civil Rights* (New York: Alfred A. Knopf, 2005), 389.

130. Quoted in Zoe Trodd and John Stauffer, eds., *Meteor of War: The John Brown Story* (Maplecrest, N.Y.: Brandywine Press, 2004), 258.

131. Ibid., 164–165.

132. See Charles Royster's chapter on the "Death of Stonewall" in *The Destructive War: William Tecumseh Sherman, Stonewall Jackson, and the Americans* (New York: Alfred A. Knopf, 1991), 213–215.

133. McPherson, *Battle Cry of Freedom,* 202–233.

134. Franny Nudelman's book *John Brown's Body: Slavery, Violence, and the Culture of War* (Chapel Hill: University of North Carolina Press, 2004) smartly argues that Brown's martyrdom and the song that celebrated it served a myriad of purposes, among them that his "example may have helped soldiers envision their own deaths as a source of collective rejuvenation: the song encouraged soldiers to believe that an individual's death might enable the larger community—the people or nation—to endure" (16). For more on Brown's body, see Laderman, *Sacred Remains,* 89–95.

2. "The Heavenly Country"

1. John M. Roberts, *A Better Country. An Association Sermon, Delivered Before the Charleston Baptist Association, at Orangeburg, (S. C.) Nov. 6th, 1809* (Charleston, S.C.: J. Hoff, 1810), 4.

2. Mrs. Sarah Gould, compiler, *The Guardian Angels, or, Friends in Heaven* (Boston: Higgins and Bradley, 1857), 214.

3. Harriett Beecher Stowe, *Uncle Tom's Cabin,* ed. Elizabeth Emmons (New York: Norton Critical Edition, 1994), 247.

4. Ibid., 254.

5. Ibid., 257.

6. Colleen McDannell and Bernhard Lang, *Heaven: A History* (New Haven: Yale University Press, 1988), 181–227.

7. Ibid., 182.

8. My reading of the antebellum evidence and the analysis that follows here suggest a very lively discussion of heavenly topics well *before* the Civil War began. I thus find myself in disagreement with the comments of Phillip Shaw Paludan in his "overview" essay, "Religion and the American Civil War," in Randall M. Miller, Harry S. Stout, and Charles Reagan Wilson, eds., *Religion and the American Civil War* (New York: Oxford University Press, 1998). Paludan argues that it was primarily *after* the Civil War that "people began to demand a more detailed view of heaven" (31). Paludan thus speculates that the carnage of the war prompted Americans to learn more about heavenly destinations. My argument tends toward the inverse proposition: that robust antebellum ideas about the afterlife may have helped Americans to stomach the carnage of war in the first place. When, in considering the antebellum period, Paludan writes that "fewer than a book a year on the subject was published in the United States" on the topic of heaven (31), I think he underestimates dramatically discussions of heaven in sermons, poetry, novels, art, and in a wide-ranging theological literature on the nature of the resurrection body. While interest in heaven may have remained intense after the war, it is simply not accurate to compare postwar abundance with prewar scarcity on this point.

9. William H. Furness, *The Kingdom of Heaven. A Sermon Preached at the Installation of Rev. John T. Sargent, as pastor of the First Congregational Church in Somerville, Mass., Wednesday, February 18, 1846* (Somerville, Mass.: Edmund Tufts, 1846), 22.

10. Augustus C. Thompson, *The Better Land; or, The Believer's Journey and Future Home* (Boston: Gould and Lincoln, 1854), 60.

11. Ibid., 68.

12. Elizabeth, Princess of Light (pseudo.), "Romance of Life in America" (ca. 1842–1865), Library of Congress, Manuscript Division.

13. Andrew Jackson Davis, *The Principles of Nature, Her Divine Revelations, and A Voice to Mankind*, 36th ed. (Rochester, N.Y.: Austin Publishing Co., 1911), xi.

14. Bret E. Carroll, *Spiritualism in Antebellum America* (Bloomington: Indiana University Press, 1997), 14.

15. Ann Braude, "News from the Spirit World: A Checklist of American Spiritualist Periodicals, 1847–1900," *Proceedings of the American Antiquarian Society* 99 (1989): 399–462.

16. Eugene D. Genovese, *Roll, Jordan, Roll: The World the Slaves Made* (New York: Vintage Books, 1976), 219f.

17. David Donald, *Lincoln* (New York: Simon & Schuster, 1995), 337.

18. Dr. Richard Emmons, *Description of Heaven. A Poem* (Philadelphia: William Emmons, 1830), Library of Congress, Rare Book Room.

19. George Wood, *Future Life; or, Scenes in Another World* (New York: Derby & Jackson, 1858), 25.

20. Ibid., 49.

21. Ibid., 54.

22. Ibid., 357.

23. Ibid.

24. Rev. H. Harbaugh, *The Heavenly Home; or, The Employments and Enjoyments of the Saints in Heaven*, 2nd ed. (Philadelphia: Lindsay & Blakiston, 1853), v.

25. Rev. H. Harbaugh, *Heaven; or, An Earnest and Scriptural Inquiry into the Abode of the Sainted Dead*, 13th ed. (Philadelphia: Lindsay & Blakiston, 1856), 35.

26. Ibid., 42.

27. Harbaugh, *Heavenly Home,* 155.

28. Harbaugh, *Heaven; or, An Earnest and Scriptural Inquiry,* 40.

29. Ibid., 41.

30. Harbaugh, *Heavenly Home,* 167.

31. Rev. Rufus W. Clark, *Heaven and Its Scriptural Emblems* (Boston: John P. Jewett and Co. Cleveland, Ohio: Jewett, Proctor & Worthington, 1853), 80.

32. Ibid., 81.

33. Harbaugh, *Heavenly Home,* 173.

34. Ibid., 174.

35. Clark, *Heaven and Its Scriptural Emblems,* 148.

36. Ibid., 148–149.

37. See esp., among a large body of work, James M. McPherson, *For Cause and Comrades: Why Men Fought in the Civil War* (New York: Oxford University Press, 1997), 104–116.

38. Caroline Walker Bynum, *The Resurrection of the Body in Western Christianity, 200–1336* (New York: Columbia University Press, 1995). As will be observed, this volume has shaped my thinking in important ways.

39. Bynum, *Resurrection of the Body,* 33 and passim.

40. Harbaugh, in *Heavenly Home,* explicitly invokes Tertullian, Augustine, and others on 223. Beyond these brief acknowledgments, it is clear that antebellum writers were keenly aware of the arguments and theological conundrums faced by their ancestors in the first centuries of the Church.

41. Samuel Drew, *An Essay on the Identity and General Resurrection of the Human Body: in which the evidences of these important subjects are considered, in relation both to Philosophy and Scripture* (Philadelphia: Joseph Whetham, 1837), 357.

42. Ibid., 358.

43. See George Bush, *The Resurrection of Christ; in answer to the question, whether he rose in a spiritual and celestial, or in a material and earthly body* (New York: J. S. Redfield, 1845); George Bush, *The Soul; or, an inquiry into the scriptural psychology, as developed by the use of the terms soul, spirit, life, etc., viewed in its bearings on the doctrine of the resurrection* (New York: J. S. Redfield, 1845); George Bush, *Anastasis: or the doctrine of the Resurrection of the Body, rationally and scripturally considered* (New York and London: Wiley and Putnam, 1845).

44. George Bush, *Anastasis,* 70.

45. Ibid., 78.

46. Harbaugh, *Heavenly Home,* 184.

47. Bush, *Anastasis,* 80.

48. Ibid.

49. Bush, *Anastasis,* 80–81.

50. Jason Lewis, *The Anastasis of the Dead: or, Philosophy of Human Immortality, as deduced from the teachings of the scripture writers, in reference to "The Resurrection."* (Boston: A. Tompkins, 1860), 115.

51. Ibid.

52. Ibid., 116.

53. Ibid., 122.

54. Harbaugh, *Heavenly Home,* 184.

55. Ibid.

56. Ibid., 185.

57. Ibid., 179.

58. Richard Mant, D.D., *The Happiness of the Blessed Considered as the Particulars of Their State: their recognition of each other in that state; and its difference of degrees. To which*

are added, musings on the church and her services (New York: Stanford and Swords, 1847), 46–47.

59. George Burgess, D.D., *The Last Enemy; Conquering and Conquered,* (Philadelphia: H. Hooker, 1850), 314; see also Harbaugh, *Heavenly Home,* 189.

60. Harbaugh, *Heavenly Home,* 187.

61. Burgess, *Last Enemy,* 313.

62. Walt Whitman, *Complete Poetry and Collected Prose,* ed. Justin Kaplan (New York: Library of America, 1982), 88. I am indebted to Dr. Martha Sledge for calling this passage to my attention. On Whitman's concern with organic images of decay and redemption, see Franny Nudelman, *John Brown's Body: Slavery, Violence, and the Culture of War* (Chapel Hill: University of North Carolina Press, 2004), 71–102.

63. N. W. Hodges, *A Sermon on The Resurrection, Delivered at the Gilgal Camp-Meeting, August, 1837* (Charleston, S.C.: James S. Burges, 1838), 9.

64. Ibid.

65. Ibid., 10.

66. Ibid., 11.

67. Thompson, *Better Land,* 216.

68. Calvin Kingsley, *The Resurrection of the Dead: A Vindication of the Literal Resurrection of the Human Body; in Opposition to the work of Professor Bush* (New York: Carlton & Phillips, 1853), 41.

69. Ibid., 41–42.

70. Benjamin T. Onderdonk, *The Change at the Resurrection: A Sermon Preached in St. Philip's Church, New York, on Tuesday, October 20, 1840 at the Funeral of the Rev. Peter Williams* (New York: Published by request of the Wardens and Vestrymen of St. Philip's Church, 1840), 11.

71. Mant, *Happiness of the Blessed,* 41f.

72. Burgess, *Last Enemy,* 313.

73. Harbaugh, *Heavenly Home,* 224.

74. Whitman, *Complete Poetry and Collected Prose,* 744–745, 763, 767–768, 771–772, and passim.

75. Russell Duncan, ed., *Blue-Eyed Child of Fortune: The Civil War Letters of Robert Gould Shaw* (Athens: University of Georgia Press, 1992), 240.

76. T. J. Jackson Lears, *No Place of Grace: Antimodernism and the Transformation of American Culture 1880–1920* (New York: Pantheon, 1981), 4. See also Bertram Wyatt-Brown, *The Shaping of Southern Culture: Honor, Grace, and War, 1760s–1880s* (Chapel Hill: University of North Carolina Press, 2001), 255 for the same quotation.

77. Wyatt-Brown, *Shaping of Southern Culture,* 250.

78. Steven E. Woodworth, *While God Is Marching On: The Religious World of Civil War Soldiers* (Lawrence: University of Kansas Press, 2001), 43.

79. Bynum, *Resurrection of the Body,* 50.

80. See Drew Gilpin Faust, "The Civil War Soldier and the Art of Dying," *Journal of Southern History* 67 (February 2001): 3–38; Gary Laderman, *The Sacred Remains: American Attitudes toward Death, 1799–1883* (New Haven: Yale University Press, 1996), 136–143 esp.

81. Daniel Sharp, *Recognition of Friends in Heaven; a Discourse* (Boston: John Putnam, Printer, 1844), 10; Rev. J. Duncan, *The Mourner's Friend; or, Recognition of Friends in Heaven* (Lowell, Mass.: N. L. Dayton, 1850), 11.

82. Sharp, *Recognition of Friends in Heaven,* 7.

83. William Mountford, *Euthanasy; or Happy Talk Towards the End of Life* (Boston: Wm Crosby and H. P. Nichols; New York: D. Appleton and Co., 1849), 462.

84. Rev. James Miller Killen, *Our Friends in Heaven; or, the Mutual Recognition of the Redeemed in Glory Demonstrated* (Cincinnati: L. Swomstedt & A. Poe, 1857), 169.

85. Ibid., 189.

86. Duncan, *Mourner's Friend*, 35.

87. F. W. P. Greenwood, D.D., *Sermons of Consolation* (Boston: William D. Ticknor & Co., 1842), 209.

88. Ibid., 250.

89. Wood, *Scenes in Another World*, 27.

90. Clark, *Heaven and Its Scriptural Emblems*, 252.

91. Ibid., 253.

92. Quoted in James M. McPherson, *For Cause and Comrades: Why Men Fought in the Civil War* (New York: Oxford University Press, 1997), 71.

93. Drew Gilpin Faust, "Christian Soldiers: The Meaning of Revivalism in the Confederate Army," *Journal of Southern History* 53 (February 1987): 63–90.

94. Quoted in Charles Royster, *The Destructive War: William Tecumseh Sherman, Stonewall Jackson, and the Americans* (New York: Alfred A. Knopf, 1991), 193.

95. Ibid., 196.

96. Ibid., 230.

97. James B. Ramsey, *True Eminence Founded on Holiness. A Discourse Occasioned by the Death of Lieut. Gen. T. J. Jackson. Preached in the First Presbyterian Church of Lynchburg, May 24th, 1863* (Lynchburg, Va.: Virginian "Water Power Presses" Print, 1863), 8–9. (Electronic version from the University of North Carolina website "Documenting the American South," http://docsouth.unc.edu.ramsey/html.)

98. Alice Fahs, *The Imagined Civil War: Popular Literature of the North and South 1861–1865* (Chapel Hill: University of North Carolina Press, 2001), 94.

99. Ibid., 100, and see her chapter on "The Sentimental Soldier" more generally, 93–119.

100. Augusta Jane Evans, *Macaria; or, Altars of Sacrifice*, ed., Drew Gilpin Faust (Baton Rouge: Louisiana State University Press, 1992), 328.

101. Ibid., 329.

102. Ibid.

103. Ibid., 402.

104. Ibid., 403.

105. Laderman, *Sacred Remains*, 162.

106. Quoted in Shelby Foote, *The Civil War: A Narrative*, vol. 3, *Red River to Appomattox* (New York: Random House, 1974), 1048.

107. Woodworth, *While God Is Marching On*, 51. See also Faust, "Civil War Soldiers," 37; Laderman, *Sacred Remains*, 132–133, on how antebellum religious convictions, especially the idea of heavenly reunion, may have bolstered the Civil War generation to fight on in the face of horrible losses.

108. Peter L. Berger, *The Sacred Canopy: Elements of a Sociological Theory of Religion* (New York: Anchor Books, 1969), 51.

3. "Melancholy Pleasure"

1. Quoted in Blanche Linden-Ward, *Silent City on a Hill: Landscapes of Memory and Boston's Mount Auburn Cemetery* (Columbus: Ohio State University Press, 1989), 191.

2. See Stanley French, "The Cemetery as Cultural Institution: The Establishment of Mount Auburn and the 'Rural Cemetery' Movement," *American Quarterly* 26 (March 1974): 45–46.

3. Joseph Story, *An Address Delivered on the Dedication of the Cemetery at Mount Auburn, September 24, 1831* (Boston: Joseph T. & Edwin Buckingham, 1831), 7.

4. Ibid., 10.

5. Ibid., 15.

6. Ibid., 18. On the importance of liminality in the rural cemetery and its connection to the Greek revival, see Gary Wills, *Lincoln at Gettysburg: The Words That Remade America* (New York: Simon & Schuster, 1992), 74.

7. Story, *Mount Auburn*, 14.

8. David Schuyler quoted in David Charles Sloane, *The Last Great Necessity: Cemeteries in American History* (Baltimore: Johns Hopkins University Press, 1991), 65.

9. See French, "Cemetery as Cultural Institution," on this point.

10. Story, *Mount Auburn*, 17.

11. Ibid., 18.

12. Ibid., 19.

13. Leo Marx, *The Machine in the Garden: Technology and the Pastoral Ideal in America* (New York: Oxford University Press, 1981), 103 and 73–144 more generally.

14. Story, *Mount Auburn*, 7.

15. Ibid., 20.

16. Ibid., 21.

17. Quoted in French, "Cemetery as Cultural Institution," 53. On the pervasiveness of the rural cemetery, see also Sloane, *Last Great Necessity*, 56.

18. Quoted in Linden-Ward, *Silent City on a Hill*, 167.

19. *Sketch of the Loudon Park Cemetery: Its Dedication, and Address of the Hon. Charles F. Mayer, Delivered on that Occasion* (Baltimore: Printing Office, Sun Iron Building, 1853), 15.

20. Bellamy Storer, Esq., *An Address, Delivered at the Consecration of the Linden Grove Cemetery, Covington, Kentucky, September 11, 1843* (Cincinnati: E. Morgan and Co., 1843), 9.

21. James L. Orr, "Development of Southern Industry," *De Bow's Review* 19 (July 1855): 7.

22. *Second Report of the Board of Managers to the Proprietors and Lot-holders of the Green Mount Cemetery* (Baltimore: John D. Troy, 1848), 31.

23. Quoted in Sybil F. Crawford, *Jubilee: Mount Holly Cemetery, Little Rock, Arkansas: Its First 150 Years* (Little Rock: Mount Holly Cemetery Association, 1993), 2.

24. Richard L. Bushman, *The Refinement of America: Persons, Houses, Cities* (New York: Alfred A. Knopf, 1992), xix and passim. Although Bushman does not include the rise of the rural cemetery movement in his overall argument, it fits snugly with his overall theory of refinement.

25. Ibid.

26. Orr, "Development of Southern Industry," 7.

27. *Proceedings of the Members of the Holly-wood Cemetery Company, at their first annual meeting, held in the City of Richmond, May 1st. With a description of the Plan of the Cemetery, and other documents relating thereto* (Richmond: MacFarlane & Fergusson, Printers, 1849), 19 for quotation. See also 4 on the issue of Notman's hire. See also Mary H. Mitchell, *Hollywood Cemetery: The History of a Southern Shrine* (Richmond: Virginia State Library, 1985), 12–16.

28. Charles Fraser, *Address Delivered at the Dedication of Magnolia Cemetery, on the 19th November, 1850* (Charleston, S.C.: Steam Press of Walker and James, 1850), 18.

29. Quoted in Linden-Ward, *Silent City on a Hill*, 132–133.

30. See the website for the Old Gray Cemetery at http://www.korrnet.org/oldgray/history.htm.

31. John H. B. Latrobe, *Dedicatory Services at the Opening of the Mount Olivet Cemetery, July 16, 1849, with a Prospectus, Terms of Subscription, etc.* (Baltimore: Armstrong & Berry, 1849), 12.

32. *The Monument Cemetery of Philadelphia. (Late Pere La Chaise.) Containing Several Scientific Essays on the Subject of Rural Cemeteries, with a Lithographic Plan* (Philadelphia: John A. Elkinton, M.D., Publisher, 1837), 13.

33. Levi Lincoln, *An Address Delivered at the Consecration of the Worcester Rural Cemetery, September 8, 1838* (Boston: Dutton and Wentworth, Printers, 1838), 6.

34. *Report of The Trustees of Green Lawn Cemetery: with the Articles of Association, the Regulations, and the Dedication Addresses, &c. &c.* (Columbus: Ohio State Journal Print. 1849), 41.

35. *Second General Report of the Managers,* 29.

36. *Laurel Grove Cemetery! An Account of Its Dedication, with the Poem of the Hon. Robert M. Charlton, and the Address of the Hon. Henry Jackson, Delivered on the 10th November, 1852, to which are added the Ordinances Establishing and Regulating the Cemetery* (Savannah, Ga.: George N. Nichals, Beck, and [?] Printer, 1853), 13.

37. John McLean, *Cemetery of Spring Grove: Its Charter, Rules, and Regulations, and also An Address delivered at the Consecration, by the Hon. John M'Lean and a Catalogue of the Proprietors on the 1st of May 1849* (Cincinnati: Gazette Office, Wright, Fisher & Co., 1849), 26.

38. Ibid.

39. Edward P. Humphrey, *An Address, Delivered on the Dedication of the Cave Hill Cemetery, near Louisville: July 25, 1848* (Louisville, Ky.: Printed at the Courier Job-Room, 1848), 4.

40. See Jefferson's design in Merrill Peterson, ed., *Jefferson: Writings* (New York: Literary Classics of the U.S., 1984).

41. William Clark, *Dedication of Mount Hebron Cemetery, in Winchester, Virginia, June 22, 1844; The Act of Incorporation by the Legislature of Virginia in 1844, and the Constitution and By-Laws of the Mount Hebron Cemetery Company* (Winchester: Printed at the Republican Office, 1845), 14–15.

42. Fraser, *Magnolia Cemetery,* 9.

43. E. B. Wilson, *An Address Delivered at the Consecration of the Riverside Cemetery in Grafton, April 29, 1851* (Boston: John Wilson & Son, 1851), 7.

44. *The Picturesque Pocket Companion, and Visitor's Guide, through Mount Auburn: Illustrated with Upwards of Sixty Engravings on Wood* (Boston: Otis, Broaders and Co., 1839).

45. Daniel Appleton White, *An Address at the Consecration of the Harmony Grove Cemetery, in Salem, June 14, 1840* (Salem: Printed at the Gazette Press, 1840), 11.

46. Latrobe, *Dedicatory Services at the Opening of Mount Olivet Cemetery,* 16.

47. Ibid., 17.

48. *First Report of the Managers of the Allegheny Cemetery, Together with the charter of the corporation; its Rules, Regulations, Lot Holders, etc., also a Funeral Address on the occasion of re-interring the remains of Com. Joshua Barney & Lieut. Jas. L. Parker. By Wilson M'Candless, Esq.* (Pittsburgh: Printed by Johnston and Stockton, 1849), 44–45.

49. Humphrey, *An Address, Delivered on the Occasion of the Cave Hill Cemetery,* 5.

50. French, "Cemetery as Cultural Institution," 59.

51. See esp. Colleen McDannell, "The Religious Symbolism of Laurel Hill Cemetery," in *Material Christianity: Religion and Popular Culture in America* (New Haven: Yale University Press, 1995), 103–131.

52. *Address Delivered at the Opening Ceremonies of Every Green Cemetery, Gettysburg, Pa., November 7, 1854. By Rev. J. H. C. Dosh, Pastor of Methodist Episcopal Church. Also*

A Discourse Delivered at the Laying of the Corner Stone of Gateway and Lodges at Cemetery, Sept. 1, 1855 (Gettysburg: H. C. Neinstadt, 1855), 4.

53. McLean, *Cemetery of Spring Grove,* 38.

54. Bellamy Strorer, Esq., *An Address, Delivered at the Consecration of the Linden Grove Cemetery,* 12.

55. *Exposition of the Plan and Objects of the Green-wood Cemetery, An Incorporated Trust Chartered by the Legislature of the State of New York* (New York: Printed by Narine & Co., 1839), 16.

56. *Picturesque Pocket Companion,* 24.

57. French, "Cemetery as Cultural Institution," 45.

58. Ibid.

59. *Dedication of Mount Hebron Cemetery,* 31.

60. Linden-Ward, *Silent City on a Hill,* 96.

61. Alfred F. Young, *The Shoemaker and the Tea Party: Memory and the American Revolution* (Boston: Beacon Press, 1999).

62. Linden-Ward, *Silent City on a Hill,* 148.

63. McDannell, *Material Christianity,* 112.

64. *Monument Cemetery of Philadelphia,* 24–25.

65. *Picturesque Pocket Companion,* 15.

66. White, *Harmony Grove Cemetery,* 30.

67. Lincoln, *Worcester Rural Cemetery,* 14.

68. Clark, *Mount Hebron Cemetery,* 20.

69. W. Gilmore Simms, *The City of the Silent. A Poem. Delivered at the Consecration of Magnolia Cemetery, November 19, 1850* (Charleston: Walker & James Publishers, 1850), 24–25.

70. *First Report of the Managers of Allegheny Cemetery,* 31–41, quotation on 41.

71. Fraser, *Magnolia Cemetery,* 21.

72. Story, *Mount Auburn,* 21.

73. *Laurel Grove Cemetery,* 17.

74. Ibid., 18.

75. *Exposition of the Plan and Object of the Green-wood Cemetery,* 18.

76. In this analysis I am indebted to the work of Caroline Winterer, *The Culture of Classicism: Ancient Greece and Rome in American Intellectual Life 1780–1910* (Baltimore: Johns Hopkins University Press, 2002).

77. Winterer, *Culture of Classicism,* 68.

78. Ibid., 77.

79. Ibid., 81.

80. Ibid., 78.

81. Herodotus, *The Histories,* trans. Aubrey De Selincourt (Penguin Classics, 1972), 52. I am grateful to my colleague Dr. Rebecca Resinski for directing me to this citation and for help in understanding ancient Greek ideas about the "beautiful death" (*kalos thanatos*) in general.

82. Caroline Winterer, "From Royal to Republican: The Classical Image in Early America," *Journal of American History* 91 (March 2005): 1274.

83. Ibid., 1277.

84. Winterer, *Culture of Classicism,* 88.

85. Stephen Crane, *Poetry and Prose,* ed. J. C. Levenson (New York: Library of America, 1984), 83.

86. My analysis here leans heavily on Jean-Pierre Vernant's essay "A 'Beautiful Death' and the Disfigured Corpse in Homeric Epic," in *Mortals and Immortals: Collected Essays,* ed.

Froma I. Zeitlin (Princeton: Princeton University Press, 1991), 50–74. I thank Dr. Rebecca Resinski for bringing this essay to my attention.

87. Homer, *The Iliad,* trans. Robert Fagles (New York: Penguin Classics, 1990), 7:152–153.

88. Ibid., 7:178–179.

89. Ibid., 9:501.

90. Ibid., 22:84–89.

91. See Vernant, "A 'Beautiful Death,' " 64.

92. Ibid., esp. 72–74.

93. Fagles, *The Iliad,* 24:925–945.

94. Wills, *Lincoln at Gettysburg,* 42.

95. Robert B. Strassler, ed. *The Landmark Thucydides: A Comprehensive Guide to The Peloponnesian War* (New York: Free Press, 1996), 115.

96. James M. McPherson, *For Cause and Comrades: Why Men Fought in the Civil War* (New York: Oxford University Press, 1997), 77.

97. Strassler, *Landmark Thucydides,* 115.

98. Ibid., 117.

99. See McPherson, *For Cause and Comrades;* and James M. McPherson, *What They Fought For 1861–1865* (Baton Rouge: Louisiana State University Press, 1994).

100. Edward L. Ayers, *In the Presence of Mine Enemies: The Civil War in the Heart of America, 1859–1863* (New York: W. W. Norton, 2004), 151. The cultural force of the Greek revival in the South is verified by Elizabeth Fox-Genovese and Eugene D. Genovese, *The Mind of the Master Class: History and Faith in the Southern Slaveholders' Worldview* (New York: Cambridge University Press, 2005), see esp. the chapter "In the Shadow of Antiquity," 249–304.

101. See Mark E. Neely Jr., "Wilderness and the Cult of Manliness: Hooker, Lincoln, and Defeat," in *Lincoln's Generals,* ed. Gabor S. Boritt (New York: Oxford University Press, 1994), 70.

102. Emory M. Thomas, *Robert E. Lee, A Biography* (New York: W. W. Norton, 1995), 332.

103. Ibid., 333.

104. Wills, *Lincoln at Gettysburg,* 41–62 esp.

105. Ibid., 69.

106. Quoted in Wills, 75.

107. *Address Delivered at the Opening Ceremonies of Ever Green Cemetery,* 11.

108. Ibid.

109. Ibid.

110. See Wills, *Lincoln at Gettysburg,* 121–147; David Herbert Donald, *Lincoln* (New York: Simon & Schuster, 1995), 460–466 esp.

111. *Lincoln, Speeches and Writings 1859–1865,* ed. Don E. Fehrenbacher (New York: Library of America, 1989), 224.

112. *Address Delivered at the Opening Ceremonies of Evergreen Cemetery,* 4.

113. David Donald, *Lincoln* (New York: Simon & Schuster, 1995), see 15, 337, 354.

114. *Address Delivered at the Opening Ceremonies of Evergreen Cemetery,* 5.

115. Wills, *Lincoln at Gettysburg,* 71.

4. "A Voice from the Ruins"

1. *Southern Literary Messenger* 13 (February 1847): 109–110. The poet in question, who was sometimes known as "Susan of Richmond" or Susan of "Henrico," may be Susan

Archer Talley of Hanover County, Virginia. For a brief biography of her writing and career, see Rufus Wilmot Griswold, *The Female Poets of America* (New York: James Miller, 1874), 311–315. Because poets sometimes published under multiple names, it is difficult to pin down Susan's identity with certainty.

2. A reading of this monthly journal over a fifteen-year span (1844–1859) unearthed a total of at least 135 poems with death as a central subject.

3. The phrase "cultural work" acknowledges the approach of Jane Tompkins in *Sensational Designs: The Cultural Work of American Fiction, 1790–1860* (New York: Oxford University Press, 1985).

4. See Philippe Ariès, *The Hour of Our Death,* trans. Helen Weaver (New York: Oxford University Press, 1981), 409–474, on the early nineteenth century as "The Age of the Beautiful Death." See also Susan Sontag's *Illness as Metaphor* (New York: Farrar, Straus and Giroux, 1978), 30–31 esp.

5. For an older but still useful interpretation of "Thanatopsis," see Albert McLean Jr., *William Cullen Bryant* (New Haven, Conn.: College & University Press, 1964), 65–84.

6. Thomas H. Johnson, ed., *The Complete Poems of Emily Dickinson* (New York: Little, Brown, 1960), 350.

7. David S. Reynolds, *Walt Whitman's America: A Cultural Biography* (New York: Alfred A. Knopf, 1995), 240.

8. Caroline May, *The American Female Poets; with Biographical and Critical Notices* (Philadelphia: Lindsay & Blakiston, 1849); Rufus Wilmot Griswold, *The Poets and Poetry of America* (Philadelphia: Parry and McMillan, 1856).

9. See William Gilmore Simms, *Poems Descriptive, Dramatic, and Legendary and Contemplative,* vols. 1 and 2 (New York: Arno Press, 1972); Mrs. Rebecca S. Nichols, *Songs of the Heart and The Hearth-Stone* (Philadelphia: Thomas, Cowperhthwaite & Co.; Cincinnati: J. F. Desilver, 1851).

10. For a fine example of a memory book by an African American woman, see Amy Matilda Cassey, "Original and Selected Poetry," Manuscripts, Library Company of Philadelphia. For a white woman's copy album, see "Drawing Album" (circa 1855), Manuscripts, Library Company of Philadelphia. I am indebted to Phillip S. Lapsansky, chief of reference, and to Cornelia S. King, reference librarian, for bringing these sources to my attention.

11. *Southern Literary Messenger* 20 (June 1854): 337. Hereafter, *Southern Literary Messenger* is cited as *SLM*.

12. *SLM* 20 (October 1854): 604.

13. See Gary Laderman, *The Sacred Remains: American Attitudes toward Death, 1799–1883* (New Haven: Yale University Press, 1996), 26–27 and passim.

14. Alice Fahs, *The Imagined Civil War: Popular Literature of the North & South 1861–1865* (Chapel Hill: University of North Carolina Press, 2001), 100 and more generally 93–119.

15. *SLM* 11 (January 1845): 30.

16. *SLM* 21 (April 1855): 220.

17. *SLM* 14 (May 1848): 280.

18. *SLM* 13 (May 1847): 315.

19. *SLM* 18 (April 1852): 224.

20. *SLM* 12 (September 1846): 540.

21. *SLM* 22 (May 1856): 388.

22. On how poetry could address this vexing issue, see Fahs, *Imagined Civil War,* 96.

23. Griswold, *Female Poets of America,* 260–262.

24. *SLM* 13 (November 1847): 646–647.

25. *SLM* 14 (March 1848): 167. For a biographical sketch of Eames, see Griswold, *Female Poets of America*, 246–249.

26. *SLM* 20 (September 1854): 564–565.

27. *SLM* 23 (October 1856): 289–290.

28. *SLM* 19 (June 1853): 343–344.

29. *SLM* 10 (February 1844): 88.

30. *SLM* 16 (March 1850): 161.

31. *SLM* 25 (December 1857): 426.

32. Fahs, *Imagined Civil War,* 103.

33. Emily N. Radigan, ed., *"Desolating This Fair Country": The Civil War Diary and Letters of Lt. Henry C. Lyon, 34th New York* (Jefferson, N.C.: McFarland & Co., 1999), 122.

34. Quoted in Laderman, *Sacred Remains,* 136.

35. Quoted in Carol Reardon, *Pickett's Charge in History & Memory* (Chapel Hill: University of North Carolina Press, 1997), 28.

36. Robert Hunt Rhodes, ed., *All For the Union: The Civil War Diary and Letters of Elisha Hunt Rhodes* (New York: Orion Books, 1985), 84.

37. James M. McPherson, *Crossroads of Freedom: Antietam* (New York: Oxford University Press, 2002). 126.

38. William C. Davis, ed., *Diary of a Confederate Soldier: John S. Jackman of the Orphan Brigade* (Columbia: University of South Carolina Press, 1990), 69.

39. Kent Gramm, *Gettysburg: A Meditation on War and Values* (Bloomington: Indiana University Press, 1997), 199. See also 219 on Confederate General Dorsey Pender's appreciation of the "beauty" of the fighting at Sharpsburg.

40. Russell Duncan, ed., *Blue-Eyed Child of Fortune: The Civil War Letters of Colonel Robert Gould Shaw* (Athens: University of Georgia Press, 1992), 231.

41. Earl Schenck Miers, ed., *When the World Ended: The Diary of Emma LeConte* (Lincoln: University of Nebraska Press, 1987), 99–100.

42. *SLM* 12 (February 1846): 81–82.

43. *SLM* 21 (January 1855): 59.

44. *SLM* 20 (July 1854): 395–396.

45. *SLM* 11 (November 1845): 689–690.

46. *SLM* 23 (August 1856): 131–132.

47. *SLM* 22 (June 1856): 442.

48. *SLM* 13 (August 1847): 472.

49. *SLM* 12 (July 1846): 400.

50. *SLM* 19 (May 1853): 306–307.

51. *SLM* 20 (April 1854): 253.

52. *SLM* 12 (February 1846): 74.

53. *SLM* 12 (November 1846): 699.

54. *SLM* 14 (August 1848): 485–486.

55. *SLM* 28 (August 1859): 306.

56. Rev. J. William Jones, D.D, *Christ in the Camp or Religion in the Confederate Army* (Harrisonburg, Va.: Sprinkle Publications, 1986); originally published in 1887.

57. On Jones's role in the making of the "Lost Cause" ideology in the postwar South, see the suggestive passages in David W. Blight, *Race and Reunion: The Civil War in American Memory* (Cambridge, Mass.: Harvard University Press, 2001), 78 and 166.

58. Drew Gilpin Faust, "Christian Soldiers: The Meaning of Revivalism in the Confederate Army," *Journal of Southern History* 53 (February 1987): 87.

59. Jones, *Christ in the Camp,* 402.

60. Ibid., 408.

61. Ibid., 409.

62. Ibid., 418.

63. Ibid., 418–419.

64. Ibid., 421.

65. Ibid., 407.

66. Ibid., 447.

67. Ibid., 449.

68. Ibid., 418.

69. *SLM* 18 (April 1852): 217.

70. Elizabeth Varon, *We Mean to Be Counted: White Women and Politics in Antebellum Virginia* (Chapel Hill: University of North Carolina Press, 1998), 117.

71. *SLM* 14 (March 1848): 139–140.

72. *SLM* 15 (August 1849): 501.

73. *SLM* 26 (March 1858): 184–187.

74. Rayburn S. Moore, ed., *A Man of Letters in the Nineteenth-Century South: The Selected Letters of Paul Hamilton Hayne* (Baton Rouge: Louisiana State University Press, 1982), 12.

75. *SLM* 14 (November 1848): 696–697.

76. *SLM* 15 (June 1849): 335.

77. Bertram Wyatt-Brown, *Southern Honor: Ethics and Behavior in the Old South* (New York: Oxford University Press, 1982); Wyatt-Brown, *The Shaping of Southern Culture: Honor, Grace, and War, 1760s–1880s* (Chapel Hill: University of North Carolina Press, 2001).

78. *SLM* 16 (September 1850): 552.

79. *SLM* 24 (March 1857): 207–209.

80. *SLM* 29 (October 1859): 276.

81. *SLM* 11 (October 1845): 608.

82. Quoted in Rayburn, *Man of Letters*, 53.

83. This brief biography is taken from *Poems of Paul Hamilton Hayne. Complete Edition with Numerous Illustrations* (Boston: D. Lothrop and Co., 1882), v–viii; both quotations from vii.

84. *Poems of Paul Hamilton Hayne,* 65–86.

85. Ibid., 65–66.

86. Ibid., 85–86.

87. Ibid., 70.

88. Ibid., 71–72, 77–78, 78–79.

89. Ibid., 71–72.

90. Lorien Foote, *Seeking the One Great Remedy: Francis George Shaw and Nineteenth Century Reform* (Athens: Ohio University Press, 2003), 119. See esp. her chapter on the memorialization of Robert Gould Shaw, 101–127. I am also indebted to Professor Foote for bringing to my attention the extraordinary document, *Memorial: RGS* (Cambridge, Mass.: University Press, 1864), and for sharing her complete photocopy with me.

91. Donald Yacovone, ed., *A Voice of Thunder: The Civil War Letters of George E. Stephens* (Chicago: University of Illinois Press, 1997), 246.

92. Quoted in Foote, *Seeking the One Great Remedy*, 120.

93. See also Steven Axelrod, "Colonel Shaw in American Poetry: "'For the Union Dead' and Its Precursors," *American Quarterly* 24 (October 1972): 523–537.

94. Foote, *Seeking the One Great Remedy,* 121.

95. *Memorial: RGS.*

96. Foote, *Seeking the One Great Remedy*, 125.

97. *Memorial: RGS*, 85.

98. Ibid., 73.

99. Ibid., 123.

5. "Better to Die Free, Than to Live Slaves"

1. Donald Vacovone, ed., *A Voice of Thunder: The Civil War Letters of George E. Stephens* (Chicago: University of Illinois Press, 1997), 4–25.

2. Vacovone, *Voice of Thunder*, 229.

3. C. Peter Ripley et al., ed., *The Black Abolitionist Papers*, vol. 3, *The United States, 1830–1846* (Chapel Hill: University of North Carolina Press, 1991), 403–412. All quotations for the Henry Highland Garnet speech are from these pages. See Sterling Stuckey's chapter "Henry Highland Garnet: Nationalism, Class Analysis, and Revolution," in his *Slave Culture: Nationalist Theory and the Foundations of Black America* (New York: Oxford University Press, 1987), 138–192.

4. Ripley, *Black Abolitionist Papers*, 405.

5. Ibid.

6. Ibid., 406.

7. Ibid.

8. Ibid., 410.

9. W. E. B. DuBois, "Black Reconstruction in America: An Essay Toward a History of the Part Which Black Folk Played in the Attempt to Reconstruct Democracy in America, 1860–1880," in *Studies in American Negro Life*, ed. August Meier (1935; repr., New York: Atheneum, 1962), 55–83.

10. Ripley, *Black Abolitionist Papers*, 408.

11. Ibid., 409.

12. Ibid., 409–410.

13. Orlando Patterson, *Slavery and Social Death: A Comparative Study* (Cambridge, Mass.: Harvard University Press, 1982).

14. Robert J. Allison, ed., *The Interesting Narrative of the Life of Olaudah Equiano, Written by Himself*, Bedford Series in History and Culture (1791; repr., New York: St. Martin's Press, 1995), 54.

15. Ibid., 55.

16. Ibid., 57.

17. Ibid.

18. Ibid., 10–11.

19. Philip D. Morgan, *Slave Counterpoint: Black Culture in the Eighteenth-Century Chesapeake & Lowcountry* (Chapel Hill: University of North Carolina Press, 1998), 443–444.

20. Peter Kolchin, *American Slavery, 1619–1877*, 1st rev. ed. (New York: Hill and Wang, 2003), 22–23. See also the collection of articles on the slave trade in the *William and Mary Quarterly* 63, 3rd ser. (January 2001), especially the finely grained study by Herbert S. Klein, Stanley L. Engerman, Robin Haines, and Ralph Shlomowitz, "Transatlantic Mortality: The Slave Trade in Comparative Perspective," 93–118.

21. Ira Berlin, *Many Thousands Gone: The First Two Centuries of Slavery in North America* (Cambridge, Mass.: Harvard University Press, 1998), 184–185.

22. Ibid., 186.

23. Morgan, *Slave Counterpoint*, 445.

24. Ibid.

25. Jeffrey R. Young, "Ideology and Death on a Savannah River Rice Plantation, 1833–1867: Paternalism amidst 'a Good Supply of Disease and Pain,'" *Journal of Southern History* 59 (November 1993): 689.

26. Ibid., 691.

27. The slave narratives considered in this section are drawn from the University of North Carolina's online collection, "Documenting the American South," http://docsouth.unc.edu/neh.

28. See John Wood Sweet, *Bodies Politic: Negotiating Race in the American North, 1730–1830* (Baltimore: Johns Hopkins University Press, 2003), esp. 64–97, where Sweet directly treats the 1768 narrative of Arthur we are about to consider.

29. *The Life, and Dying Speech of Arthur, a Negro Man: Who Was Executed at Worcester, October 20, 1768. For a Rape Committed on the Body of One Deborah Metcalfe*, electronic ed., p. 5 of 6, http://docsouth.unc.edu/neh/arthur/arthur.html.

30. *The Last Words and Dying Speech of Edmund Fortis, a Negro Man, Who Appeared to Be Between Thirty and Forty Years of Age, but Very Ignorant. He Was Executed at Dresden, on the Kennebec River, on Thursday the Twenty-Fifth Day of September, 1974, for a Rape and Murder, Committed on the Body of Pamela Tilton, a Young Girl of About Fourteen Years of Age, Daughter of Mr. Tilton of Vassalborough, in the County of Lincoln*, electronic ed., p. 5 of 6., http://docsouth.unc.edu.neh/fortis/fortis.html.

31. *Life, Last Words and Dying Speech of Stephen Smith, a Black Man, Who Was Executed at Boston This Day Being Thursday, October 12, 1797 for Burglary*, electronic ed., p. 3 of 4, http://docsouth.unc.edu/neh/smithste/smithste.html.

32. *Confession of John Joyce, Alias Davis, Who Was Executed on Monday, the 14th of March, 1808. For the Murder of Mrs. Sarah Cross; With an Address to the Public and People of Colour. Together with the Substance of the Trial, and the Address of Chief Justice Tilghman, on His Condemnation. Confession of Peter Mathias, Alias Matthews, Who Was Executed on Monday, the 14th of March, 1808. For the Murder of Mrs. Sarah Cross; With an Address to the Public and People of Colour. Together with the Substance of the Trial, and the Address of Chief Justice Tilgman, on His Condemnation*, electronic ed., p. 1 of 21, http://docsouth.unc.edu/neh/joyce/joycehtml.

33. William E. Cain, ed., *William Lloyd Garrison and the Fight Against Slaver: Selections from The Liberator*, Bedford Series in History and Culture (New York: St. Martin's Press, 1995), 36.

34. Harriet A. Jacobs, *Incidents in the Life of a Slave Girl, Written by Herself*, ed. Jean Fagan Yellin (1861; repr., Cambridge, Mass.: Harvard University Press, 1987), 62.

35. From the *Narrative of William Wells Brown, a Fugitive Slave, Written by Himself*, in *Puttin' on Ole Massa: The Slave Narratives of Henry Bibb, William Wells Brown, and Solomon Northrup*, ed. Gilbert Osofsky (New York: Harper & Row, 1969), 218.

36. Charles M. Wiltse, ed., *David Walker's Appeal to the Coloured Citizens of the World, but in particular, and very expressly, to those of the United States of America* (1829; repr., New York: Hill and Wang, 1965), 71–72.

37. Frederick Douglass, *My Bondage and My Freedom*, ed. Philip S. Foner (1855; repr., New York: Dover Publications, 1969). All subsequent citations are from this edition.

38. William S. McFeely, *Frederick Douglass* (New York: W. W. Norton, 1991), 180.

39. Cited in Vacovone, *Voice of Thunder*, 31.

40. Douglass, *My Bondage and My Freedom*, 57.

41. Ibid., 122–123.

42. Kolchin, *American Slavery*, 129–131.

43. Ibid., 131.

44. Ibid., 131–132.

45. Douglass, *My Bondage and My Freedom*, 247.

46. Ibid.

47. Ibid., 95.

48. Ibid., 284.

49. Ibid.

50. Ibid., 297.

51. Ibid., 301–302.

52. *Frederick Douglass Paper*, April 15, 1853. This citation and other references to African American newspapers in this chapter were drawn from the electronic subscription source Accessible Archives (http://www.accessible.com), available at the Library Company of Philadelphia.

53. *Frederick Douglass Paper*, August 26, 1853.

54. McFeely, *Frederick Douglass*, 15.

55. *Frederick Douglass Paper*, February 24, 1854.

56. *Provincial Freeman*, April 26, 1856.

57. *Provincial Freeman*, July 19, 1856.

58. *Frederick Douglass Paper*, November 18, 1853.

59. *Frederick Douglass Paper*, October 5, 1855.

60. *Frederick Douglass Paper*, July 6, 1855.

61. W. E. B. DuBois, *The Souls of Black Folk*, introduction by John Edgar Wideman (1903; repr., New York: Library of America, 1990), 145.

62. "Questions and Answers," *National Era* 4, no. 198 (October 17, 1850): 166.

63. "A Letter to the American Slaves from those who have fled from American Slavery," *North Star*, September 5, 1850.

64. Humanitas, *Reflections on Slavery; With Recent Evidence of Its Inhumanity. Occasioned by the Melancholy Death of Romain, A French Negro* (Philadelphia, 1803).

65. Ibid., 13.

66. Ibid.

67. Ibid., 14.

68. Ibid.

69. Jesse Torrey, *A Portraiture of Domestic Slavery, in the United States: with the reflections on the practicability of restoring the moral rights of the slave, without impairing the legal privileges of the possessor; and a project of a colonial asylum for free persons of colour: including memoirs of facts on the interior traffic in slaves, and on Kidnapping. Illustrated with engravings* (Philadelphia: published by the author, 1817).

70. Ibid., 21.

71. Ibid., 30.

72. Ibid., 42.

73. Ibid., 43–44.

74. Ibid., 44.

75. Ibid., 45, for all examples.

76. "Slavery in the District of Columbia," *Freedom's Journal*, January 16, 1829.

77. "The Slave Trade," *National Era* 2, no. 96 (November 2, 1848).

78. *Provincial Freeman*, October 20, 1855.

79. William Wells Brown, *Clotel; or, The President's Daughter: A Narrative of Slave Life in the United States*, ed. Robert S. Levine, Bedford Cultural Editions (New York: St. Martin's Press, 2000). All subsequent citations are to this edition.

80. See ibid., chap. 25, "Death Is Freedom," 204–209. Illustration on 206.

81. Ibid., 207.

82. Ibid.

83. Russ Castronovo, *Necro Citizenship: Death, Eroticism, and the Public Sphere in the Nineteenth-Century United States* (Durham, N.C.: Duke University Press, 2001), 36. See also 34–45.

84. Brown, *Clotel*, 207.

85. "Liberty or Death," *National Era* 2, no. 75 (June 8, 1848): 91, for all quotes regarding this incident.

86. *The North Star*, April 20, 1849, for all quotes regarding this incident.

87. "What has the North to do with Slavery?," *The Colored American*, February 17, 1838, for all quotes regarding this incident.

88. *Frederick Douglass Paper*, March 11, 1853.

89. "Doings in Maryland," *The North Star*, July 14, 1848, for all quotes regarding this incident. On October 13, 1848, *The North Star* published, under a section entitled "Verses," a poem regarding Redden's suicide.

90. "Give Me Liberty, or Give Me Death," *Provincial Freeman*, April 11, 1857.

91. Steven Hahn, *A Nation Under Our Feet: Black Political Struggles in the Rural South from Slavery to the Great Migration* (Cambridge, Mass.: Belknap Press of Harvard University Press, 2003), 64.

92. On the question of runaways, see John Hope Franklin and Loren Schweninger, *Runaway Slaves: Rebels on the Plantation* (New York: Oxford University Press, 1999), 282. By 1860, the authors calculate, "the number of runaways annually would exceed 50,000."

93. See the classic article by Harvey Wish, "American Slave Insurrections Before 1861," *Journal of Negro History* 22 (July 1937): 299–320 and 308 for quotation. See also Willie Lee Rose, ed., *A Documentary History of Slavery in North America* (New York: Oxford University Press, 1976), 99–101 and 97–134 more generally.

94. Wish, "American Slave Insurrections Before 1861," 308.

95. On the Stono Rebellion, see Peter H. Wood, *Black Majority: Negroes in Colonial South Carolina from 1670 through the Stono Rebellion* (New York: W. W. Norton), 308–326.

96. Douglas R. Egerton, "A Peculiar Mark of Infamy: Dismemberment, Burial, and Rebelliousness in Slave Societies," in *Mortal Remains: Death in Early America*, ed. Nancy Isenberg and Andrew Burstein (Philadelphia: University of Pennsylvania Press, 2003), 150.

97. Kenneth S. Greenburg, ed., *The Confessions of Nat Turner and Related Documents*, Bedford Series in History and Culture (New York: St. Martin's Press, 1996), 19–20.

98. On Fort Pillow, see Ira Berlin, ed., Joseph P. Reidy and Leslie Rowland, assoc. ed., *Freedom: A Documentary History of Emancipation, 1861–1867*, series 2, *The Black Military Experience* (New York: Cambridge University Press, 1982), 539–548. On the Poison Spring massacre, see Gregory Urwin, "'We Cannot Treat Negroes...as Prisoners of War': Racial Atrocities and Reprisals in Civil War Arkansas," *Civil War History* 42, no. 3 (1996): 193–210.

99. Gary B. Nash, *Race and Revolution* (Madison, Wis.: Madison House Publishers, 1990), 57.

100. Sylvia R. Frey, *Water From the Rock: Black Resistance in a Revolutionary Age* (Princeton: Princeton University Press, 1991), 108–142.

101. Ibid., 169.

102. Douglas R. Egerton, *Gabriel's Rebellion: The Virginia Slave Conspiracies of 1800 & 1802* (Chapel Hill: University of North Carolina Press, 1993), 51.

103. Historians have engaged in spirited debate regarding the most basic facts in the received wisdom regarding the Denmark Vesey conspiracy. For a useful starting point,

see Michael P. Johnson, "Denmark Vesey and His Co-Conspirators," *William and Mary Quarterly* 63, 3rd ser. (October 2001): 915–976; and the reactions to Johnson's article in "The Making of a Slave Conspiracy, Part II" in *William and Mary Quarterly* 59, 3rd ser. (January 2002): 135–202.

104. Melton A. McLaurin, *Celia, A Slave* (New York: Avon Books, 1993), 56.

105. Ibid., 135.

106. Winthrop D. Jordan, *Tumult and Silence at Second Creek: An Inquiry into a Civil War Slave Conspiracy* (Baton Rouge: Louisiana State University Press, 1993).

107. Ibid., 5.

108. Ibid., 11.

109. Ibid., 5.

110. Du Bois, *Black Reconstruction in America,* 104.

111. This account of the battle of Fort Hudson leans heavily on Lawrence Lee Hewitt's essay "An Ironic Route to Glory: Louisiana's Native Guards at Port Hudson," in *Black Soldiers in Blue: African American Troops in the Civil War Era,* ed. John David Smith (Chapel Hill: University of North Carolina Press, 2002), 78–106.

112. Edwin S. Redkey, *A Grand Army of Black Men: Letters from African-American Soldiers in the Union Army, 1861–1865* (New York: Cambridge University Press, 1992), 137.

113. Hewitt, "Ironic Route to Glory," 96.

114. Ibid., 95.

115. Redkey, *Grand Army of Black Men,* 137–138.

116. Berlin, *Black Military Experience,* 584–585.

117. Ibid., 528–529.

118. Quoted in Dudley Taylor Cornish, *The Sable Arm: Negro Troops in the Union Army, 1861–1865* (New York: W. W. Norton, 1966), 143.

119. Ibid., 144.

120. Hewitt, "Ironic Route to Glory," 98–100 for divergent contemporary accounts of the battle.

121. Yacovone, *Voice of Thunder,* 243–250.

122. Virginia Matzke Adams, ed., *On the Altar of Freedom: A Black Soldier's Civil War Letters from the Front, Corporal James Henry Gooding* (Boston: University of Massachusetts Press, 1991), 38.

123. Berlin, *Black Military Experience,* 536–538.

124. Yacovone, *Voice of Thunder,* 246.

125. William Glenn Robertson, "From the Crater to New Market Heights: A Tale of Two Divisions," in *Black Soldiers in Blue,* ed. John David Smith, 186 and 169–199.

126. Ibid.

127. Stuckey, "Henry Highland Garnet," 188.

128. Ibid.

6. "The Court of Death"

1. On the concept of "thick description," see Clifford Geertz, *The Interpretation of Cultures: Selected Essays* (New York: Basic Books, 1973), 3–30.

2. All lithographs in this chapter may be found in the collections of the American Antiquarian Society, Worcester, Mass. I am especially indebted to Georgia Brady Barnhill, Andrew W. Mellon Curator of Graphic Arts, at the Antiquarian Society for her energy and insight in helping me explore this topic. Her articles "Keep Sacred the Memory of

Your Ancestors: Family Registers and Memorial Prints," and "Checklist of Printed Family Registers and Memorial Prints, 1790–1900," in *The Art of Family: Genealogical Artifacts in New England,* ed. D. Brenton Simons and Peter Benes (Boston: New England Historic Genealogical Society, 2002) were invaluable to me. All lithographs discussed in this chapter may be located in the "Checklist" piece.

3. See here Jay Ruby, *Secure the Shadow: Death and Photography in America* (Cambridge, Mass.: MIT Press, 1995), 49–111 esp.

4. Barnhill, "Keep Sacred the Memory of Your Ancestors," 63.

5. Bryan F. Le Beau, *Currier & Ives: America Imagined* (Washington, D.C.: Smithsonian Institution Press, 2001), 21.

6. Ibid., 26.

7. American Antiquarian Society, Graphics Department.

8. Barnhill, "Checklist," 295.

9. Le Beau, *Currier & Ives,* 35.

10. Karen Halttunen, *Confidence Men and Painted Women: A Study in Middle Class Culture in America, 1830–1870* (New Haven: Yale University Press, 1982), 124.

11. For a taste of the memorial paraphernalia available to antebellum Americans, see Martha V. Pike and Janice Gray Armstrong, eds., *A Time to Mourn: Expressions of Grief in Nineteenth Century America* (Stony Brook, N.Y.: Museums at Stony Brook, 1980), 127–188. These pages contain the catalog and images from a museum exhibition dedicated to the topic.

12. Barnhill, "Checklist," 284.

13. Barnhill, "Keep Sacred the Memory of Your Ancestors," 72.

14. On the diversity of American religious experience in this era, see Nathan O. Hatch, *The Democratization of American Christianity* (New Haven: Yale University Press, 1989); Jon Butler, *Awash in a Sea of Faith: Christianizing the American People* (Cambridge, Mass.: Harvard University Press, 1990).

15. Drew Gilpin Faust, "The Civil War Soldier and the Art of Dying," *Journal of Southern History* 67 (February 2001): 3–38.

16. The emergence of abstract notions of nationhood during the Civil War is fruitfully examined by Franny Nudelman's book *John Brown's Body: Slavery, Violence, and the Culture of War* (Chapel Hill: University of North Carolina Press, 2004), 6 and passim.

17. Barnhill, "Keep Sacred the Memory of Your Ancestors," 68.

18. Ibid., 72.

19. Quoted in Alan Trachtenberg, ed., *Classic Essays on Photography* (New Haven, Conn.: Leete's Island Books, 1980), 13.

20. Quoted in Trachtenberg, *Classic Essays,* 38.

21. Nathan G. Burgess, "The Value of Daguerreotype Likenesses," *Photographic and Fine Art Journal* 8 (1855): 19.

22. Alan Trachtenberg, "Albums of War: On Reading Civil War Photographs," *Representations* 9, special issue, *American Culture Between the Civil War and World War I* (Winter 1985): 6.

23. Dr. Oliver Wendell Holmes, "The Stereoscope and the Stereograph," *Atlantic Monthly* 3 (June 1859): 738.

24. Ibid., 744.

25. Ruby, *Secure the Shadow,* 110.

26. Nathan G. Burgess, "Taking Portraits After Death," *Photographic and Fine Arts Journal* 8 (1855): 80.

27. See Ruby, *Secure the Shadow,* 63–74.

28. From the collections of the Historical Society of Pennsylvania, Philadelphia.

29. Ruby, *Secure the Shadow*, 32.

30. Philippe Ariès, *Western Attitudes toward Death from the Middle Ages to the Present* (Baltimore: Johns Hopkins University Press, 1974), 24–25.

31. See Nudelman, *John Brown's Body*, 109, 122, 128, and passim on this point.

32. William A. Frasanito, *Antietam: The Photographic Legacy of America's Bloodiest Day* (Gettysburg, Penn.: Thomas Publications, 1978), 30–32, for example.

33. See Alexander Gardner, *Gardner's Photographic Sketchbook of the Civil War* (New York: Dover Publications, 1959).

34. On the popularity of Shakespearean drama in antebellum America (and of Hamlet in particular), see Lawrence W. Levine, "William Shakespeare in America," in *Highbrow/ Lowbrow: The Emergence of Cultural Hierarchy in America* (Cambridge, Mass.: Harvard University Press, 1988), 13–81.

35. *Gardner's Photographic Sketchbook,* plates 40 and 41, and the text accompanying the plates.

36. See especially Constance Sullivan, ed., *Landscapes of the Civil War: Newly Discovered Photographs From the Medford Historical Society* (New York: Alfred A. Knopf, 1995), 107; Nudelman, *John Brown's Body,* 128.

37. Timothy Sweet, *Traces of War: Poetry, Photography, and the Crisis of the Union* (Baltimore: Johns Hopkins University Press, 1990), 109.

38. George N. Barnard, *Photographic Views of Sherman's Campaign* (New York: Dover Publications, 1977).

39. Susan Sontag, *Regarding the Pain of Others* (New York: Farrar, Straus and Giroux, 2003), 75–76.

40. Nudelman, *John Brown's Body,* 103–131.

41. "Brady's Photographs: Pictures of the Dead at Antietam." *New York Times,* October 20, 1862, 5, cols. 3 and 4.

42. Ibid.

43. "Photographic Phases," *New York Times,* July 21, 1862, 5.

44. "Brady's Photographs. Pictures of the Dead at Antietam."

45. Dr. Oliver Wendell Holmes, "Doings of the Sunbeam," *Atlantic Monthly* 12 (July 1863): 12.

46. Trachtenberg, "Albums of War," 16.

47. Holmes, "Doings of the Sunbeam," 11.

48. Ibid., 12.

49. Evidence regarding the enormous popularity of "The Court of Death" is gleaned from Ellen Hickey Grayson, "Art, Audiences, and the Aesthetics of Social Order in Antebellum America: Rembrandt Peale's Court of Death" (Ph.D. diss., George Washington University, 1995), esp. 407–564.

50. Peale quoted in Carol Eaton Soltis, " 'In Sympathy with the Heart': Rembrandt Peale, an American Artist and the Traditions of European Art" (Ph.D. diss., University of Pennsylvania, 2000), 376. See also 375–430 more generally for a brilliant analysis of the painting.

51. See Lillian B. Miller, *In Pursuit of Fame: Rembrandt Peale, 1778–1860* (Washington, D.C.: National Portrait Gallery, Smithsonian Institution in association with the University of Washington Press, 1992), 129–138.

52. Peale composed a number of tracts explaining *The Court of Death* and its impact during the antebellum era. The quotations in this paragraph are drawn from Rembrandt Peale, *History of the Painting, in a Letter from the Artist to a Friend in New-York,* 5–6 (1845), American Antiquarian Society.

53. *History of the Painting,* 5.

54. Quoted in Soltis, "'In Sympathy with the Heart,'" 392.

55. See William T. Oedel, "The Reward of Virtue: Rembrandt Peale and Social Reform," in *The Peale Family: Creation of a Legacy 1770–1870,* ed. Lillian B. Miller (New York: Abbeville Press, 1996), 151–167.

56. *Great Moral Picture, The Court of Death, Painted by Rembrandt Peale* (1820?), 2, American Antiquarian Society.

57. *History of the Painting,* 4.

58. *Great Moral Picture,* 2.

59. *History of the Painting,* 5.

60. Quoted in Oedel, "Reward of Virtue," 161.

61. See Jean-Pierre Vernant, "A 'Beautiful Death' and the Disfigured Corpse in Homeric Epic," in his *Mortals and Immortals: Collected Essays* (Princeton: Princeton University Press, 1991), 50–74. The classic treatment of the age of the "beautiful death" in the nineteenth century is Philippe Ariès, *The Hour of Our Death,* trans. Helen Weaver (New York: Oxford University Press, 1991), 409–474.

62. See Sweet, *Traces of War,* 107–137.

63. Mary Panzer, *Mathew Brady and the Image of History* (Washington, D.C.: Smithsonian Institution Press, 1997), 7.

64. *History of the Painting,* 5.

65. *Great Moral Picture,* 2.

66. *Description of the Court of Death,* broadside sheet, 1859, American Antiquarian Society.

67. Miller, *In Pursuit of Fame,* 123.

68. *Description of the Court of Death,* broadside sheet, 1859, American Antiquarian Society.

Epilogue

1. See Tony Horwitz, *Confederates in the Attic: Dispatches from the Unfinished Civil War* (New York: Vintage Books, 1999), 10.

2. Ulysses S. Grant, *Memoirs and Selected Letters* (New York: Library of America, 1990), 247. See also Horwitz's chapter on Shiloh, 157–189, for a nice summary of the interpretive issues surrounding the battlefield.

Index

Page numbers in italics refer to figures.